DISABILITY, CULTURE

Alfredo J. Artiles, *Series Editor*

Published by Teachers College Press® 1234 Amsterdam Avenue, New York, NY 10027

Copyright © 2022 by Teachers College, Columbia University

Front cover art by David J. Connor. Front cover icons (left to right): Signing hands by National Park Service, Brain by Arafit Uddin, Wheelchair by Linseed Studio, Guide dog by Mark Caron, Occluded eye by Bluu, TTY machine by Ivan Colic, and Prosthetic leg by lastspark, all via Noun Project.

All rights reserved. No part of this publication may be reproduced or transmitted in any form or by any means, electronic or mechanical, including photocopy, or any information storage and retrieval system without permission from the publisher. For reprint permission and other subsidiary rights requests, please contact Teachers College Press, Rights Dept.: tcpressrights@tc.columbia.edu

Library of Congress Cataloging-in-Publication Data is available at loc.gov

ISBN 978-0-8077-6634-7 (paper)
ISBN 978-0-8077-6635-4 (hardcover)
ISBN 978-0-8077-8072-5 (ebook)

Printed on acid-free paper
Manufactured in the United States of America

DisCrit Expanded

Reverberations, Ruptures, and Inquiries

EDITED BY

Subini A. Annamma
Beth A. Ferri
David J. Connor

TEACHERS COLLEGE PRESS

TEACHERS COLLEGE | COLUMBIA UNIVERSITY
NEW YORK AND LONDON

To
My chosen family, I am here because you have held me
—Subini
My doctoral students who keep me learning
and loving my work
—Beth
Carmen Rose Curran, in friendship
—David

Contents

PART II: INWARD INQUIRIES

PART III: MARGIN TO MARGIN

The Future(s) of Disability

Of Complementary Representations, Heteroglossic Communities, and Moral Leadership

The production of the volume *DisCrit Expanded: Inquiries, Reverberations, and Ruptures* is taking place at an unprecedented time in the history of the United States; in fact, of the entire world. This is a moment in history recently described by Ford Foundation President Darren Walker as "a season of suffering" (10th paragraph). In his words,

> . . . America faces a pandemic of pandemics: Fear and fire and fury that betray corruption and climate catastrophe and callous indifference to 400 years of a racialized caste system; a lethal virus and subsequent economic fallout that lay bare the profoundly unequal ways in which we survive or succumb—in which we live and die. (Walker, 2020, 3rd paragraph)

The pandemic has made inequality disturbingly visible all around us—in the employment, housing, and health sectors but particularly in education. Because isolation and social distancing were logical prescriptions to stop the spread of the virus, school systems quickly moved to online delivery, but this well-intentioned response amplified preexisting structural inequalities. Scarcity of hardware and uneven access to high-speed connectivity hit particularly hard the most vulnerable groups of students—low-income, students of color, learners with disabilities. "Shame on us for asking students—some 12 million kids across the United States—to click into classrooms from the parking lots of fast-food restaurants," Darren Walker (2020) admonished us. Inequality slipped deeper into these communities' and families' lives.

The current crisis is changing irrevocably the ways we live and educate future generations of citizens. A corollary of this historical moment is that more than ever we need interdisciplinary resources to understand and change the evolving complexities of educational injustices. Few ideas in the education field embody so neatly the contemporary complexities of inequity as disability. Disability has been at the epicenter of educational equity battles and projects ranging from struggles for rights and access to inclusive programs to unsettling entanglements with race, social class, gender, and language. Historian Henri-Jacques Stiker (2009) described disability as a state of affairs. In a sense, disability is a universal condition, for all human beings will experience it in one way or another throughout their life span. As we find ourselves imagining and constructing better futures for/with people with disabilities in the global age of unequal differences, multifaceted and historically loaded notions such as disability demand alternative conceptualizations, creative methods of inquiry, and multiple representational languages and modalities to describe it. These investments require a renewed commitment to moral leadership in the academy (Artiles, 2019). However, as described later, the majority of education research on disability has been narrowly framed around biology and cognition. Alternative frames in disability studies, sociology, anthropology, and related disciplines are available, though these bodies of knowledge have evolved predominantly in parallel fashion, with relatively little enrichments across scholarly communities.

Scholars have called for theoretical and methodological diversity in the production of disability scholarship (Artiles, 2003; Connor et al., 2011), and we are witnessing a growing plurality of disability frameworks in the main square of education. For instance, disability studies (and its iterations) have become increasingly visible in journals outside their community and in research organizations such as the American Educational Research Association. These are encouraging developments.

It is in this context of emerging theoretical and methodological diversification that *DisCrit Expanded* enters the grand conversation about disability in the education field. *DisCrit Expanded* pursues an ambitious project to illuminate how "racism and ableism are mutually constitutive and collusive—always circulating across time and context in interconnected ways" (Connor et al., 2021, p. 4). The foundations of Disability Critical Race Theory (DisCrit) are located in the tradition of Critical Race Theory (CRT) and disability studies (DS), and its contributions are indispensable for the interdisciplinary refinement of the idea of disability in education. I contextualize in this foreword the importance of this project for its potential contributions to complementary representations and multiple standpoints about disability. I close with a brief reflection about the moral leadership that this scholarly work requires from us.

GRAND ASPIRATIONS: COMPLEMENTARY REPRESENTATIONS AND ALTERNATIVE STANDPOINTS ABOUT DISABILITY

Disability has been predominately framed through medical and psychological lenses. The disability narratives accumulated by these disciplines have dominated research, policy, and practice in the United States. Disciplinary narratives are concerned with canon formation and thus represent the commonsense history of a field, what Rorty (1984) described as doxographies. "A doxography of [disability] assumes that the key topics and scholars in [such] field are timeless and uncontestable, and it does not acknowledge that societal changes and transformations in [disability] theory and research are perennially taking place" (Artiles, 2004, pp. 551–552). Indeed, disciplinary narratives are unstable (Goodman, 2003).

The canonical narrative that emerged from generations of medical/psychological scholarship represents disability as an objective deficit feature of individuals. These canonical representations assume that individuals' actions and decisions are stripped of historical and structural influences, and the intersections of disability with other difference markers (e.g., race, gender, social class, language) are regarded as negligible—merely background noise that ought to be statistically controlled. In addition, canonical disability representations are expected to reflect continuity and progress, which brings a sense of direction, thus bridging the past with the present and the future (Levine & Nathan, 1995).

DisCrit joins a few other scholarly communities to destabilize canonical views of disability. As the breadth of alternative disability representations grows across these communities, we should anticipate that "boundary work" (Gieryn, 1999) may be enforced to contest the legitimacy of each other's theoretical formulations and findings and ultimately compete for credibility and resources. Scholarly communities maintain their credibility by claiming *epistemic authority*—"the legitimate power to define, describe, and explain bounded domains of reality" (Gieryn, 1999, p. 1). Some communities maintain their epistemic authority, while others have it denied. Although medical and psychological representations of disabilities have enjoyed significant epistemic authority, alternative frameworks also hold considerable clout. DisCrit may inevitably get embroiled in boundary work with other scholarly communities, particularly medical and psychological models, but it may also accrue greater epistemic authority as its knowledge base grows and matures.

DisCrit has several chief characteristics that contribute to this evolution. For instance, similar to CRT and cultural historical critical approaches (Artiles, 2011; Crenshaw, 1989; Gutierrez, 2008), DisCrit represents disability in its sociohistorical contexts. In this model, biological impairments are examined through the cultural work done in the space between the individual and society—Dis/ability. DisCrit, therefore, assumes that identities have historical baggage (Hall, 1990). Rather than fixed facts, cultural identities such as disability or race are *produced*; they constitute processes of becoming (Artiles, 2004; Erevelles, 2011). To wit: ". . . like everything which is historical, [identities] undergo constant transformation. Far from being externally fixed in some essentialized past, they are subject to the continuous play of history, culture, and power" (Hall, 1990, p. 225). Therefore,

DisCrit implicitly calls for "'the end of innocence' . . . the end of the innocent notion of the essential Black subject" (Hall, 1995, pp. 224–225) or the quintessential Black male with disabilities. I further argue that we must expose and disrupt the use of an insidious form of innocence, namely white innocence (Gotanda, 2004; Ross, 1990). Institutions invoke white innocence when inequities are revealed (Artiles, 2011). This is the innocence individuals or institutions claim in "aha! moments" when confronted with evidence about injustices; nonetheless, they sever these wrongs from the historical collusion of institutions and technologies that created and maintained the injustices in the first place (Gotanda, 2004). For example, aha! moments materialized when evidence about racial disparities in special education was legitimized by the National Academy of Sciences report (Donovan & Cross, 2002). White innocence has been maintained since that time by diluting the multifaceted historical and structural nature of racial disparities down to technical debates about measurement quarrels and policy surveillance of statistical thresholds (Skiba et al., 2016). The media and scholarly community have succumbed to the allure of such abstractions, thus disregarding the inequities that can unwittingly emerge from the equity efforts of special education and that disproportionality affect students of color (Artiles, 2019).

In brief, canonical disability representations are unstable, and DisCrit's standpoint—with its attention to history, context, and power—affords new vocabularies and analytical opportunities to deepen our understanding of disability's common sense by integrating insights from the social model of disability with CRT's intersectional power.

Another strength of the DisCrit framework that contributes to its development is the refusal to align with long-standing binaries such as theory versus activism. On the one hand, theoretical work is construed as a sign of the academy's elitism that manufactures the language of *Othering*— theory "produce[s] rather than reflect[s] [its] objects of reference" (Bhabha, 1988, p. 7). On the other hand, activism is concerned with inciting changes in institutions or structures to advance a political project while rejecting abstract language that erases the materiality of people's everyday lives. DisCrit aspires to build a parsimonious language that is mindful of regularities and patterns while it delves into the contingencies of local everyday experiences—I sense a desire for contributing to a material philosophy of disability (Graeber & da Col, 2011). The challenge for DisCrit, therefore, is to continue mapping disability's moving pieces and contradictions. This cartographic project ought to bear in mind that one of the most critical assets of theory is the power to name, but what is DisCrit to do, since so much surrounding disability has been named? Is it possible to advance a theory that subverts and replaces *at the same time*? Can a theory name what has not been named? (Bhabha & Stierstorfer, 2015). The chapters in this volume begin to address these questions.

I would also like to suggest that DisCrit needs to saturate its scholarly practices with various forms of self-critique—that is, make reflexivity a distinctive feature of its scholarly culture. This practice will arguably enhance DisCrit's epistemic authority and propel the production of more nuanced representations of disability. In fact, reflexivity is urgently needed across scholarly communities as we observe the unprecedented changes taking place in the cultures of knowledge production and the academy. There are indeed growing incentives for pursuing personal fame and external funding to study issues often defined by third parties. In a 2016 opinion piece published in the *Proceedings of the National Academy of Sciences*, Donald and Stuart Geman (2016) identified this cultural shift in the worlds of research reflected in their article's title, "Science in the age of selfies." The new regimes of incentives and rewards and the pressures from faster, more efficient technologies have altered the everyday lives of scientists. "Prolonged focusing is getting harder" (p. 9385), and an anxiety for public exposure (e.g., through "citation-fishing") (Lawrence, 2007, p. 583) is increasingly influencing career advancement. The Gemans added, "Even the elite scientific journals seem too favorable to observations of patterns in new [often big] data, even if . . . *utterly lacking any supporting theory*" (2016, p. 9386, emphasis added). In these rapidly changing times, some scholars are taking unsettling shortcuts, such as the "game of concept-of-the-month . . . 'fast-food' theory, piecemeal reading, the assembl[ing] of micro excerpts and fishing for catchy concepts" (Col & Graeber, 2011, pp. xii, xiii). The relentless hunt for the spotlight and the growing demand for theorizing findings from new data lay out perilous topographies for DisCrit's future knowledge production efforts.

DisCrit scholars must veer away from these ploys and make reflexivity a routine practice in the development of this scholarly community, and the impetus for this volume is precisely to begin confronting these trends. DisCrit aims to avert a tourist gaze and document what happens when a body of knowledge creates epistemological distance from canonical narratives of disability. Where does DisCrit take us when inquiries push to the epistemological edges of canonical narratives? (Bhabha, 1988).

Annamma, Ferri, and Connor invited contributors to document inquiries grounded in DisCrit as well as record *reverberations* and *ruptures* stemming from this work. *Reverberations* (or what the editors describe as outward inquiries) are concerned with the repercussions of this framework across topics and areas of study; the goal is to trace the continuing effects of these ideas. This volume reveals reverberations in the study of identities in the contexts of activism and collective resistance (Banks et al., ch. 6), applications to American law (Morgan, ch. 1), and the need to free schools from police presence (Payne-Tsoupros & Johnson, ch. 7). Contributors also examine disability intersections with race and gender (Miller et al., ch. 3), language and migration status (Migliarini et al., ch. 4; Phuong & Cioè-Peña, ch. 8), levels in the education system (higher education) (Shallish et al., ch. 2), and disability classifications (deaf, students with significant support needs) (Clark et al., ch. 10).

This volume is also designed to take up what the editors describe as *ruptures*, which signal breaks or disturbances of harmonious conditions. Annamma and colleagues are interested in inward (essential questions of ourselves) and margin-to-margin (driven by questions that look sideways—across differences and divides) inquiries. The contributing authors instill reflexivity in DisCrit's narrative by asking compelling questions about the usefulness of the framework in the Global South (Sarkar et al., ch. 5), juxtaposing it with scholarship from the Latinx Global South (Padilla, ch. 9) or challenging scholars to ground their work in community knowledges (Banks et al., ch. 6). Moreover, authors point out areas in need of further analyses, missing parts, and silences in the DisCrit community. These contributions put in conversation CRT's idea of whiteness as property (Harris, 1993), denounce the invisibility of race in the education of learners with "severe disabilities" (Clark et al., ch. 10), and suggest crossfertilizations with decolonial ideas.

Inquiries, reverberations, and ruptures are essential nourishments for the maturity of all theoretical perspectives and scholarly communities. The work represented in this volume opens opportunities to fashion—following Vygotsky (1978)—a sort of leading activity in the development of DisCrit, an activity that creates optimal conditions for the refinement of the theory in the present, while it sets the foundation for the movement of ideas to the next stage of development. Specifically, a sustained engagement with inquiries, reverberations, and ruptures makes possible the formation of a heteroglossic DisCrit community (Bakhtin, 1981) in which a variety of points of view coexist within an overarching critical language about disability. In turn, DisCrit's representational practices and languages need to continue conversing with other programs of scholarship that also aim to destabilize canonical narratives of disability, such as CRT, DS, and critical cultural historical models—including formative interventions (Artiles, 2003; Bal et al., 2018) and critical studies of disability and inclusive education in the Global South (Grech & Soldatic, 2016; Singal & Muthukrishna, 2014). Cross-pollinations with other representational traditions and languages of disability can forge complementarities and contradictions with DisCrit's knowledge base. In turn, these epistemological spaces can seed the potential for more nuanced interdisciplinary and historically grounded representations of disability, which we so urgently need to expand educational equity scholarship (Artiles, 2019).

I alluded in the opening of this foreword to the unparalleled present moment in the history of the United States. Ibram X. Kendi (2020) declared that American society is "living in the midst of an anti-racist revolution" as a result of being confronted with "the racism still coursing through the country, [as well as] *the reflex to deny that reality*" (Section I, para. 8, emphasis added). I argue that this moment in time demands that scholars generate complementary disability representations to interrupt denials of the inequalities suffered by individuals and communities living in the liminal spaces of marked categories and pave the way for solutions. "Is not the least we owe the sufferings of the past a full and frank accounting of them?" (Smith, 2020, p. 13). DisCrit's project aspires to engage these exigencies.

Scholars enjoy the privilege of access to theories and methodological tools to craft new knowledge. However, we must reflect on the nature of representations we create in our scholarly work, for "[r]epresentations of science . . . have less to do with the cultural realities they supposedly depict, and more to do with the cultural realities they sustain" (Gieryn, 1999, p. xii). This realization imposes an ethical responsibility in our scholarship and calls for new ways in the preparation of the next generation of scholars. It invokes new forms of moral leadership in the academy that should be guided by a long-term vision for a more just society (Walker, 2020). The moral leadership represented in this volume will contribute to a pressing educational equity project in this beleaguered point in history.

—*Alfredo J. Artiles*

REFERENCES

Artiles, A. J. (2003). Special education's changing identity: Paradoxes and dilemmas in views of culture and space. *Harvard Educational Review, 73*(2), 164–202.

Artiles, A. J. (2004). The end of innocence: Historiography and representation in the discursive practice of learning disabilities. *Journal of Learning Disabilities, 37*(6), 550–555.

Artiles, A. J. (2011). Toward an interdisciplinary understanding of educational equity and difference: The case of the racialization of ability. *Educational Researcher, 40*(9), 431–445.

Artiles, A. J. (2019). Reenvisioning equity research: Disability identification disparities as a case in point. *Educational Researcher, 48*(6), 325–335.

Bakhtin, M. (1981). *The dialogical imagination: Four essays*. University of Texas Press.

Bal, A., Afacan, K., & Cakir, H. I. (2018). Culturally responsive school discipline: Implementing learning lab at a high school for systemic transformation. *American Educational Research Journal, 55*(5), 1007–1050.

Bhabha, H. K. (1988). The commitment to theory. *New Formations, 5*(1), 5–23.

Bhabha, H. K., & Stierstorfer, K. (2015). Diaspora and home: An interview with Homi K. Bhabha. In F. Kläger & K. Stierstorfer (Eds.), *Diasporic constructions of home and belonging* (pp. 11–20). De Gruyter.

Connor, D. J., Ferri, B. A., & Annamma, S. A. (2021). From the personal to the global: Engaging with and enacting discrit theory across multiple spaces. *Race Ethnicity and Education, 24*(5), 597–606. doi: 10.1080/13613324.2021.1918400

Connor, D. J., Gallagher, D., & Ferri, B. A. (2011). Broadening our horizons: Toward a plurality of methodologies in learning disability research. *Learning Disability Quarterly*, *34*(2), 107–121.

Crenshaw, K. (1989). Demarginalizing the intersection of race and sex: A Black feminist critique of antidiscrimination doctrine, feminist theory, and antiracist politics. *University of Chicago Legal Forum*, *1989*(10), 139–167.

Donovan, M. S., & Cross, C. T. (Eds.). (2002). *Minority students in special and gifted education*. National Academy Press.

Erevelles, N. (2011). *Disability and difference in global contexts: Enabling a transformative body politic*. Palgrave Macmillan. http://dx.doi.org/10.1057/9781137001184

Geman, D., & Geman, S. (2016). Opinion: Science in the age of selfies. *Proceedings of the National Academy of Sciences*, *113*(34), 9384–9387.

Gieryn, T. F. (1999). *Cultural boundaries of science: Credibility on the line*. University of Chicago Press.

Goodman, D. J. (2003). Introduction: Narratives, geistesgeschichtes, and the history of social history. In G. Ritzer (Ed.), *The Blackwell companion to major classical social theorists* (pp. 1–12). Blackwell.

Gotanda, N. (2004). Reflections on Korematsu, brown, and white innocence. *Temple Political and Civil Rights Law Review*, *13*, 663–674.

Graeber, D., & da Col, G. (2011). The return of ethnographic theory. *HAU: Journal of Ethnographic Theory*, *1*(1), vi–xxxv.

Grech, S., & Soldatic, K. (Eds.). (2016). *Disability in the Global South: The critical handbook*. Springer.

Gutierrez, K. D. (2008). Developing a sociocritical literacy in the third space. *Reading Research Quarterly*, *43*(2), 148–164.

Hall, S. (1990). Cultural identity and diaspora. In J. Rutherford (Ed.), *Identity, community, culture, difference*. Lawrence & Wishart.

Hall, S. (1995). New ethnicities. In B. Ashcroft, G. Griffiths, & H. Tiffin (Eds.), *The post-colonial studies reader* (pp. 223–227). Routledge.

Harris, C. I. (1993). Whiteness as property. *Harvard Law Review*, *106*(8), 1707–1791.

Kendi, I. X. (2020, September). The end of denial. *The Atlantic*. https://www.theatlantic.com/magazine/archive/2020/09/the-end-of-denial/614194/

Lawrence, P. A. (2007). The mismeasurement of science. *Current Biology*, *17*(15), 583–585.

Levine, D. N., & Nathan, L. D. (1995). *Visions of the sociological tradition*. University of Chicago Press.

Rorty, R. (1984). The historiography of philosophy: Four genres. In R. Rorty, J. B. Schneewind, & Q. Skinner (Eds.), *Philosophy in history: Essays on the historiography of philosophy* (pp. 49–75). Cambridge University Press.

Ross, T. (1990). The rhetorical tapestry of race: White innocence and black abstraction. *William & Mary Law Review*, *32*(1), 1–40

Singal, N., & Muthukrishna, N. (2014). Education, childhood and disability in countries of the South: Re-positioning the debates. *Childhood*, *21*(3), 293–307.

Skiba, R. J., Artiles, A. J., Kozleski, E. B., Losen, D. J., & Harry, E. G. (2016). Risks and consequences of over-simplifying educational inequities: A response to Morgan et al. (2015). *Educational Researcher*, *45*(3), 221–225.

Smith, Z. (2020, February). What do we want history to do to us? *The New York Review of Books, 67*(3), 10–14.

Stiker, H. J. (2009). *A history of disability.* University of Michigan Press.

Vygotsky, L. S. (1978). *Mind in society.* Harvard University Press.

Walker, D. (2020, October 7). *The imperative of moral leadership.* Ford Foundation Equals Change Blog. https://www.fordfoundation.org/ideas/equals-change-blog/posts/the-imperative-of-moral-leadership/?utm_medium=email&utm_campaign=DW_Annual

Acknowledgments

As editors, we want to share our deepest gratitude to all contributors to this book, authors who pushed themselves and DisCrit to be responsive to the needs of multiply marginalized communities. We thank the scholars who have worked with us in developing DisCrit throughout the years since its inception and recently with other projects, including David Gillborn for his guidance with a special edition of *Race Ethnicity & Education*, Michelle Knight-Manuel for her support of a special edition of *Teachers College Record*, and Alfredo Artiles for including us in the edited *Disability, Culture, and Equity Series* of Teachers College Press, and Elizabeth Kozleski.

From the beginning of my academic career, I (Subini) have been nurtured by some incredible scholars and humans. Janette Klingner was the first to see me in my master's program and tell me that my expertise and voice were needed in the academy, and she kept telling me that throughout. Linda Mizell, Elizbeth Dutro, Reiland Rabka, Kris Gutierrez, Susan Jurow, and many others supported me in developing my theoretical, axiological, and methodological commitments; and those who have ridden hard for DisCrit and me from the jump, including Dave Stovall, Leigh Patel, David Gillborn, Nirmala Erevelles, Zeus Leonardo, Elizabeth Kozleski, Marvin Lynn, Larry Parker, Danny Solorzano, and others have opened doors for me. Scholar family like Maxine McKinney de Royston, Angela Booker, Jamelia Morgan, Darrell Jackson, Ruth Lopez, JaeRan Kim, Josh Childs, Omaris Zamora, Darren Canady, Charlesia McKinney, Rita Kohli, Déana Scipio, Veronica Velez, Carrie Sampson, Greg Prieto, and Betina Hsieh who support me continually. Activist homies like Alice Wong and Vilissa Thompson who inspire me. Colleagues who have welcomed me so completely, including Arnetha Ball, Guadalupe Valdes, Alvin Pearman, Jenny Langer-Osuna, Mike Hines, Ramón Martinez, Farzana Saleem, Antero Garcia, Jonathan Rosa, Adam Banks, and Bryan Brown among others and the doctoral students who have kept learning, teaching, and building, including Sylvia Nygenye, Brian Cabral, Kristen Jackson, Rubén González, Kyalamboka Brown, Alexandros Orphanides, Courtney Wilt, Jennifer Wilmot, Brianna Harvey, Neida Ahmad and Annie Le. Also thanking the incarcerated and formerly incarcerated youth I collaborate with at the Walkout! Lab for Youth Justice. Finally, I want to thank David Connor and Beth Ferri. The further I get in this academic game, the more I realize how rare our collaboration really is and that what we have built together is better than anything we could have done individually.

I (Beth) also want to acknowledge with gratitude our many collaborators and contributors (past and present), the rich legacy of scholars who informed (and are informing) DisCrit, as well as the gift of this collaboration with David and Subini, which has been both generative and transformative.

I (David) want to thank my family for their ongoing support and encouragement, and finally—last but not least—my collaborators on this book.

DisCrit Expanded

Reflecting on DisCrit

Subini Annamma, Beth A. Ferri, & David Connor

In September 2020, as we prepared this book for submission, a whistle-blower complaint was filed concerning, "the rate at which hysterectomies are performed on immigrant women under ICE custody" (Project South, 2020, p. 2). Many, including lawmakers and the Mexican government, have called for or begun investigations of these forced and coerced sterilizations (Jayapal et al., 2020; Ducey, 2020; Klar, 2020). What quickly became clear was the fact that multiple women and others who can become pregnant,[1] a majority who were Black and Latinx immigrants, were undergoing forced or coerced hysterectomies in U.S. Immigration and Customs Enforcement (ICE) detention. Those "who say they underwent or were pressured to undergo unnecessary treatments has risen to 57," though the number may be much higher given that access to detainees has been limited by ICE (Washington & Olivares, 2020). According to the complaint, many of the detained immigrant women and others who can become pregnant did not know what procedures they were going in for and did not know until later they had been part of this eugenicist project (Project South, 2020).

This most recent use of forced or coerced sterilization is part of a long legacy of reproductive violence in policies and practices that was explicitly directed at Black and Indigenous Women and others of Color who can become pregnant. In California between 1997–2013, almost 1,400 women, again mainly Black and Latinx, were forcefully sterilized in prisons (McKay, 2020). Through the 1960s and 1970s, it is estimated that up to 25% of all Indigenous girls and women between the ages of 15–44 were sterilized, many coerced or without their knowledge (Lawrence, 2000). From the 1930s to the 1970s, one-third of Puerto Rican women were sterilized (Andrews, 2017). Latinx women were also targeted for sterilizations in Los Angeles during the 1960s and 1970s (ibid). Forced sterilization rates rose along with desegregation when Black women became specific targets. From 1937 to 1966, large numbers of Black women were forcibly sterilized in North Carolina, with dramatic increases coinciding with desegregation orders (Minna Stern, 2020). Forced sterilizations became so common that Fannie Lou Hamer, who had been forcibly sterilized herself, publicly shared her own experiences with and fought against what she coined the Mississippi appendectomy (Hamer, 1964). Connecting the emergence of forced hysterectomies at ICE facilities with a longer historical context of targeting Black, Indigenous, and Women of Color, and others who can become pregnant—many who were also disabled[2]—for state violence in the form of forced and coerced sterilizations reveals the long-standing reverberations of eugenic-based violence.

DisCrit was created to address the connections between racism and ableism, and nowhere are these connections clearer than in eugenicist projects such as forced sterilizations. Rooted in the eugenicist belief that society can wipe out those of lesser intelligence, learning, and behavior by cutting out the possibility of reproducing, these sterilizations are not simply an egregious violation of bodies through state violence, they are also a human rights abuse, stealing babies from their mothers and cutting off futures. As Dorothy Roberts (1999) writes in *Killing the Black Body*,

> I turn to a discussion of eugenics because this way of thinking helped to shape our understanding of reproduction and permeates the promotion of contemporary policies that regulate Black women's childbearing. Racist ideology, in turn, provided fertile soil for eugenic theories to take root and flourish. (p. 98)

Roberts' text clearly lays out how eugenicist thinking relies upon ableism and racism, grounded in the belief that race is located in genetics and that genetics prescribed future capabilities.

Ultimately, the goal of DisCrit was to create a theory that was responsive to the immense inequities occurring in daily life, one that centered those pushed to the margins even in conversations about justice. When we conceptualized DisCrit, we were hoping that critical disability scholars would substantially integrate racism into their analyses while race scholars would do the same with ableism. In 2020, along with the eugenicist projects of forced sterilizations, we experienced a global pandemic whose devastating effects were exacerbated by a governmental response that sacrificed disabled people, old people, incarcerated people, low-income people, many who were multiply marginalized Black people, Indigenous people, and other People of Color. In 2020, we also experienced an onslaught of extrajudicial murders by police and other white vigilantes against Black people—another eugenicist project with a history of targeting multiply marginalized Black people, Indigenous people, and other People of Color. Mentally ill and/or disabled[3] Black men (Walter Wallace Jr., Daniel Prude, Elijah McClain, Miciah Lee, LaQuan McDonald), Black women (Michelle Cusseaux, Natasha McKenna, Tanisha Anderson, Deborah Danner), Black queer, trans and nonbinary people (Kawaski Trawick, Layleen Xtravaganza Cubilette-Polanco, Tony McDade), Indigenous people (Jeanetta Riley, Benjamin Whiteshield, Loreal Tsingine, Paul Castaway), and other People of Color (Magdiel Sanchez,

Christopher Torres, Melissa Ventura, Anthony Nuñez, Freddy Centeno, Daniel Pham, Jazmyne Ha Eng) who have frequently been the victims of police violence. Ultimately, both the pandemic response and the extrajudicial murders are eugenicist projects, illustrating that this ideology continues to animate state-sponsored violence, segregation, and eradication of multiply marginalized people.

What was equally as powerful was the robust resistance that people engaged when faced with seemingly unending and compounding inequities that the pandemic produced and exacerbated and multiple forms of unceasing racial violence (extrajudicial murders, brutality in and outside detention of immigrants, allowing the pandemic to rampage through prisons and nursing homes). Dawn Wooten, the whistleblower who exposed ICE's human rights abuses of forced and coerced sterilization, who is a Black woman nurse, discussed on *Democracy Now* the multiple reasons she came forward about forced hysterectomies and the horrendous conditions in the facility in response to COVID-19.

> You have several detainees that would come up, and they would be symptomatic. But I was told that everybody reads the news, everybody sees the news, they know how to present the symptoms coming across the news. It was inhumane. And it was not justifiably correct. I live by you treat people how you want to be treated. You don't treat people as if they don't exist. And they were ignored. (Goodman, 2020)

Wooten simply could not participate in the inhumane treatment of immigrants who were detained in response to a pandemic. Additionally, in the same interview, Wooten noted her own health conditions played a role.

> I am a mother with an underlying condition. I have underlying conditions. And once the terms came to, "Hey, there's COVID-19 inside of this facility," they were not reporting to the health department. They were not reporting to the CDC. So, there were cases in the beginning that were not accounted for. They were not justified. And I became in fear not just for myself, but for the lives of others that were around me, as well as my children. (Goodman, 2020)

Wooten's resistance was informed by multiple truths, both that the conditions were inhumane and that those conditions put herself and her family at direct risk. Wooten, like Fannie Lou Hamer before her, fought against racism and ableism because it was directly impacting her, *and* she was witnessing the harm to a vulnerable population. Wooten's politic reflects the Combahee River Collective Statement (1977), where the authors state, "Our politics initially sprang from the shared belief that Black women are inherently valuable, that our liberation is a necessity not as an adjunct to somebody else's may because of our need as human persons for autonomy" (p. 2). Her own rights to survival as a Black woman with a chronic health issue requires her own safety be centered in the discussion, because "the personal is political" (Combahee River Collective Statement, 1977, p. 3). Simultaneously, Wooten's protection would have meant the protection of all the immigrants in detention (Combahee River Collective Statement, 1977, p. 4).

The grounding assumption that undergirds Disability Critical Race Theory (DisCrit) is that racism and ableism are mutually constitutive and collusive—always circulating across time and context in interconnected ways. Consequently, DisCrit has been a theory that fundamentally exposes and examines eugenicist projects. Though fewer people currently assess the quality of one's genes to argue for their eradication—though this line of thinking certainly has not been eliminated[4]—in other ways, many have creatively blamed societal and school failure collectively and individually on multiply marginalized Black people, Indigenous people, and other People of Color. A central and defining argument that is central to DisCrit is that deficit thinking about Black people, Indigenous people, and other People of Color is deeply rooted in the mutually constitutive nature of racism and ableism.

Additionally, the power of DisCrit lies in its commitments to centering both the injustices that those from the margins experience *and* the resistance that they engage. DisCrit centers the multiply marginalized, the oppressions they experience, and the ways they resist with savvy and ingenuity. In developing DisCrit, we hoped to highlight stories like Dawn Wooten's, one where those with disabilities and/or chronic health conditions play fundamental roles in fighting against the collusive power of racism and ableism. We sought to refuse the erasure of historical and present-day freedom fighters who are reduced to race or gender and their disability and/or chronic health conditions are ignored. Ultimately, we engaged more substantive conversations that recognized that chronic health conditions were essential parts of the stories of Black, Indigenous, and People of Color. In fact, disability and/or chronic health conditions often shaped and informed their resistance, as it did for Fannie Lou Hamer.

Individually and collectively, we three authors and co-editors have advanced DisCrit empirically and theoretically in books, chapters, and journal articles. Subini's work continues to focus on Black girls (Wilmot et al., 2021) and Girls of Color in public schools and youth prisons (Annamma et al., 2020), tracing their education trajectories and experiences with debilitating practices, highlighting the ways they resist structural hegemony, and reconceptualizing justice (Annamma & Handy, 2021). Beth's recent work has begun to incorporate critical spatial analyses as well as archival research to look at the long-standing effects of redlining and white supremacy on disabled students of color in urban schools (Ashby et al., 2020; White et al., 2019). David's work has focused upon critiquing the field of special education's denial of overrepresentation of children and youth of color in soft disability categories and restrictive placements (Cavendish et al., 2020) and its highly problematic color evasiveness (Connor et al., 2019), as well as the value of intersectionality in social justice pedagogy across the curriculum (Connor & Gabel, 2010; Connor, in review), yet what has been most powerful to witness is how DisCrit has been engaged, expanded, and evolved by others taking up the tenets of DisCrit in their own work.

In a recent critical literature review, we found DisCrit had traversed a myriad of spaces, crossing disciplinary boundaries and geographic borders (Gillborn et al., 2016; Migliarini, 2018). DisCrit's intellectual lineage[5] is one that temporally reaches back to Anna Julia Cooper (1892) and W.E.B. DuBois (1920) to work explicitly examining multiple oppressions (Combahee River Collective, 1977; Lorde, 1984; Anzaldúa, 1987) to more recent work manifestly questioning the connections between racism and ableism (Artiles, 2013; Leonardo & Broderick, 2011) and forward into the present. Recently, scholars have used DisCrit to critically analyze how instruction and labels impact emergent bilinguals labeled as disabled (Cioè-Peña, 2021; Phuong, 2019); how Positive Behavioral Intervention and Supports (PBIS) reifies racism and ableism (Adams, 2015); how students of color understand multiple identities and negotiate a myriad of oppressions (Iqtadar et al., 2020); how teacher education relies on conceptions of whiteness and ability for white teachers (Beneke, 2021); how teachers of color understand disability, race, and culture (Kulkarni, 2015); how disabled Scholars of Color experience the academy (Cannon, 2019); how school turnaround can employ narratives of racism and ableism (Pazey, 2020); how education leadership can address racism and ableism in practice (DeMatthews, 2020); how disabled medical students reveal their disability strategically during their education (Jain, 2020); how a disabled Latina experiences and resists white supremacy and ableism during the pandemic (Torres, 2021), and more. Beyond traditional academic spaces, DisCrit has been taken up through poetry (Atakpa, 2018) and in a play tracing the lives of incarcerated Black girls (Canady, 2018). In tracing these engagements, we are struck by the ways DisCrit has been expanded upon and used as a jumping off point for further creative articulations. The dynamic landscape of scholarship taking up DisCrit reflects its role in fostering a transgressive space that has generated critical questions looking outward, inward, and across differences and divides.

This second volume of DisCrit begins with a foreword by Alfredo Artiles, one of DisCrit's intellectual forebearers, who describes the power, path forward, and cautions as DisCrit becomes more firmly established. Artiles's words are a necessary launching point, as DisCrit would not exist without his work that broke ground for our own conceptualizations and the way he encourages us to proceed with both courage and contemplation. In subsequent chapters, authors expand and engage DisCrit to address a myriad of issues, contexts, and concerns. Each contributor responded to our call seeking reverberations (where authors trace the ways DisCrit has been taken up and how this work echoes along lines of temporalities, shaking what we know and building new knowledges), ruptures (where writers build knowledge by diving into the fault lines of tension within DisCrit through asking questions of the theory, themselves, and society to create something more generative), and inquiries (where contributors dialogue across divides by speaking to and through rigorous engagements of DisCrit as a theoretical and/or analytical tool). We purposefully drew from a range of authors who were at different points in their careers, who claimed different positionalities, and engaged with different types of methods and analysis. The result is what you hold in your hand, a carefully curated project of robust engagements with DisCrit across disciplines, geographies, and temporalities.

Witnessing how DisCrit has been taken up over the last seven years has been remarkable. We are humbled. We are thrilled. We are cautious. We continue to encourage scholars and practitioners to engage both racism and ableism as interdependent and build their understandings of inequities and justice from that theoretical grounding. When one does that, the result is what is in the book, chapters filled with clarity around how racism and ableism circulate across spaces, temporalities, and disciplines. We invite you to conversate with these brilliant authors who we were honored to work with and learn from in the process of creating this book. Ultimately, we hope you find within these pages both clarity around what we are fighting against and what we are fighting for, and that anyone who uses DisCrit does so in order to dismantle the eugenicist projects of racism and ableism and move towards abolition. That is what theory is all about and what DisCrit was created to do—name inequities more precisely and build resistance individually and collectively, so that we can move toward more generative futures.

—Subini, Beth, & David

NOTES

1. We use the term women and others who can become pregnant to recognize that not everyone with a uterus identifies as a woman and that reproductive justice directly is about protecting everyone, including nonbinary and transgender people. When citing literature, we use the language of the literature but acknowledge that data collection has historically been limited to binary notions of gender identity.

2. There were many white disabled women who were also forcibly sterilized in American history. Disabled women of all races—and particularly those who were poor, those who got STIs or who got pregnant—were forcibly sterilized with impunity in congregant settings. Often, these sterilizations were a precondition for their release because eugenics was rooted in the commitments to target those unworthy of reproduction. In this chapter, our focus is on the ways racism and ableism intersect with other oppressions, such as misoynoir and sexism. To read more about forced sterilizations of disabled white women, see Lombardo (2008) and Burch & Joyner (2007).

3. We draw from Annamma & Morrison (2018) who listen to the disability community to use identity-first language, "Using disabled students instead of students with disabilities is a purposeful language choice . . . which many in the disability community have repeatedly called . . . if we imagine disability as a political identity with immense possibilities, instead of a deficit, then we do not need to say, "person with a disability" (p. 13). Consequently, we used disabled as an identity marker.

4. See, for example, "The Last Children of Down Syndrome" in *The Atlantic*, with the subtitle of: Prenatal testing is changing who gets born and who doesn't. This is just the beginning. https://www.theatlantic.com/magazine/archive/2020/12/the-last-children-of-down-syndrome/616928/

5. We will never have enough room to note all of the voices that contributed to our conceptualization around DisCrit. Similar to the first book, this introduction continues our truncated genealogy of DisCrit.

REFERENCES

Adams, D. (2015). *Implementation of school-wide positive behavior supports in the neoliberal context in an urban elementary school* (Doctoral dissertation, Syracuse University). https://surface.syr.edu/etd/300/

Andrews, K. (2017, October 30). *The dark history of forced sterilization of Latina women.* Panoramas. https://www.panoramas.pitt.edu/health-and-society/dark-history-forced-sterilization-latina-women

Annamma, S. & Morrison, D. (2018). DisCrit classroom ecology: Using praxis to dismantle dysfunctional education ecologies. *Teaching and Teacher Education*, 73(1), 70–80.

Annamma, S., Handy, T., Miller, A. L., & Jackson, E. (2020). Animating discipline disparities through debilitating practices: Girls of color and inequitable classroom interactions. *Teachers College Record*, 122(5), 1–46. https://www-tcrecord-org.stanford.idm.oclc.org/library

Annamma, S. A. & Handy, T. (2021). Sharpening justice through DisCrit: A contrapuntal analysis of justice. *Educational Researcher*, 50(1), 41–50 https://doi.org/10.3102/0013189X20953838

Anzaldúa, G. (1987). *Borderlands/la frontera: The new mestiza.* Aunt Lute Books.

Artiles, A. J. (2013). Untangling the racialization of disabilities: An intersectionality critique across disability models. *Du Bois Review: Social Science Research on Race*, 10(2), 329–347.

Ashby, C., White, J. M., Ferri, B., Li, S., & Ashby, L. (2020). Enclaves of privilege: Access and opportunity for students with disabilities in urban K-8 schools. *History of Education Quarterly*, 60(3), 407–429.

Atakpa, R. (2018). *Their eyes were watching.* https://spencerart.ku.edu/sites/default/files/rachel%20atakpa.pdf

Beneke, M. R. (2021). Mapping socio-spatial constructions of normalcy: whiteness and ability in teacher candidates' educational trajectories. *Whiteness and Education*, 6(1), 92–113.

Canady, D. (2018). *Black butterflies.* https://news.ku.edu/2018/02/15/book-explores-how-girls-color-disabilities-are-criminalized-form-ecology-resistance

Cannon, M. A. (2019). *Because I am human: Centering Black women with dis/abilities in transition planning from high school to college.* [Doctoral dissertation, Indiana University-Purdue University Indianapolis]. ProQuest Dissertatios and Thesis Global.

Cavendish, W., Connor, D., Gonzalez, T., Jean-Pierre, P., & Card, K. (2020). Troubling "the Problem" of racial overrepresentation in special education: A commentary to call to rethink research. *Educational Review, 72*(5), 567–582.

Cioè-Peña, M. (2021). Raciolinguistics and the education of emergent bilinguals labeled as disabled. *The Urban Review, 53*(3), 443–469.

Combahee River Collective. (1977). "A Black feminist statement." In B. Guy-Sheftall (Ed.), *Words of fire: An anthology of African American feminist thought* (1995 pp. 232–40). New Press.

Connor, D. J. (in review). Revamping a graduate course to (in)fuse disability studies: The politics of representation in "The study of learning disabilities in children and adolescents." *Journal of Teaching Disability Studies.*

Connor, D. J. & Gabel, S. L. (2010). Welcoming the unwelcome: Disability as diversity. In N. Hobbel & T. Chapman (Eds.), (2nd ed.) *Social justice pedagogy in the United States: The practice of freedom* (pp. 217–238). Routledge.

Connor, D., Cavendish, W., Gonzalez, T., & Jean-Pierre, P. (2019). Is a bridge even possible over troubled waters? The field of special education negates the overrepresentation of minority students: A DisCrit analysis. *Journal of Race, Ethnicity & Education, 22*(6), 723–745.

Cooper, A. J. (1892/2000). Woman vs. Indian. In C. Lemert, & E. Bhan (Eds.), *The voice of Anna Julia Cooper: Including a voice from the South and other important essays, papers, and letters* (pp. 88–108). Rowman & Littlefield Publishers.

DeMatthews, D. (2020). Addressing racism and ableism in schools: A DisCrit leadership framework for principals. *The Clearing House: A Journal of Educational Strategies, Issues and Ideas, 93*(1), 27–34.

DuBois, W. E. B. (1920). The souls of white folk. In *Darkwater: Voices from within the veil.* Courier Corporation.

Ducey, K. (2020, September 23). *ICE whistleblower: Mexico investigating US immigrant 'sterilisations.'* BBC. https://www.bbc.com/news/world-latin-america-54265571

Gillborn, D., Rollock, N., Vincent, C., & Ball, S. (2016). The black middle classes, education, racism, and dis/ability: An intersectional analysis. In D. Connor, B. Ferri, & S. A. Annamma (Eds.), *DisCrit: Critical conversations across race, class, & dis/ability* (pp. 35–54). Teachers College Press.

Goodman, A. (September 22, 2020). *Whistleblower Nurse in ICE Jail Alleges Forced Sterilization & Neglect Amid 8th COVID Death.* Democracy Now. https://www.democracynow.org/2020/9/22/dawn_wooten_ice_forced_sterilization

Hamer, F. L. (1964). Testimony before a select panel on Mississippi and Civil Rights, Washington D.C. June 8, 1964. In M. P. Brooks & D. W. Houck (Eds.), *The speeches of Fannie Lou Hamer: To tell it like it is* (2011). University Press of Mississippi.

Iqtadar, S., Hernández-Saca, D. I., & Ellison, S. (2020). "If it wasn't my race, it was other things like being a woman, or my disability": A qualitative research synthesis of disability research. *Disability Studies Quarterly, 40*(2).

Klar, R. (2020, September 15). *Democratic lawmakers call for an investigation into allegations of medical neglect at Georgia ICE facility.* The Hill. https://thehill .com/homenews/house/516567-democratic-lawmakers-call-for-an-investigation -into-allegations-of-medical

Kulkarni, S. S. (2015). *Beliefs about disability, race, and culture of urban special education teachers and their retention decisions.* [Doctoral dissertation, The University of Wisconsin-Madison]. ProQuest Dissertations and Theses Global.

Jain, N. R. (2020). Political disclosure: resisting ableism in medical education. *Disability & Society, 35*(3), 389–412.

Jayapal et al. (2020). *Letter from Pramila Jayapal et al., 168 members of Congress to Joseph V. Cuffari Inspector General Department of Homeland Security.* Congress of the United States. http://jayapal.house.gov/wp-content/uploads /2020/09/DHS-IG-Letter-9.15.pdf

Lawrence, J. (2000). The Indian health service and the sterilization of Native American women. *American Indian Quarterly, 24*(3), 400–419.

Leonardo, Z., & Broderick, A. (2011). Smartness as property: A critical exploration of intersections between whiteness and disability studies. *Teachers College Record, 113*(10), 2206–2232.

Lorde, A. (1984). *Sister outsider: Essays and speeches.* Crossing Press.

McKay, H. (2020, June 15). *New documentary highlights the forced sterilization of women in California prison.* Fox News. https://www.foxnews.com /entertainment/new-documentary-illuminates-the-forced-sterilization-of -women-in-california-prison

Migliarini, V. (2018). 'Colour-evasiveness' and racism without race: the disablement of asylum-seeking children at the edge of fortress Europe. *Race Ethnicity and Education, 21*(4), 438–457.

Minna Stern, A. (2020, August 26). *Forced sterilization policies in the US targeted minorities and those with disabilities—and lasted into the 21st century.* The Conversation. https://theconversation.com/forced-sterilization-policies-in-the-us-targeted -minorities-and-those-with-disabilities-and-lasted-into-the-21st-century-143144

Pazey, B. L. (2020). ¡Ya basta! Countering the effects of neoliberal reform on an urban turnaround high school. *American Educational Research Journal, 57*(4), 1868–1906.

Phuong, J. (2019). What is normal in educational linguistics? *Working Papers in Educational Linguistics (WPEL), 34*(1), 7.

Project South. (2020). *Whistleblower complaint: Lack of medical care, unsafe work practices, and absence of adequate protection against COVID-19 for detained immigrants and employees alike at the Irwin County Detention Center.* Project South. https://projectsouth.org/wp-content/uploads/2020/09/OIG-ICDC-Complaint -1.pdf

Roberts, D. (1997). *Killing the black body: Race, reproduction, and the meaning of liberty.* Pantheon.

Torres, L. E. (2021). Straddling death and (re)birth: A disabled Latina's meditation on collective care and mending in pandemic times. *Qualitative Inquiry, 27*(7), 895–904.

Washington, J., & Olivares, J. (2020, October 27). *Number of women alleging misconduct by ICE gynecologist nearly triples.* The Intercept. https://theintercept .com/2020/10/27/ice-irwin-women-hysterectomies-senate/

White, J. M., Ferri, B., Ashby, C. E., Bern, P. H., & Ashby, L. (2020). Mapping access and opportunity for students with disabilities: Urban K-8 schools as pockets of privilege. *The Educational Forum*, 84(4), 356–376.

White, J. M., Li, S., Ashby, C. E., Ferri, B., Wang, Q., Bern, P., & Cosier, M. (2019). Same as it ever was: The nexus of race, ability, and place in one urban school district. *Educational Studies*, 55(4), 453–472.

Wilmot, J. M., Migliarini, V., & Annamma, S.A. (2021). Policy as punishment and distraction: The double helix of racialized sexual harassment of Black girls. *Educational Policy*, 35(2), 347–367. https://journals.sagepub.com/doi/full/10.1177/0895904820984467

Part I

OUTWARD INQUIRIES

CHAPTER 1

Toward a DisCrit Approach to American Law

Jamelia N. Morgan

In their groundbreaking article, "Dis/ability Critical Race Studies (DisCrit): Theorizing at the Intersections of Race and Dis/ability" (2013), Subini Ancy Annamma and colleagues ask, "How might DisCrit further expand our knowledge (or understanding) of race and dis/ability?" I take up this question and offer a set of responses geared toward the field of American law. Given the ongoing discrimination, marginalization, and violence against disabled people of color, and the inability of existing federal disability laws, policies, and practices to fully protect against these harms or adequately remedy them, I argue that it is time for a DisCrit approach to American law.

It has been over 30 years since Congress passed the Americans with Disabilities Act (ADA). The passage of the ADA was a testament to the determination, organizing, and mobilization of members of the disability rights movement. This movement for access, inclusion, and equal rights for all disabled people[1] traces its origins to the independent living movements that started in Berkeley, California, Section 504 protests that pushed for the government to enact regulations implementing that section of the Rehabilitation Act of 1973. In the 1980s, American Disabled for Attendant Programs Today (ADAPT) led protests that pressed for transportation access (Kendall, 2015; Pangrazio, 2020; Shapiro, 1994). The movement is also attributable to countless other direct actions that catalyzed the political will that eventually led to the passage of the ADA (Kendall, 2015; Pangrazio, 2020; Shapiro, 1994). By enacting the ADA, Congress expressed a firm commitment "to provide a clear and comprehensive national mandate for the elimination of discrimination against individuals with disabilities," and "to provide clear, strong, consistent, enforceable standards addressing discrimination against individuals with disabilities" (42 U.S.C. § 12101).

The backlash to the ADA came almost immediately (Krieger, 2010), aided in part by a string of Supreme Court decisions that narrowed the definition of disability, limiting protections and remedies for disabled people (*G. Albertsons, Inc. v. Kirkingburg*, 1999; *Murphy v. United Parcel Service*,

1999; *Sutton v. United Airlines*, 1995). There were some victories in the same period; the Supreme Court's 1999 *Olmstead* decision, which held that unjustified institutionalization amounted to discrimination under the act, and the amendments to the ADA in 2008 that broadened the definition of disability are two of the most significant ones during the first 20 years of the Act's existence (*Olmstead v. L.C.*, 1999). Under the Obama administration, the Department of Justice ramped up enforcement of federal disability rights laws, which signaled a firm commitment on the part of the executive branch to protecting the rights of disabled people, yet in recent years, once again the ADA is under attack, along with important protections for disabled people under the Affordable Care Act (Arnold & Jansen, 2019). Most recently, the ongoing COVID-19 crisis has revealed yet another example of just how unprotected disabled people are, whether they are held in nursing homes and group homes, or whether they are living in states that have adopted rationing systems that label disabled people as low priority for certain life-saving treatments and therapies like ventilators (Alabama Disabilities Advocacy Program, 2020; Mizner, 2020). Ultimately, though there have been tremendous gains made in the protection of civil rights for disabled people, the passage of the ADA has not led to dramatic changes to the material conditions that impact the daily lives of disabled people.

An intersectional approach to and examination of disability law reveals how the ADA, despite its broad protections, leaves disabled people of color in particular underprotected. The nationwide housing crisis has rendered disabled people homeless—a large percentage of whom are Black—leaving them to fend for food and shelter in public spaces that are highly policed. Generations of divestment in mental health funding in communities has contributed not only to conditions of poverty but also homelessness and an increased reliance on law enforcement as components of mental health responses, whether emergency or civil commitment orders, responding to individuals in mental crisis. Cities and localities continue to pursue aggressive policing strategies, whether through zero tolerance, broken windows, or quality-of-life policing strategies that target disabled people of color in public spaces. These systematic divestments from community mental health care, housing and social benefits programs, along with aggressive policing strategies have led to the twin problems of overpolicing and overcriminalization, which have, in turn, led to high rates of disability in local jails and state and federal prisons (Bronson et al., 2015). For whatever gains have been made, it is clear to see that equal access, social inclusion, and freedom from discrimination are not rights guaranteed to all disabled people, particularly multiply marginalized disabled people of color.

Underinclusive approaches to disability, or laws, policies, and practices that lack an intersectional lens, may not protect the rights of all disabled people. For example, proposals that seek to set up databases that track disabled people within a particular police precinct may render vulnerable Black and trans disabled people even more vulnerable to police surveillance, harassment, and even violence. Jurisdictions that rely on state criminal laws, municipal ordinances, and the ADA to police public space can put unsheltered disabled people at risk of criminalization, even if one of the stated goals is to keep sidewalks clear for wheelchair users. What can the law do to protect multiply marginalized disabled people of color? Are there existing methodologies within legal scholarship that can more adequately protect those situated at the intersection of multiple axes of oppression?

Existing methods within critical legal scholarship are promising but have not yet been able to adequately address the ongoing rights violations and, more broadly, the needs and the vulnerabilities of multiply marginalized disabled people of color. As is discussed, existing silos between critical scholars discussing issues of race and those discussing disability explain part of this inattention. This chasm is being narrowed through promising scholarly engagements with race and disability. However, at present, there is a need for deeper critical inquiry and analysis.

One of the principal contributions of Critical Race Theory (CRT) is the theoretical foundation and the legal and doctrinal support for the notion that race is a social construction and that law constructed racial categories largely through defining and delineating the boundaries between and among white and Black, Indigenous, Latinx, and Asian racial groups (Lopez, 1996). In the process, laws and legal doctrine (hence, legal construction) not only constructed race but worked to uphold white supremacy, in part by assigning advantages and disadvantages based on these racial classifications (*Lum v. Rice*, 1927; *Ozawa v. United States*, 1922; *United States v. Thind*, 1923). CRT scholars have yet to substantively engage with disability as a lens for analysis, although legal scholars have noted potential opportunities for engagement (Asch, 2001; Ribet, 2010).

Similarly, disability law scholars have applied central tenets from disability studies to demonstrate that disability is a social construction and to reject medical and biological models of disability. As Kantor and Ferri (2013) explain, "When disability is defined as a social category rather than as an individual characteristic, it is no longer the exclusive domain of medicine, rehabilitation, special education, physical or occupational therapy, and other professions oriented toward the cure, prevention, or treatment of disease, injury, or physical or mental impairment" (p. 2). In this way, disability studies emphasize that disabled people are not defective persons or victims but, rather, are limited by social and environmental barriers. In a recent essay, legal scholars Doron Dorfman and Rabia Belt write that a social model of disability contrasts with a biological one in that the former focuses not just on "impairment" but the social meanings that attach to impairments (Belt & Dorfman, 2020). The social model of disability affirms a legal scholarship approach to civil rights protections for disabled people that focuses on social barriers and not individual deficiencies (Areheart, 2008; Bagenstos, 2000; Rovner, 2004; Scotch, 2000; Stein, 2004).

The social model of disability is an important critical legal intervention, as medicalized notions of disability tend to operate as a limit to relief for disabled plaintiffs (Schlesinger, 2014). Further, the medical model may be inconsistent with what Congress intended when it passed the ADA in 1990. Consistent with disability studies, legal scholars advancing this position have maintained that the ADA was intended to address the forms of social discrimination that created barriers to inequality, inclusion, and access for disabled people. They have argued that disabled people are a subordinated group—akin to other minority groups on account of disability (Bagenstos, 2000, 2003). As with CRT and issues of disability, within disability legal studies, though a number of prominent disability law scholars apply disability studies in their work, few engage extensively with issues pertaining to race or Critical Race Theory, though here, too, early engagements are a step in the right direction (Ocen, 2010; Perez, 2019; Ribet, 2010). Here also, there is less engagement with how law worked to construct disability in ways that reinforced the subordination of disabled people, and in particular, multiply marginalized disabled Black, Indigenous, and People of Color.

As the foregoing suggests, what has yet to be fully explored is how race and disability were co-constituted, informed, and motivated by the intent not only to uphold racial hierarchy/white supremacy but also to uphold the related racial project of ableism. Lewis (2021) defines ableism as

> a system that places value on people's bodies and minds based on societally constructed ideas of normalcy, intelligence, excellence, and productivity. These constructed ideas are deeply rooted in anti-Blackness, eugenics, colonialism, and capitalism. This form of systemic oppression leads to people and society determining who is valuable and worthy based on a person's appearance and/or their ability to satisfactorily [re]produce, excel and "behave." You do not have to be disabled to experience ableism.

As critical disability scholars have argued, ableism is reinforced by white supremacy, and "notions of dis/ability continually shift over time according to the social context" (Annamma et al., 2013, p. 3). At the same time, disability and race bear an important relationship because disability as a social construction is informed by race. Annamma et al. (2013) write:

> Racism and ableism are normalizing processes that are interconnected and collusive. . . . Racism validates and reinforces ableism, and ableism validates and reinforces racism. . . . Racism and ableism are so enmeshed in the fabric of our social order, they appear both normal and natural to people in this culture. (p. 6)

This chapter further explores the interconnected relationship between racism and ableism.

I argue that Disability Critical Race Theory offers a theoretical framework for understanding how laws function to construct not just racial categories but also construct the definition and boundaries of disability (Annamma et al., 2013). Beyond this, DisCrit provides an analytical tool to examine how law not only co-constructed disability but has contributed to the historic and, I argue, ongoing subordination of Black, Indigenous, and People of Color with disabilities. In the sections that follow, I discuss how some of DisCrit's central tenets offer a basis for critical and intersectional approaches to American law. This project is both exploratory and a call for subsequent engagements. It offers opportunities for future critical projects that engage with race and disability across American legal history and across various sites of American law.

DisCrit's first tenet "focuses on the interdependent ways that racism and ableism shape notions of normalcy." Taken together, DisCrit offers a lens from which to examine the ways in which racism and ableism are "mutually constitutive processes [that] are enacted through normalizing practices . . . [that] reinforce[e] the unmarked norms of whiteness" (Annamma et al., p. 11). Racial ideology provided justifications for legally sanctioned enslavement of Black people and the violent dispossession of Indigenous people from their lands. Ableism also undergirded the profound violence central to the enslavement of Black people. To extract profits, enslavers extracted value from Black bodies—and minds—and assigned value to Black bodies that were assessed and exchanged through market-based transactions. Profits were based on the amount of value that could be derived from the productivity extracted from the forced labor of enslaved Black people. Productivity potential was derived from assessments of the physical health and the vitality of enslaved Blacks as well as mental stability (Boster, 2012; Davis, 1983). Enslaved Black people were literally assigned monetary value in markets based on size, strength, and reproductive capabilities for enslaved women. Disabilities, whether in the form of physical attributions or conditions labeled as illness or defect, not only discounted the value of Black bodies but formed the basis for disputes involving breach of warranty where the buyer alleged that the enslaved person who was purchased was defective (Boster, 2012).

Courts, through judicial opinions in the early years of the American republic, created and assigned property rights to whites in uninhabited lands, while refusing to recognize property interests in land held by Native Americans (Harris, 1993). Scholars of settler colonialism have acknowledged the role of race and its function as part of a broader scheme to violently dispossess Native Americans of their land. As Lytle Hernandez (2017) explains, "settler societies strive to block, erase, or remove racialized outsiders from their claimed territory" (pp. 7–8). Law provided legitimacy to the

appropriation of Indigenous lands while delegitimizing existing property regimes and customary practices. In *Johnson v. M'Intosh*, where the Supreme
Court adopted the doctrine of discovery, rather than recognizing that tribes
had legal entitlement as original owners of the land, the Court simply re-
classified the tribe's property interest from one of owner to one of occupant
(right of occupancy). Underlying the Supreme Court's reasoning was the
notion that Native Americans did not use the land efficiently and should
therefore not be permitted to own the land (*Johnson v. M'Intosh*, 1823).

Ableism also featured in massive dispossession and displacement. As
historian Evelyn Nakano Glenn (2015) argues, white settler property interests structured racial and gender classifications and characterization of
Indigenous and enslaved peoples. With respect to race–gender constructions, as Professor Glenn argues, "masculine whiteness" became central to
settler identity, as status was closely tied to ownership of property and political sovereignty. Heteropatriarchy rendered white manhood supreme with
respect to control over property and self-rule and presumed that "heteropa-
triarchal nuclear-domestic arrangements, in which the [white] father is both
protector and leader should serve as the model for social arrangements of
the state and its institutions" (p. 58). In the view of white settlers, "the fact
that Indian women did heavy physical labor and were ignorant of modern
housekeeping methods accounted for Indian men's laziness and disinterest
in material progress" (p. 57). Although it may not at first glance appear to
reinforce the subordination of disabled people, the construction of Native
American men as lazy is an ableist trope; to designate a body as lazy is to assign meaning to real or perceived productivity. Ableist tropes of Indigenous
people as lazy or ignorant justified violent dispossession and displacement.

These legacies of ableism and racism continue to this day and are acknowledged in legal scholarship. A number of legal scholars have recognized
the law's complicity in upholding race-based subordination in their discussions of the juvenile justice system, school-to-prison pipeline, and enforcement under the Individuals with Disabilities Education Act (Baldwin Clark,
2018; Henning, 2012; Nanda, 2012, 2019). Some, but not all, of these accounts center critical approaches to disability as an analytical lens. DisCrit
offers an approach for examining how normalizing practices are perpetu-
ated by policing practices and enforcement policies that target Black and
Latinx students as disorderly, disruptive, and at risk, warranting additional
criminal sanction. DisCrit may also shed light on why limited acknowledged cultural capital disadvantages Black parents seeking to advocate for
their children's rights under the Individuals with Disabilities Education Act
(IDEA), to draw from the work of Latoya Baldwin Clark (2018).

In my own research on criminal law and enforcement, I have identified
the ways in which criminal laws operate to marginalize disabled people of
color. Examining disorderly conduct laws, I found that courts tend to ignore the ways in which the notion of disorder itself is rooted in racialized,

gendered, and ableist notions of order, which in turn track racialized, gen-dered, and ableist notions of normalcy (Morgan, 2020). Relying on Susan Schweik's (2010) work on the so-called "ugly laws," I discuss how those laws historically targeted not only disabled people with physical disabilities, disfigurement, or so-called deformities but, as Schweik recounts, disabled people of color amid a broader effort to regulate property and labor while criminalizing poverty.

DisCrit's tenet two acknowledges "multidimensional identities," in-stead of "singular notions of identity, such as race, dis/ability, social class, or gender" (Annamma et al., 2013, p. 2). Scholars have argued that the Americans with Disabilities Act is consistent with antidiscrimination law and antisubordination principles (Bagenstos, 2000). These scholars, like critical race scholars, have demonstrated that anticlassification princi-ples pose a threat to robust statutory protections for disabled people—protections that are consistent with Congress's expansive goal of removing historic and ongoing social barriers to equality, access, and inclusion for disabled people (Arehcart, 2011). These scholarly interventions are aimed at protecting the Americans with Disabilities Act to ensure its longevity and ward off rollbacks to its substantive protections. An intersectional ap-proach to disability strengthens these arguments by demonstrating how disability and historically marginalized identities and statutes interact to render some disabled persons even more vulnerable to disability discrimi-nation and how recognizing that acts in favor of strengthening legal protec-tions under the ADA.

There is some engagement with intersectionality in extant disability law scholarship (Morgan, 2019; Perez, 2019). For example, activist and scholar Kat Perez relies on a critical race and disability legal studies approach to immigration law and policy to shed light on the experiences of disabled people of color and center these lived experiences and disability in the im-migration reform debate. As Perez (2019) writes, her work aims to "present the work of the National Coalition for Latinxs with Disabilities (CNLD) as an exemplar of how grassroots disability justice movements are complicat-ing our understanding of disability and proscribing more complex solutions to the immigration debate." As Perez cautions, "progressive immigration reform can only take place when we consider the unique ways in which racism and ableism interact to permeate our immigration system." Further intersectional analysis relying on DisCrit principles can enhance legal and policy reforms and transformative change proposals relating to additional areas of law, such as antidiscrimination law, education law, voting rights, environmental law, and criminal law and punishment, to name a few.

Tenet three "rejects the understanding of both race and dis/ability as primarily biological facts and recognizes the social construction of both as society's response to 'differences' from the norm" (Annamma et al., 2013, p. 12). As noted, disability law scholars have adopted the model of disability as a social construction not rooted in biological traits and conditions or medicalized definitions but rather rooted in societal norms, attitudes, prejudices, and architectural barriers (Schlesinger, 2014). However, there is little engagement with race and how both disability and race were "socially constructed in tandem" (Annamma et al. 2013, p. 13). The lack of engagement with race and disability contributes to the failure to adequately protect disabled people of color who are policed, imprisoned, undocumented, unsheltered, and enduring in conditions of poverty. To illustrate, I'll provide two examples from constitutional law. First, disability as an identity is not centered as a lens in Amendment IV analysis, leaving disabled people of color vulnerable to stops, frisks, arrests, and even detention for disability-related behaviors. By erasing any discussion of race or disability in legal doctrine, the Supreme Court effectively constructs a normative bodymind, "the intertwinement of the mental and the physical" (Schalk, 2018) deserving of constitutional protection against unreasonable searches and seizures. Such constructions are apparent in legal tests that fail to consider whether disability has informed an officer's basis for a stop, or whether an individual with a disability has voluntarily consented to a search. Second, weak protections against the criminalization of status under Amendment VIII can result in individuals with disabilities—particularly those who are low or no income and unsheltered—vulnerable to criminal sanction on account of their disabilities. Amendment VIII protects against cruel and unusual punishment, and in a case called *Robinson v. California*, the Supreme Court held that the amendment protected against what was termed "status-based crimes" (*Robinson v. California*, 1962). Ongoing litigation around constitutional protections against the criminalization of status show federal courts divided on whether conduct inextricably linked to status (here, disability) cannot be criminalized (*Manning v. Caldwell*, 2018; *Martin v. Boise*, 2019). This means that conduct—from public intoxication to sleeping in public to disorderly conduct—linked to disability in some cases does not constitute status-based offenses, and, thus, Amendment VIII offers no protection against punishment for such crimes. Given that Amendment VIII jurisprudence also does not address questions of race (such claims fall under Amendment XIV, and there, plaintiffs face the high burden of intentional discrimination) and does not adequately address issues of disability, without centering race and disability, disabled people of color are again rendered vulnerable to aggressive policing and punishment.

Tenet four "disrupt[s] the tradition of ignoring the voices of traditionally marginalized groups and instead privileges insider voices" (Annamma et al., 2013, p. 13). The notion of outsider jurisprudence as a way to disrupt master narratives and produce counternarratives is rooted in Critical Race Theory and specifically the work of Mari Matsuda (1989). Legal doctrine and the legal profession have historically ignored and continue to ignore the experiences of those most vulnerable to state violence (Crenshaw, 1989). As discussed, legal doctrine contains depictions of disability that are rooted in the medical model of disability, reflect paternalism, and reinforce associations between disability and criminality and other ableist ideologies. For example, Amendment VIII jurisprudence requires advocates to reinforce medicalized notions of disability that center the violence and harms stemming from imprisonment in the bodies and minds of the disabled incarcerated people *rather than* in the systems and the structures that contribute to their disablement. This leads to pleadings, briefs, and legal opinions that reify constructions of disability—particularly psychiatric disabilities—as pathological, tormented, uncontrollable, violent, and deviant.

It goes without saying that the role of the lawyer may at times conflict with the autonomy of a client the attorney is representing. This may lead to clients feeling that they are being silenced by their own counsel. For example, though clients can set the objectives for legal representation, it is the duty of counsel to come up with the appropriate legal strategy. This may mean that clients (e.g., those facing criminal charges or even the death penalty) and their counsel may have conflicts over how to best mount a defense. As argued elsewhere, in cases where the client and the client's counsel differ on whether and how to present disability or disablement as a mitigating condition, clients may feel disempowered, ignored, and marginal in their own case (Morgan, 2019). Again, such disagreements may not be rooted in the intentional misconduct of lawyers but may instead reflect what is required to prevail on particular legal claims. This analysis centers the cause of such disempowerment in the doctrine and not simply the individual prejudices of the attorney.

Finally, existing rules of professional ethics provide little guidance to lawyers looking to adequately represent the interests of disabled clients. To date, the Model Rules of Professional Conduct (MRPC) address disability either as a category of discrimination, which is prohibited, or by reference to clients "with diminished capacity" (American Bar Association, 2020). The MRPC requires that lawyers maintain a normal client–lawyer relationship with clients labeled as having diminished capacity. This attempt to manage and measure the efficacy of legal representation based on what is termed a normal client relationship does not provide adequate protection for disabled people, nor does it require that their voices be included in what law and legal advocates say about their lived experiences as disabled people. It simply requires a normal relationship and by so doing provides no guidance for avoiding paternalism and ableism from seeping into the attorney–client relationship.

DisCrit's tenet five "considers legal, ideological, and historical aspects of dis/ability and race and how both have been used separately and together to deny the rights of certain citizens" (Annamma et al., 2013, p. 14). Eugenics and compulsory sterilization feature prominently in discussions on race and disability in legal scholarship, but few discussions address how both have been deployed to subordinate disabled people and disabled people of color in contemporary times.

White supremacy as a racial project (Omi & Winant, 2015) grounds whiteness as the dominant normative racial identity, accompanied by privileges and entitlements such as those that confer status and legal rights (Harris, 1993). During the period of eugenics when racist pseudoscience was propagated to justify the superiority of the white race, the predominant notion of disability was that disability distorted not only the *normalized* white bodymind, but the *ideal* white bodymind (Bridges, 2019). That is because under the racist logics of eugenics, disability corrupted the *purity* of the white race by introducing mental and physical defects that detracted from eugenicist conceptions of whiteness as physically fit, intelligent, industrious, and moral.

By contrast, negatively racialized groups were positioned as lacking in those desirable and, under common eugenicist conceptions, inheritable traits. Conceptions of Black men as unintelligent or infantile, Native Americans as lazy, and Chinese women as servile and gullible were attempts to construct racial categories and boundaries through physical and mental attributes and group-based stereotypes that distinguished white from non-white. Though historically these conceptions have long existed to dehumanize racial others, the period of eugenics represents a dramatic expansion of state power to regulate *white* bodies (to prevent reproduction or to incapacitate in state institutions) and minds (also through institutionalization) and to prevent the racial mixing that was regarded as a threat to white racial purity. Forced sterilizations, the birth of state mental hospitals, and the proliferation of anti-miscegenation laws demonstrate a coordinated state policy designed to whiten the increasingly racially and ethnically diverse American society.

In *Buck v. Bell*, the Supreme Court decided that the forcible sterilization of Carrie Buck did not deprive her of the right to equal protection and due process under Amendment XIV (*Buck v. Bell*, 1927). Carrie Buck was 17 years old when she was labeled by the state of Virginia as feebleminded and sent to the State Colony for Epileptics and Feebleminded. In 1924, the Colony's superintendent, Dr. Albert Priddy, selected Carrie Buck as the first person to be sterilized pursuant to a Virginia law passed that same year (Cohen, 2016). The law professed that the "health of the patient and the welfare of society may be promoted in certain cases by the sterilization of mental defectives," and permitted sterilization of men and women where the procedure could be safely performed "without serious pain or substantial danger to life" (*Buck v. Bell*, 1927, p. 205). Virginia justified such invasive and drastic action as necessary to protect society from would-be menaces who, if released, would procreate and, consistent with the eugenics logic of the period, transmit such undesirable traits like insanity and imbecility (*Buck v. Bell*, 1927, p. 206).

The eugenics period also marks the height of state-sponsored efforts to localize social problems within *racialized* bodies and minds labeled as defective, ill, insane, disordered, and feeble. Once social problems became linked to defective, ill, insane, disordered, and feeble bodies and minds, those individuals could be more readily managed and controlled pursuant to the state's police power. Once linked with immorality, criminality, and promiscuity, such traits, supported by pseudoscientific evidence, formed legal bases and justification for institutionalization. Once institutionalized, women so labeled were then forcibly sterilized on the grounds that the state had an interest in preventing women from reproducing children with these undesirable traits who were presumed to be public charges or an eventual strain on the public purse.

A DisCrit approach explains why forced sterilization as a practice fell within the ambit of state power. Stated differently, a race-disability lens provides theoretical grounding for examining the pervasiveness of forms of state control over the reproductive capacities of women and in particular low-income Black, Latinx, and Indigenous women. Racialized constructions of gender are also ableist racialized constructions of gender. By constructing Black, Latinx, and Indigenous women as lazy, pathological, and incompetent, state entities could more readily construct legal justifications for laws, policies, and practices that deprived these women of their reproductive and parental rights and criminalize them when they are held in conditions of poverty. A DisCrit approach provides a way to center race, gender, *and* disability in issues relating to reproductive justice, criminalization of poverty, and parental rights.

DisCrit tenet number six draws from the groundbreaking work of Cheryl Harris and her article *Whiteness as Property* (1993) to recognize that "whiteness and Ability" function as "property, conferring economic benefits to those who can claim whiteness and/or normalcy and disadvantages for those who cannot lay claim to these identity statuses" (Annamma et al., 2013, p. 16). Laws enacted and as interpreted by courts historically delineated and defined racial categories for the purposes of designating Black people as enslaved persons and nonwhites as free. Property law, as Harris explains, did not recognize the property rights of Indigenous people. Early legal doctrines designated Native lands as uninhabited and, therefore, open to appropriation by white settlers. Under the Treaty of Guadalupe Hidalgo, following the Mexican American War, Mexican nationals were classified as white and, therefore, eligible for citizenship, but their whiteness was a liminal status, as it did not entitle them to property rights that public and private individuals were bound to respect. Whiteness also conferred the right to exclude those from membership in the nation and thus members of the body politic. In *Ozawa* and *Thind*, the Supreme Court arbitrarily determined that Mr. Ozawa, an American of Japanese ancestry, and Mr. Thind, an immigrant from India, were both nonwhite and thus ineligible for citizenship (*Ozawa v. United States*, 1922; *United States v. Thind*, 1923). When 5-year-old Martha Lum sought to attend public school in segregated Mississippi in the early 1920s, the district court deciding her case held that Chinese Americans were not white and, therefore, not entitled to attend white, segregated schools (*Gong Lum v. Rice*, 1927). Such examples demonstrate how whiteness functions as a type of property right, with courts as its primary agent of administration.

Whiteness as property functions to assign and deny rights and privileges along the axis of disability. Racialized notions of disability and its influence on immigration laws provide a useful example. In the late 19th and early 20th century, as the numbers of immigrants increased, eugenicists allied themselves with other interest groups to provide biological arguments to support immigration restriction (Silber, 1997). During this period, immigration laws reflected a clear objective of keeping disabled people—termed as defectives—out of the country (Baynton, 2005). The law provided that "it shall also be unlawful for any such person to bring to any port of the United States any alien afflicted with any mental defect other than those above specifically named, or physical defect of a nature which may affect his ability to earn a living" (Immigration Act of 1917). The list of those included is long: the deaf, blind, epileptic, and mobility impaired; people with curved spines, hernias, flat or clubfeet, missing limbs, and short limbs; those unusually short or tall; people with intellectual or psychiatric disabilities; intersexuals; men of "poor physique" and men diagnosed with "feminism." The law also provided that "it shall also be unlawful for any such person to bring to any port of the United States any alien who is excluded by the provisions of section 3 of this Act because unable to read. . . ." In statements in support of the Immigration Act of 1924, one representative leading efforts to pass the bill noted: "it has become necessary that the United States cease to become an asylum" (Immigration Act of 1924). Not only were disabled individuals excluded, but particular races and nationalities were also identified as undesirable based on their supposed susceptibility to mental, moral, and physical defects. As Douglas Baynton (2005) notes, "The desire to keep out immigrants deemed defective was not an isolated development, but rather was one aspect of a trend toward the increasing segregation of disabled people into institutions and the sterilization of the 'unfit' and 'degenerate' under state eugenic laws" (p. 32).

Negatively racialized groups were often characterized as desirable immigrants based on their fitness or capacity for manual labor, as these groups filled gaps within the labor market (Glenn, 2015). However, as Professor Natalie Molina (2006) observes, "Because immigrants were considered advantageous only to the extent they filled critical gaps in the labor market, physical fitness was central to gauging a group's desirability." Moreover, when, as demonstrated by the treatment of Chinese immigrants in the late 19th century, when the labor demands subsided, the incidents of violence

rose, as did xenophobia and efforts to restrict Chinese labor from entering the country. These efforts culminated in the passage of the Chinese
Exclusion Act of 1882.

Finally, tenet seven affirms DisCrit's support for "activism and . . .
diverse forms of resistance" (Annamma et al., 2013, p. 17). DisCrit stands
alongside movement-based activism led by and for disabled people of color,
like disability justice. Disability justice provides a framework for developing
multidimensional consciousness. A disability justice approach recognizes
that "able-bodied supremacy has been formed in relation to intersecting
systems of domination and exploitation," and that it is impossible to "comprehend ableism without grasping its interrelations with heteropatriarchy,
white supremacy, colonialism and capitalism, each system co-creating an
ideal bodymind built upon the exclusion and elimination of a subjugated
'other.'" Central to the disability justice framework is the notion that "all
bodies are unique and essential, that all bodies have strengths and needs that
must be met" (Berne, 2015).

CONCLUSION

The future of disability rights law is to move from disability rights (central
to the ADA) to disability justice. As Critical Race theorists have long argued, there are clear limits to formal equality. A DisCrit intervention into
American law can explain why, over 30 years after the passage of the ADA,
with clear exceptions for those with privilege, disabled people remain a
subordinated group within society. It is no surprise that legal protections
against discrimination and legal remedies fail to achieve substantive equality
for historically subordinated groups.

What is interesting about the ADA is that it does not presume that
discrimination is aberrational; it presumes that barriers to inclusion are
pervasive in society and that discrimination is widespread. It confers an
affirmative duty on employers, public entities, and places of public accommodations to accommodate qualified individuals with disabilities. However,
even with that acknowledgment, the ADA still conditions relief on qualification and limits relief available where, for example, such accommodation
poses an undue hardship for employers or fundamentally alters a program,
service, or activity with public entities. It requires that employers, public
entities, and places of public accommodation provide equal access only. It
does not require altering the fundamental social conditions that produced
the inequality in the first place, including, for example, structural barriers to
employment (Bagenstos, 2003). The robust protections and obligations under the ADA are, of course, the product of political compromise, even for a
statute that passed with overwhelming approval. This may necessarily limit
the scope of protections and the remedies available. However, adopting

a DisCrit approach offers a lens through which to both identify potential limits of legal remedies and develop more robust arguments in support of broader coverage, legal protections, and legal remedies.

What would it look like to incorporate DisCrit into American law? As CRT and disability legal studies scholars have long argued, albeit separately, race and disability are social constructions, and laws have been and continue to be used to subordinate disabled people, rendering them vulnerable to ongoing forms of discrimination, exclusion, poverty, houselessness, policing, imprisonment, and premature death. As I have attempted to show, incorporating a DisCrit approach provides opportunities to better ensure legal guarantees under constitutional law and federal disability rights laws for multiply marginalized people of color. Beyond this, DisCrit provides a more complete, robust lens for critical analysis of American law.

Efforts to incorporate a DisCrit approach into American law come with tensions—one related to the issue of recognizing disability and another related to the risk of cooptation. The first is a tension that may or may not be particular to disability, whereas the second is a problem for constitutional and antidiscrimination law more broadly. So much of the work leading up to a legal case involves spotting the right issues and developing evidence to support factual allegations and legal claims. A DisCrit approach to American law is an effective method for critical engagement with issues of race and disability in legal doctrine, law, and policy, but to be truly effective, it also should inform how we empower clients to tell their stories, how lawyers develop legal claims, how courts view race/disability claims, and how policymakers understand disability-based discrimination or even ableism, less recognized in liberal and progressive reform circles, as implicating questions of racial subordination. The second tension raises the possibility that the language of DisCrit may be coopted without substantive engagement with legal remedies that address the twin evils of racism and ableism. As CRT scholars have long argued, the end to de jure segregation marked the rise of the era of so-called formal equality and colorblindness. During this era, civil rights reforms were attacked, framed as divisive or the product of identity politics, or the perpetuator of racial divisions. While seeking to roll back civil rights protections, opponents of civil rights reforms sought to use the language of equality and civil rights, often captured so eloquently in the words of Dr. Martin Luther King Jr., to support their own conservative anti-civil rights agendas. Color-evasiveness dominates constitutional equality jurisprudence to this day. As noted, conservatives have also sought to roll back civil rights protections under the ADA. A DisCrit approach to American law must consider how the theory can be protected from such co-optation—a task that is even more important in this era when the ADA and civil rights protections are under increasing scrutiny.

A DisCrit approach to American law offers a robust methodology that can be used to critique American law for the purposes of strengthening existing legal protections and ending vulnerabilities of multiply marginalized disabled people of color to private, state/structural forms of violence. The seeds of such analysis have been sewn, but more robust engagement and analysis are needed. I have sought to offer possible engagements and sites for further inquiry to spur additional expansions of this robust theoretical framework into additional areas of American law and policy.

NOTE

1. In my discussion of individuals with disabilities, I use identity-first language to refer to disabled people as a group or class (Brown, 2011).

REFERENCES

Alabama Disability Advocacy Program. (2020, March 24). *Complaint of Alabama Disabilities Advocacy Program and The Arc of the United States.* https://adap.ua.edu/uploads/5/7/8/9/57892141/al-ocr-complaint_3.24.20.pdf

Albertson's, Inc. v. Kirkingburg, 527 U.S. 555 (1999).

American Bar Association. (2020). *Model rules of professional conduct.* https://www.americanbar.org/groups/professional_responsibility/publications/model_rules_of_professional_conduct/model_rules_of_professional_conduct_table_of_contents/

Americans with Disabilities Act, 42 U.S.C. § 12101 *et seq.* (1990).

Americans with Disabilities Act Amendments Act of 2008, Publ. L. No. 110-325 (2008). https://www.dol.gov/sites/dolgov/files/OASAM/legacy/files/ADA-1990.pdf

Americans with Disabilities Act of 1990, Publ. L. No. 101-336, 104 Stat. 327 (1990). https://www.ada.gov/pubs/adastatute08.pdfAnnamma, S. A., Connor, D., & Ferri, B. (2013). Dis/ability critical race studies (DisCrit): Theorizing at the intersections of race and dis/ability. *Race Ethnicity and Education, 16*(1), 1–31.

Areheart, B. A. (2008). When disability isn't just right: The entrenchment of the medical model of disability and the Goldilocks dilemma. *Indiana Law Journal, 83*(1), 181–232.

Arnold, J., & Jansen, E. (2019). People with disabilities concerned about possible repeal of Affordable Care Act. WUSA9. https://www.wusa9.com/article/news/people-with-disabilities-concerned-about-possible-repeal-of-affordable-care-act/65-ef052be8-789f-4ecd-94d1-6aa02318e445

Asch, A. (2001). Critical race theory, feminism, and disability: Reflections on social justice and personal identity. *Ohio State Law Journal, 62*, 391–423.

Baldwin Clark, L. (2018). Beyond bias: Cultural capital in anti-discrimination law. *Harvard Civil Rights-Civil Liberties Law Review (CR-CL), 53*, 381–443.

Bagenstos, S. R. (2000). Subordination, stigma, and "disability." *Virginia Law Review, 86*(3), 397–534.

Bagenstos, S. R. (2003). "Rational discrimination," accommodation, and the politics of (disability) civil rights. *Virginia Law Review, 89*(5), 825–923.

Baynton, D. C. (2005). Defectives in the land: Disability and American immigration policy,1882–1924. *Journal of American Ethnic History*, 24(3)2, 31–44.

Belt, R., & Dorfman, D. (2020). Disability, law, and the humanities: The rise of disability legal studies. In S. Stern, M. D. Mar, & B. Meyler (Eds.), *The Oxford handbook of law and humanities*. Oxford University Press.

Berne, P. (2015, June 10). Disability justice—a working draft by Patty Berne. *Sins Invalid*. https://www.sinsinvalid.org/blog/disability-justice-a-working-draft-by -patty-berne

Boster, D. H. (2012). *African American slavery and disability: Bodies, property and power in the antebellum South, 1800–1860*. Routledge.

Bridges, K. M. (2019). White privilege and white disadvantage. *Virginia Law Review*, 105(2), 449–482.

Bronson, J., Maruscak, L. M., & Berzofsky, M. (2015). *Disabilities among prison and jail inmates, 2011–12*. U.S. Department of Justice. https://www.bjs.gov /content/pub/pdf/dpji1112.pdf

Brown, L. (2011). *Identity-first language*. Autistic Self-Advocacy Network. https:// autisticadvocacy.org/about-asan/identity-first-language/

Buck v. Bell, 274 U.S. 200 (1927).

Carmel, J. (2020, July 22). *Before the A.D.A., there was section 504*. New York Times. https://www.nytimes.com/2020/07/22/us/504-sit-in-disability-rights.html

Cohen, A. (2016). *Imbeciles: The Supreme Court, American eugenics, and the sterilization of Carrie Buck*. Penguin Press.

Crenshaw, K. (1989). Demarginalizing the intersection of race and sex: Black feminist critique of antidiscrimination doctrine, feminist theory and antiracist politics. *University of Chicago Legal Forum*, 1989(1), 139–168.

Davis, A. Y. (1983). *Women, race and class*. Knopf Doubleday Publishing Group.

Glenn, E. N. (2015). Settler colonialism as structure: A framework for comparative studies of US race and gender formation. *Sociology of Race and Ethnicity*, 1(1), 52–72.

Gong Lum v. Rice, 275 U.S. 78 (1927).

Harris, C. I. (1993). Whiteness as property. *Harvard Law Review*, 106(8), 1707–1791.

Henning, K. (2012). Criminalizing normal adolescent behavior in communities of color: The role of prosecutors in juvenile justice reform. *Cornell Law Review*, 98(2), 383–461.

Hernandez, K. L. (2017). *City of inmates: Conquest, rebellion, and the rise of human caging in Los Angeles*. University of North Carolina Press.

Immigration Act of 1917, 39 Stat. 874, 64 Cong. Ch. 29 (1917).

Johnson v. M'Intosh, 21 U.S. 543 (1823).

Kantor, A., & Ferri, B. (Eds.). (2013). *Righting educational wrongs: Disability studies in law and education*. Syracuse University Press.

Kendall, J. (2015, July 20). *Independent living: From Berkeley to the ADA to ILA*. ACL Administration for Community Living. https://acl.gov/news-and-events/ acl-blog/independent-living-berkeley-ada-ila

Lewis, T. L. (2021, January 1). *January 2021 working definition of ableism*. Talila A. Lewis. https://www.talilalewis.com/blog/january-2021-working-definition-of -ableism

Lopez, I. H. (1996). *White by law: The legal construction of race* (Vol. 21). New York University Press.

Krieger, L. H. (Ed.). (2010). *Backlash against the ADA: Reinterpreting disability rights*. University of Michigan Press.

Manning v. Caldwell, 900 F.3d 139 (4th Cir. 2018).

Martin v. City of Boise, 920 F.3d 584 (9th Cir. 2019).

Matsuda, M. J. (1989). When the first quail calls: Multiple consciousness as jurisprudential method. *Women's Rights Law Reporter*, *11*(1), 7–10.

Mizner, S. (2020, June 23). *COVID-19 deaths in nursing homes are not unavoidable — they are the result of deadly discrimination*. ACLU. https://www.aclu.org/news /disability-rights/covid-19-deaths-in-nursing-homes-are-not-unavoidable-they -are-the-result-of-deadly-discrimination/

Molina, N. (2006). Medicalizing the Mexican: Immigration, race, and disability in the early-twentieth-century United States. *Radical History Review*, *2006*(94), 22–37.

Morgan, J. (2019). Reflections on representing incarcerated people with disabilities: Ableism in prison reform litigation. *Denver Law Review, 96*(4), 973–991.

Morgan, J. (2020). Rethinking disorderly conduct. *California Law Review*, Forthcoming.

Murphy v. United Parcel Service, 527 U.S. 516 (1999).

Nanda, J. (2012). Blind discretion: Girls of color & delinquency in the juvenile justice system. *UCLA Law Review*, *59*, 1502–1520.

Nanda, J. (2019). The construction and criminalization of disability in school incarceration. *UCLA Law Review*, *9*(2), 265–321.

Ocen, P. A. (2010). Beyond analogy: A response to surfacing disability through critical race theoretical paradigm. *Georgetown Journal of Law & Modern Critical Race Perspectives, 2*(2), 255–256.

Olmstead v. L.C., 527 U.S. 581 (1999).

Omi, M., & Winant, H. (2015). *Racial formation in the United States*. Routledge.

Ozawa v. United States, 260 U.S. 178 (1922).

Pangrazio, P. (2020, June 1). *A brief history of disability rights and the ADA*. Ability360. https://ability360.org/livability/advocacy-livability/history-disability-rights -ada/

Perez, K. (2019, February 9), *A critical race and disability legal studies approach to immigration law and policy*. UCLA Law Review. https://www.uclalawreview .org/a-critical-race-and-disability-legal-studies-approach-to-immigration-law -and-policy/

Ribet, B. (2010). Surfacing disability through critical race theoretical paradigm. *Georgetown Journal of Law & Modern Critical Race Perspectives, 2*(2), 209–254.

Robinson v. California, 370 U.S. 660 (1962).

Rovner, L. L. (2004). Disability, equality, and identity. *Alabama Law Review, 55*(4), 1043, 1051–1052.

Schalk, S. (2018). *Bodyminds reimagined*. Duke University Press.

Schlesinger, L. (2014). The social model's case for inclusion: "Motivating factor" and "but for" standards of proof under the Americans with Disabilities Act and the impact of the social model of disability on employees with disabilities. *Cardozo Law Review, 35*(5), 2115–2145.

Schweik, S. M. (2010). *The ugly laws: Disability in public*. New York University Press.

Scotch, R. K. (2000). Models of disability and the Americans with Disabilities Act. *Berkeley Journal of Employment and Labor Law*, 21(1), 213–222.

Shapiro, J. P. (1994). *No pity: People with disabilities forging a new civil rights movement*. Broadway Books.

Silber, R. (1997). Eugenics, family and immigration law in the 1920's. *Georgetown Immigration Law Journal*, 11(4), 859–899.

Stein, M. A. (2004). Same struggle, different difference: ADA accommodations as antidiscrimination. *University of Pennsylvania Law Review*, 153(2), 579–673.

Sutton v. United Airlines, 527 U.S. 471 (1999).

United States v. Thind, 261 U.S. 204 (1923).

CHAPTER 2

Collusive Symbiosis

Notes on Disability as White Property in Higher Education

Lauren E. Shallish, Michael D. Smith, & Ashley Taylor

> Whiteness as property has historically and continues to function as a tool to confer social benefits, from the intangible to the material, on those who possess it and to punish those who do not. (Annamma, 2015, p. 298)

PROLOGUE

While discussing an upcoming student teaching placement with a white, cisgender student teacher, the student reported feeling anxious about teaching in a nearby urban school. At this point in their teacher education program, they had already taken a number of courses related to diversity and inclusion and participated in multiple field placements. Despite repeated discussions about (1) urban placements as centers rich with transcultural literacies, (2) the rigor of the student's preparation, (3) affirmations of the typical and expectable pre-student teaching nerves, and (4) appeals to our obligation to teach all students, the student teacher maintained their position. Being placed in *this* urban school would be too overwhelming and, well, *different*—insurmountably different. Without faculty support to transfer to an alternate teaching placement, the student was undeterred; instead, they simply changed tack. A couple of weeks later, the student submitted medical documentation of a psychiatric condition stating, "a student teaching placement at *this* school would just be too triggering for anxiety." They stated, "I've got a doctor's note and need an accommodation to be placed elsewhere." Checkmate.

As scholars of critical disability studies and teacher educators, we are dedicated to advocacy alongside and on behalf of dis/abled and historically multiply minoritized students. Because of this, we find ourselves at odds

31

with a pattern that we have increasingly noticed in our teaching and advising, namely that whiteness is deployed to commandeer the mechanisms of disability accommodation in higher education settings to serve its own white supremacist ends, and in so doing, rendering invisible the very white privilege that is being leveraged. In this chapter, we endeavor to use the theoretical framework provided by DisCrit (Annamma et al., 2013) to examine the complex ways in which whiteness and ability supremacy are entangled in disability labels, accommodations requests, and student advocacy in higher education.

We begin by applying DisCrit theorizing to institutions of higher education (broadly) and processes of higher education accommodations (specifically). In the next section, we draw on the seminal work of Sleeter (1986), Harris (1993), and Broderick and Leonardo (2016) to examine whiteness as property and how dis/ability and its attendant accommodations are deployed as yet another form of white property. We argue that the use of accommodations as property is a violent practice that repropertizes equity-based accommodations for disabled people as white capital. To this end, we describe this repropertizing practice not as a singular act but a tactic that is variously deployed and multiply motivated yet serving the same end. In our last section, we address pathways forward given this terrain and wonder aloud about the ways in which DisCrit theorizing alternately clarifies and problematizes whiteness's interactions with disability in institutional policy.

INTRODUCTION

At its core, the arguments developed within this chapter are situated between complementary foundational premises. First, while the commonsense need for (and right to) disability accommodations is uncontested within the chapter, we believe nonetheless that there is value in critical, intersectional analyses of accommodations along class, race, and disability axes, knowing that the concept itself is both embodied and relational. Social models of disability "aim to understand disability as a total experience of complex interactions between the body and physical, social, and cultural environments" (Baglieri & Shapiro, 2012, p. 25). As long as our cultural and institutional spaces are defaulted toward able-bodied/minded dominance, common sense tells us that forms of accommodation are necessary to ensure equitable access and opportunity. To this end, disabled people and their advocates must be able to articulate accommodation requests and have institutions (and their charges) respond affirmatively with good-faith efforts to either remove impediments or provide necessary assistance. Herein lies the tension. Though the unqualified good of disability accommodations makes sense, we know that there are times when we must strain to peer beyond immediate commonsense understandings, apply critical habits of mind, and consider other possibilities.

Johnson (2006) observed that many facets of our social world have been taken for granted as real, true, and thus beyond questioning, even though they've been socially constructed. The power of a socially constructed reality is that "once human beings give something a name—whether it be skin color or disability—that thing acquires a significance it otherwise would not have. More important, the name quickly takes on a life of its own as we forget the social process that created it and started treating it as 'real' in and of itself" (Johnson, 2006, p. 20). The seductiveness of some commonsense notions lies in the ways they obscure the power dynamics and asymmetric histories that led to its original establishment and broad acceptance. Mendoza and colleagues (2016) problematized commonsense complicity as they warned that, left unexamined, some applications of common sense leave open the possibility that "(1) anyone who participates in practices shaped by dominant ideology is susceptible to perpetuating inequities through common sense; (2) common sense is so grounded in social practices and dominant ideologies that good intentions alone are not a guarantee that equity work will be done; and (3) common sense is not easy to overcome, but awareness of its development can allow for shifts in understanding" (p. 77). We stand firmly between our understanding of the immeasurable good that disability accommodations bring in the context of persistent ableism and the discomfiting recognition of the ways that race and class complicate access to—and in some cases exploitation of—disability accommodations.

Second, while still recognizing the commonsense good that disability accommodations proffer to countless individuals, we cannot help but wonder about the degree to which (and manner in which) disability accommodations are often exploited as yet another tool for dominance. That is, like a tree with an invasive root system, the effects of whiteness promulgate into unseen and perhaps unexpected spaces such as the realm of disability accommodations in higher education, and in so doing, accommodations deployed through the machinations of whiteness further leverage existing advantages accrued to whiteness instead of those accommodations being used to achieve baseline access and opportunity. The analytical tools of DisCrit allow—if not demand—critical examinations of social, political, and educational institutions and the ways in which our understandings are enriched through just this type of intersectional analyses. To wit, Annamma et al. (2013) assert that "DisCrit recognizes the shifting boundary between [being constructed as] normal and abnormal, between [assigned] ability and disability, and seeks to question ways in which race contributes to one being positioned on either side of the line" (p. 10). This analysis clarifies existential and epistemological entanglements in the lived experience of dominance *and* oppression.

Taken together, problematizing accommodation policy through this intersectional lens reveals yet another space where whiteness seizes goods and services that both sate its wants and meet its demands. Annamma et al. (2013) observe that "racism and ableism are normalizing processes that are interconnected and collusive . . . racism validates and reinforces ableism, and ableism validates and reinforces racism" (p. 6). In this chapter, we describe this interconnected and collusive relationship between racism and ableism in higher education disability policy as an expression of "collusive symbiosis." In this case, collusive symbiosis describes the situation whereby whiteness exploits loopholes in institutions to make disability accommodations an unwilling and unlikely co-conspirator serving white supremacy, such that whiteness validates its ascendancy through the use of disability accommodations, and the provision of disability accommodations serves to concretize the ascendancy of whiteness. Again, checkmate.

DEPLOYING DISABILITY DIAGNOSIS AS WHITE PROPERTY

Like other policies that provide or withhold access, goods, and services, the practice of providing accommodations on the basis of disability holds the potential to be co-opted to serve majoritarian ends. Exploring policies and practices of accommodating students through the "primacy of race" (Gillborn, 2015) positions us to understand how such policies reassert white supremacy and, in many cases, evidence institutional practices of anti-Blackness (Dumas, 2016). In early 2019, the U.S. Justice Department announced the results of Operation Varsity Blues. Over 50 charges of fraud were levied against wealthy parents who were using a variety of illegal means to secure their children's admission into elite colleges. One of the mechanisms used was the falsification of learning disability diagnoses that gained students access to extended time and priority testing environments for the SAT and ACT (Shapiro & Goldstein, 2019). While the scandal has attracted enormous media attention, it is only the most recent demonstration of how intersectional race and class advantage is deployed to exploit loopholes in disability accommodations. By using their status to secure extended time on standardized testing via disability diagnoses, the mostly white parents involved in Operation Varsity Blues turned disability accommodations into what Harris (1993) calls "white property," or "the legal legitimation of expectations of power and control that enshrine the status quo as a neutral baseline, while masking the maintenance of white privilege and domination" (p. 1715). While Operation Varsity Blues is an unambiguous instance of the bad-faith use of disability accommodations to hoard resources and occupy elite higher education as white space, such a practice perhaps more regularly occurs via educational policies and structures that normalize and legitimate disability diagnoses as vehicles for white advantage. After all, whites securing advantage in bad faith is not a paradigmatic case of whiteness as property; to maintain itself, whiteness also *needs* to secure structural advantage and works parasitically to do so.

According to Harris (1993), whiteness functions as a form of economic capital whose normative intent is neutralized and legitimated via the state sanction of the law. Accordingly, whites are empowered to territorialize institutions because whiteness and property have always been synonymous within the American legal and political system. Because the mechanism by which such advantage is obtained is not only fully legal but rendered neutral through its legality, the fact that such advantage is leveraged to uphold a racist system is obscured (Harris, 1993). According to Harris (1993), "Whiteness at various times signifies and is deployed as identity, status, and property, sometimes regularly, sometimes in tandem" (p. 1725). In addition to revealing how disability diagnoses are turned into the legally legitimated property of whites, Operation Varsity Blues also demonstrates how these parents *deploy* their status via economic wealth and social capital to maintain white supremacy.

While parental advocacy has long played a crucial role in disabled students' educational access, it also operates within white supremacy to produce and maintain whites' systemic advantage. White parents and parents of color spend capital very differently, particularly because the cultural and social knowledge that is valued in educational institutions privileges white agency (Yosso, 2005). Thus, whites experience substantively different kinds of agency than parents of color in the context of disability advocacy (Gillborn, 2015; Gillborn et al., 2016). Says Gillborn (2015), "White supremacy refers to the operation of much more subtle and extensive forces that saturate the everyday mundane actions and policies that shape the world in the interests of white people" (p. 278). A clear example of this interest convergence is Sleeter's (1986) tracing of the origins of learning disability to white middle-class parent activism and more recently in Gillborn et al.'s (2016) study of Black middle-class parents in the United Kingdom. By affixing a new marker of difference to their children, white parents reclaimed access to education by dissociating from disability diagnoses that jeopardized that access. By contrast, the advocacy of parents of color worked against, rather than through, racist systems in securing educational access (Gillborn, 2015; Gillborn et al., 2016). Yosso (2005) refers to this exercise of capital as navigational capital, wherein communities of color deploy institutional maneuvering strategies to challenge injustice and to resist institutional violence. Notably, Gillborn (2015) found that when Black parents pursue privately financed assessments of their child to *counter* the racialized deficits of school-based assessments, they face obstructionist attitudes grounded in blocking access to *enabling* labels in favor of *disabling* diagnoses. Thus, while Black parents deployed their resources to equalize their child's access via a disability label and resist racist violence, "class advantage fails to protect in the face of entrenched racism" (Gillborn, 2015, p. 283).

At the K–12 level, racialized labeling practices operate alongside and compound the differential deployment of class advantage in parental advocacy. As a result, the K–12 context stratifies disability identification and experience along the lines of race, such that Black, Latinx, and Indigenous students experience disproportionate labeling in subjective or soft disability categories (Baglieri & Shapiro, 2012) and more restrictive placements on the basis of a diagnosis (Adams & Meiners, 2014). In addition, they and their families are systematically denied power and undermined in their pursuit and negotiation of positive identifications and in managing how identifications are deployed within the classroom and throughout the schooling day (Gillborn et al., 2016), as well as in securing more coveted placements within the racial, economic, and ability-stratifying web that is school choice (Waitoller & Lubienski, 2019). In their analysis of how goodness operates as a form of white property, Broderick and Leonardo (2016) describe how the repeated positioning of white students as "good"—good learners, good listeners—results in a thickening process that repeatedly and both consciously and unconsciously positions white students as more deserving of benefits and freedoms, or what Annamma (2015) calls "the intangible benefits of innocence" (p. 297). While this positioning is based primarily on racialized differences, it operates as if it is based solely on student merit, thus rendering that positioning process all but invisible.

Importantly, white students, by virtue of this thickening process, are schooled in an expression of agency that empowers them to seek, request, and expect supports. Leonardo and Broderick (2016) observed that there are clear affective and material benefits accrued to students who have been constructed as or recognized for being good and/or smart. White students are enabled to experience themselves as entitled to a whole range of educational resources and services denied to students of color on the basis of the former's cumulative positioning as deserving and the latter's cumulative positioning as undeserving. While the development of self-advocacy is important for disabled students, self-advocacy in the service of access is different from self-advocacy in service of advantage; this latter sense of advocacy is better understood as an audacious expression of agency that enables the violent hoarding of resources.

The kinds of labels that mark and overwhelmingly structure Black and Brown students' experiences of special education are those that resist the ability to accrue property. Labels such as emotional and behavioral disturbance (EBD), for example, to which Black, Latinx, and Indigenous children are disproportionately more likely than whites to be subject, are not those that position students to secure the kinds of personal supports that enable college access. Quite the opposite: "Students labeled with [emotional disturbance and other cognitive disabilities] are typically not tracked toward graduation or postsecondary education, are suspended and expelled at higher rates than students without these disabilities and are disproportionately overrepresented in juvenile justice systems and prisons" (Adams & Meiners, 2014, p. 155). Such labels clearly do not bring about increased supports or positive outcomes for students, even when students need emotional and psychological resources. They certainly do not translate into students' alternative access to the SAT and ACT, nor are they typically accompanied by a corresponding set of accommodations at the higher education level (Annamma et al., 2013).

An analysis of racialized labeling reveals that the same labels can provide very different opportunities when attached to white versus Black or Brown students (Annamma et al., 2013). White families can circumvent special education services by leveraging intersectional racial and class advantage and, in many cases, secure individualized instruction and educational access without having their child classified. The diagnoses and accommodations sought and even engineered by white families do enable access for some students in some cases; parental advocacy is a powerful tool to safeguard a student's access to needed resources. However, it is clear that the differential agency experienced by white parents by virtue of systemic power, in comparison to parents of color, works symbiotically with disability diagnoses to secure higher education access as white property. As we discuss in the next section, this collusion is both enabled and legitimated by the configurations of higher education and disability law.

THE COLLUSIVE POTENTIAL OF ACCOMMODATIONS

While often misunderstood, accommodations on the basis of documented disability are intended to provide equal access to college for students whose modes of learning, mobility, or sensory engagement differ from the imagined normal student for whom colleges are designed. In one sense, it's almost— *almost*—like accommodations recognize that colleges perform a gatekeeping role against disabled students, a gate for which accommodations are the key. However, while disability accommodations are woven into a legal system that is nominally aimed at leveling the playing field and thereby intervening upon the system of discrimination within the education system that privileges able-bodyminds, accommodations do not actually respond to discrimination.

The landscape of higher education law creates a terrain rife for the deployment of whiteness as property, particularly because it is structured on a rights model. As the debates ensued to draft both the statute and regulations of the Americans with Disabilities Act (ADA) and the Americans with Disabilities Act Amendments Act (ADAAA), these did not fully procure disability protection, as contests over alcoholism or people living with

HIV/AIDS, for example, complicated the terms of the law (Shapiro, 1994). As Congress is only appointed to regulate commerce, and given that laws themselves emerge from extensive compromise and debate, there are notable absences in both what can be considered disability under the law and in interpretations of what the regulations actually guarantee. It is for these reasons combined, among others, that transformative and radical approaches to disability regard rights frameworks as fundamentally assimilationist and, therefore, limited—if not outright counterproductive (Withers et al., 2019).

Colleges and universities largely regard disability as a technical issue (Michalko, 2002). As such, accommodations are procedural in nature, operating individually to entitle a student to a particular point(s) of access, such as increased time on an exam or adjustments of academic expectations. While perhaps appearing as a commonsense practice, these chains of transactions that take place across individuals, departments, and units have the potential to eclipse the substantive matter of the law and the ways legal regulations "draw boundaries and enforce or reorder existing regimes of power" (Harris, 1993, p. 1715). While much of the literature on disability and higher education operates from a framework assuming that impairment and disability labels (and their impacts) are monolithic and fixed (Heyward, 1998), we seek a shift to an intersectional approach that makes clear the dynamic of forces that manifest within institutional and legal frameworks. As the tenets of DisCrit compel us, we investigate how accessing the technical procurement of a reasonable accommodation in higher education can also serve to reposition the regulatory forces of white capitalist property.

Section 504 (Pub. L. 93-112) of the Rehabilitation Act of 1973 prohibited state and local governments from discriminating against disabled people with regard to access and use of programs operated by a federally funded entity. For higher education, Section 504 largely focused on discrimination in the admissions process (Evans et al., 2017). The legal definition of reasonable accommodation involves "any change in the work or school environment or in the way things are customarily done that enables an individual with a disability to enjoy equal opportunity" (U.S. Equal Employment Opportunity Commission, 2011, para. 11). Combined with the legislative powers of the ADA, specifically Title II, the Higher Education Opportunity Act of 2008 (HEOA), and the ADAAA, these regulations provide access to higher education for students, faculty, and staff writ large. Noticeably absent in these regulations is the involvement of families and educators, who in K–12 settings manage most of the decisionmaking (see Valle & Connor, 2010, p. 212). As a result, the onus in higher education is on students to advocate on their own behalf, a reality that amplifies the differential agency that whites experience relative to self-advocacy.

Disabled college students are required to oversee a number of legally mandated requirements in order to meet the thresholds for recognition as part of a protected class. Students must self-identify to the institution through the disability resource office and advocate for accommodations through a formal request vis-à-vis medical documentation and processes of disclosure. As noted earlier, these interactions are nearly inverted in nature from K–12 settings. One must first self-identify and then demonstrate that they are "otherwise qualified" and that their disability "substantially limits" a "major life activity," and then the process of reasonable accommodation can begin. While students must present medical documentation for their disability, accommodations are determined by the "*impact* of the impairment rather than the *existence* of it" (Evans et al., 2017, p. 97, our emphasis). The terms of establishing the impact of impairment are one space where white supremacy can take hold in a process of thickening, referred to earlier in the K–12 context. It may be the lever that, while enabling reasonable accommodation, also allows whiteness to reposition itself and undermine transformation more broadly.

Colleges are responsible only for accommodations and not personal services such as an organization coach or social skills role-playing, which can be provided under the legislation governing the K–12 context. The educational entitlement law guaranteeing personal services in K–12 primes white students for acts of self-advocacy that operate in the creation and the occupation of space to secure their dominance in higher education. The vacuum left by the absence of personal services in higher education invites the parasitic features of whiteness to imbue transactions that secure reasonable accommodations. The tactics demonstrated by the students are often read as laudable self-advocacy rather than a manifestation of advantage: "The relationship between expectations and property remains highly significant, as the law has recognized and protected even the expectation of rights as actual legal property" (Harris, 1993, p. 7).

ACCOMMODATIONS AS SERVICES FOR WHITE SUPREMACY

During the 2020 spring semester of the COVID-19 pandemic, a white female student with an existing letter of accommodation contacted her instructor during spring break before the move to online teaching began. In her email, she made a blanket request for extensions on all remaining assignments, stating that, "Outlined in my accommodation letter, I receive flexible deadlines for assignments. I was hoping that because of the upcoming online format we could arrange that I could receive this for all my assignments going forward. Because I am having to do my classes from home, I feel as though these extra days will allow me to take my time with my work in class." While the faculty member confirmed that they would continue to uphold the terms of the original accommodation letter and thanked the student for their open communication, the instructor also noted that it appeared the student was both rewriting and expanding the provision of reasonable accommodation without consultation from the disability services office, operating from the assumption that the forthcoming online format *automatically* necessitated expansion of accommodations *and* that the student was in the right to seek these out themselves. The instructor included the director of disability services on the email exchange as a precautionary measure. The director responded by asking the student to provide more detail about her request but stating her concern that "A blanket accommodation of extended deadlines would not be a reasonable accommodation." The student replied that she understood the faculty member and the director's concerns and was nervous about the new online format, then agreed to contact the instructor for each assignment three business days in advance to request an extension, if needed, pursuant to her original letter of accommodation. A week later the student requested weekly individual meetings with the faculty member to review each remaining assignment.

On its face, this example has the potential to be read as a student's simple self-advocacy (albeit clunky) or a need for flexibility in light of an unusual and difficult moment likely to affect mental health and concentration. However, DisCrit compels us to analyze the student's tactics in recognition of the way that whiteness confers advantage and expands the benefits. Specifically, we can observe white students' ability to occupy normative cultural standards of the able-bodied/minded despite the claim of mental distress. While earlier examples of the urban teaching placement and college admissions scandal were explicitly about utilizing accommodations in bad faith, this scenario demonstrates the porous and unstable nature of reasonable accommodation with regard to disability discrimination and the ways whiteness exploits these loopholes to secure advantage and operate parasitically upon disability law. Using DisCrit, we are able to analyze this white student's repropertizing of disability accommodations—her seeking more of them *and* on her own terms—as more than a one-off instance of a student innocently (see Annamma, 2015) advocating for additional supports within the context of an unsettling global pandemic. Certainly, the global pandemic has been disruptive and destructive on countless levels for all students, yet the institutional processes that recognize these goods and services confer recognition to more culturally valued expressions of advocacy and experience, those that are aligned with whiteness and goodness (Leonardo & Broderick, 2016). Again, whiteness validates its ascendency through accommodations, seizing goods and services for its own aims of gatekeeping and hoarding.

DisCrit allows for an analysis of this event that keeps the social construction of both ability and racial categories in tension with the acknowledgment of the "real material outcomes that emerge in terms of lived experiences" (Annamma et al., 2013, p. 9). According to Harris (1993), "In creating property rights, the law draws boundaries and enforces or reorders existing regimes of power. The inequalities that are produced and reproduced are not givens or inevitabilities but rather are conscious selections regarding the structuring of social relations" (p. 1715). This student's existing access to accommodations via the legal structure of disability services allowed her to deploy, extend, and capitalize on whiteness through a discourse of entitlement and a posture of a rightful claim to personalized supports. In a process that clearly underscores the collusive symbiosis of disability accommodations and whiteness as property, the student deployed a commonsense lever of self-advocacy to maximize her success in the course. The initial request to extend her accommodations letter, along with a set of cascading requests for individualized instruction and overall interactions from the faculty member, reveal the student's orientation toward disability accommodations as beneficial services, an orientation that reflects white students' differential access to disability diagnoses and accommodations in K–12 that align with increased opportunity and advantage.

WAYS FORWARD

Whiteness co-opting the domains of other social identity categories to compound its own advantages is not a new phenomenon. Whiteness writ large has used fundamental assumptions about (dis)ability, (il)legitimacy, and (ab)normality to violently seize and subsequently hoard privilege, status, and even the most basic freedoms associated with citizenship for generations. In this chapter, we endeavor to describe the collusively symbiotic relationship between racism and ableism in higher education disability accommodation policy. Through a DisCrit analysis, we provide a framework for understanding the institutional and structural factors that make possible and make *nearly* invisible the ways in which disability accommodations may be both possessed and deployed as white capitalist property. Against the backdrop of existing stratification in K–12 labeling, parental advocacy, and access to personalized services via diagnosis, white students are positioned to accrue additional advantage through the deployment of audacious agency, as we described earlier. However, the mechanisms of higher education law render securing white privilege all but invisible, as it allows cascading interconnected streams of systematic advantage to masquerade as mere equal access to a neutrally and mutually available good. The examples discussed in the chapter illustrate different facets of this phenomenon. Bad-faith actors who are, more or less, attempting to cover illegitimate ends with disability accommodation's legitimate means are relatively easily identified and straightforwardly addressed. The final vignette presents a more subtle case wherein the student's intention is less clear, but the practice of advocacy and posture of entitlement act in the service of white advantage, nonetheless.

The path forward is as it ever was for all of us who focus our professional and personal energies toward increasing equitable access and outcomes for historically marginalized groups—strewn with potholes to progress, uncomfortable conversations, internal deliberation, and yet the resolve to persist anyway. In "A Pedagogy of Discomfort," Boler (1999) cautions that "the path of understanding, if it is not to 'simplify,' must be tread gently. Yet if one believes in alternatives to the reductive binaries of good and evil, 'purity and corruption,' one is challenged to invite the other, with compassion and fortitude, to learn to see things differently, no matter how perilous the course for all involved" (pp. 175–176). Given the collusive symbiosis between whiteness and disability policy in higher education, what is one to do? The unsatisfying and uncomfortable answer, of course, is that it depends on the situation and one's sphere of influence. That said, responses that would occasion faculty and staff to second guess, constrain, and resist *all* disability accommodation requests for fear of complicity with whiteness represent an overcorrection and create collateral damage by reifying the marginalization of disabled people while only marginally constraining this exercise of white dominance. Accommodations are low-hanging fruit, as it is much easier to direct one's ire and energies toward the hard target that is disability policy than to address the amorphousness of institutional engagement with dismantling white power. In fact, policing disabled people's access avoids addressing white violence for what it is, thereby colluding with white supremacy, and again, disability is made an unwilling and unlikely co-conspirator with whiteness.

As Annamma et al. (2016) argue, DisCrit propels scholars to "examine the processes in which students are simultaneously raced and dis/abled" (p. 13). We believe that DisCrit principles have numerous applications for (re)considering the many ways institutional policies press on individuals and the asymmetric outcomes that fall along racial, ability, and socioeconomic lines. In particular, the DisCrit framework allows us to examine those instances in which white disabled students' demands for access appear both common sense and exploitative of systemic advantage. At the same time, DisCrit intentionally guards *against* interpretations grounded in dysconscious ableism (Broderick & Lalvani, 2017) that would dismiss concerns about pervasive academic ableism (see Dolmage, 2017). Dysconscious ableism, or the "impaired or distorted way of thinking about dis/ability" (Broderick & Lalvani, 2017, p. 2), creates reverberations that move outwardly in destructive, parasitic ways, including by emboldening faculty to debate the merits of *any* accommodations sought by their students. In utilizing the tools of DisCrit to expand upon the collusion of race and ability in higher education inequality, we hope to demonstrate that it is whiteness's gray areas that are perhaps most difficult to observe, most difficult to dismantle, and nevertheless most in need of analysis.

REFERENCES

Adams, D., & Meiners, E. (2014). Chapter nine: Who wants to be special? Pathologization and the preparation of bodies for prison. *Counterpoints*, *453*, 145–164.

Americans with Disabilities Act Amendments Act (2008).

Americans with Disabilities Act of 1990, Pub. L. No. 101-336, 104 Stat. 328 (1990).

Annamma, S. A. (2015). Whiteness as property: Innocence and ability in teacher education. *The Urban Review*, *47*(2), 293–316.

Annamma, S. A., Connor, D., & Ferri, B. (2013). Dis/ability critical race studies (DisCrit): Theorizing at the intersections of race and disability. *Race Ethnicity and Education*, *16*(1), 1–31

Baglieri, S., & Shapiro, A. (2012). *Disability studies and the inclusive classroom: Critical practices for creating least restrictive attitudes*. Routledge.

Boler, M. (1999). *Feeling power: Emotions and education*. Routledge.

Broderick, A., & Lalvani, P. (2017). Dysconscious ableism: Toward a liberatory praxis in teacher education. *International Journal of Inclusive Education*, *21*(9), 894–905.

Broderick, A. A., & Leonardo, Z. (2016). What a good boy: The deployment of "goodness" as ideological property in schools. In D. J. Connor, B. A. Ferri, & S. A. Annamma (Eds.), *DisCrit: Disability studies and critical race theory in education* (pp. 55–67). Teachers College Press.

Dolmage, J. T. (2017). *Academic ableism: Disability and higher education*. University of Michigan Press.

Dumas, M. J. (2016). Against the dark: Antiblackness in education policy and discourse. *Theory into Practice*, *55*(1), 11–19.

Evans, N. J., Broido, E. M., Brown, K. R., & Wilke, A. K. (2017). *Disability and higher education: A social justice approach*. Jossey-Bass.

Gillborn, D. (2015). Intersectionality, critical race theory, and the primacy of racism: Race, class, gender, and disability in education. *Qualitative Inquiry*, *21*(3), 277–287.

Gillborn, D., Rollock, N., Vincent, C., & Ball, S. (2016). The Black middle classes, education, racism, and dis/ability: An intersectional analysis. In D. J. Connor, B. A. Ferri, & S. A. Annamma (Eds.), *DisCrit: Disability studies and critical race theory in education* (pp. 35–54). Teachers College Press.

Harris, C. I. (1993). Whiteness as property. *Harvard Law Review*, *106*(8), 1707–1791.

Heyward, S. (1998). *Disability and higher education: Guidance for Section 504 and ADA compliance*. LRP Publications.

Higher Education Opportunity Act of 2008, Public Law No. 110-315 (2008).

Johnson, A. G. (2006). *Power, privilege, and difference*. Mayfield.

Leonardo, Z., & Broderick, A. A. (2016). What a good boy. In D. J. Connor, B. A. Ferri, & S. A. Annamma (Eds.), *DisCrit: Disability studies and critical race theory in education* (pp. 55–67). Teachers College Press.

Mendoza, E., Paguyo, C., & Gutierrez, K. (2016). Understanding the intersection of race and dis/ability: Common sense notions of learning and culture. In D. J. Connor, B. A. Ferri, & S. A. Annamma (Eds.), *DisCrit: Disability studies and critical race theory in education* (pp. 71–86). Teachers College Press.

Michalko, R. (2002). *The difference that disability makes*. Temple University Press.

Section 504 of the Rehabilitation Act of 1973, Pub. L. No. 93-112 (1973).

Shapiro, E., & Goldstein, D. (2019, March 14). *Is the college cheating scandal the "final straw" for standardized tests?* New York Times. https://www.nytimes.com/2019/03/14/us/sat-act-cheating-college-admissions.html

Shapiro, J. (1994). *No pity: People with disabilities forging a new civil rights movement.* Random House Publishing.

Sleeter, C. E. (1986). Learning disabilities: The social construction of a special education category. *Exceptional Children, 53*(1), 46–54.

U.S. Equal Employment Opportunity Commission. (2011). *The Americans with Disabilities Act: Applying performance and conduct standards to employees with disabilities.* https://www.eeoc.gov/facts/performance-conduct.html

Valle, J. W., & Connor, D. J. (2010). *Rethinking disability: A disability studies approach to inclusive practices.* McGraw Hill.

Waitoller, F. R., & Lubienski, C. (2019). Disability, race, and the geography of school choice: Toward an intersectional analytic framework. *AERA Open, 5*(1), 1–12.

Withers, A. J., Ben-Moshe, L., Brown, L. X., Erickson, L., da Silva Gorman, R., Lewis, T. A., McLeod, L., & Mingus, M. (2019). Radical disability politics. In R. Kinna & U. Gordon (Eds.), *Routledge handbook of radical politics* (pp. 178–193). Routledge.

Yosso, T. J. (2005). Whose culture has capital? A critical race theory discussion of community cultural wealth. *Race ethnicity and education, 8*(1), 69–91.

CHAPTER 3

Disrupting Dominant Modes of Expression: Illuminating the Strengths and Gifts of Two Disabled Girls of Color

Amanda Miller, Sylvia Nyegenye, & Rose Mostafa-Shoukry

Disabled girls of color[1] have unique school experiences that reveal multiple intersecting oppressions at macrosociopolitical (e.g., ableism, linguicism, racism) and microinteractional (e.g., access to curriculum, classroom interaction) levels (Erevelles & Minear, 2010). Macrosociopolitical oppressions are woven throughout the fabric of society (Anzaldúa, 1990; hooks, 1989) and, therefore, exist in education (Ladson-Billings, 1998). In schools, disabled youth of color are measured against whiteness or what is considered "normal" (Annamma et al., 2013a) in regard to learning, talking, and being. Schooling mechanisms that label disabled youth of color as deficient and different (re)produce exclusionary practices, such as segregated classrooms (de Valenzuela et al., 2006) and harsh discipline (Suarez, 2017). Such exclusionary practices deny disabled girls of color opportunities to learn with peers or engage meaningfully in learning activities that represent them (Cowley, 2013). Moreover, disabled girls of color may be funneled from exclusionary schooling practices (e.g., withholding communication and learning supports) as youth to exclusionary experiences (e.g., few opportunities for meaningful employment, lack of access to reproductive rights and health care, limited housing options) in adulthood. However, knowing the outcomes is not the same as knowing how the processes occur that produce those inequities (Annamma et al., 2020). Because the school experiences of disabled girls of color are underrepresented in education research (Sinclair et al., 2018) and are often hidden or unrecognized by school systems, a more complete storyline is necessary, as inequitable educational opportunities lead to damaging outputs for disabled girls of color (Erevelles, 2011).

This chapter examines how two disabled girls of color honor their discursive practices and reposition themselves (Davies & Harré, 1990), refusing to accept academic and social inequities in schools and classrooms. We seek to understand how hegemonic modes of expression (e.g., talk, English) influence their learning. We explore how two multiply marginalized focal participants, one disabled 8th-grade Afghan girl in middle school and one disabled Latina girl in a high school postsecondary program, discursively navigate general and special education classrooms through their varied modes of expression and communicative mediums (e.g., eye gaze, facial expressions, gestures). First, we discuss how scholars have used discursive practices (e.g., talk, actions) as analytical tools in general and special education classrooms. Then, we outline our theoretical framing: Disability Critical Race Theory (DisCrit; Annamma et al., 2013b) to uncover how teaching practices impact opportunities for two disabled girls of color. We close by examining how the focal participants use their discursive practices as strengths in the classroom, and how schools burden them with carrying the discursive load of showing their knowledge predominantly with hegemonic modes of expression (e.g., talk, English).

DISCURSIVE PRACTICES AS ANALYTICAL TOOLS

Discursive practices (e.g., talk, actions) produce societal ideologies and distribute power (Wodak, 2016). For example, discursive practices can mediate relationships through interaction and knowledge sharing as social and cultural tools. Through interactions, meaning is constructed among groups and distributed (Foucault, 1972). Depending on how power is produced or withheld, new or modified relationships and ideas may form over time through discursive practices. Schools, as social systems, mediate relationships and knowledge and, therefore, (re)produce societal ideologies. A focus on discursive practices in schools can help in understanding how power and dominant ideologies operate through interactions between students and teachers (Rogers, 2011).

Educational Settings

Extant scholarship has revealed how teachers' discursive practices position disabled youth in general education classrooms. For example, teachers have disregarded students' opinions (Hinchman & Young, 2001) or used particular words to describe "other" youth (Orsati & Causton-Theoharis, 2013). School staff used the words "wild" or "trying me out" when describing unwanted or noncompliant behaviors (Orsati, 2015, p. 130). Such discursive practices carried meaning and revealed how teachers' positioning of students impacted the students' identity and participation, including whether students were physically excluded from classroom environments (Orsati & Causton-Theoharis, 2013). However, little is known about the discursive practices of disabled girls of color in general education classrooms.

Existing scholarship has also examined teachers' discursive practices in special education classrooms. Kurth and colleagues (2016) identified that adults frequently controlled the classroom discourse by talking often, while youth had few opportunities to talk. Pennington and Courtade (2015) found that teachers in segregated schools and self-contained classrooms provided students few opportunities to respond and gave minimal feedback. Often, students' responses were unidirectional (e.g., answering questions, following directions). In another study, Causton-Theoharis and colleagues (2011) observed disrespectful talk among teachers and students in self-contained classrooms, yet few studies have examined the discursive practices of disabled girls of color through a multimodal (Jewitt, 2008) lens.

Youth's Discursive Practices

While teachers play a role in (re)producing discursive practices in the classroom (Cazden & Beck, 2003), youth also contribute. For example, disabled youth of color subtly claimed discursive power by asking questions (Collins, 2011a). Disabled girls of color have resisted individual and societal marginalization by refusing to answer questions directly to protect themselves or others (Annamma, 2017). However, more research is needed to understand how disabled girls of color who use talk and actions (e.g., eye gaze, facial expressions) reposition in learning contexts. Therefore, one question guided this inquiry: How are academic and social opportunities afforded or constrained by discursive practices (e.g., talk, actions) for disabled girls of color?

CONCEPTUAL FRAMEWORK

We drew on DisCrit (Annamma et al., 2013b) to uncover how two disabled girls of color were discursively honored and positioned in classrooms. First, we utilized DisCrit tenet one to explain how racism and ableism operate interdependently to marginalize particular groups of people while simultaneously constructing normalcy (Erevelles, 2002). We examined how the discursive practices of two disabled girls of color were positioned as lesser than due to assumptions about race and ability. These judgements pathologize difference and position disabled girls of color and their modes of expression as outside what is normal, and therefore problematic (Erevelles et al., 2006).

Second, we employed DisCrit tenet six to show how whiteness (Harris, 1993) and ability afforded access to property rights for white students while withholding those same rights from the focal participants. Goodness and smartness (Broderick & Leonardo, 2016) are allocated to white students as property rights, while schools withhold those same rights from disabled girls of color. For example, school practices afford disabled white youth more opportunity to learn in general education classrooms (Blanchett et al., 2009) and more access to communication supports (Lindsay & Tsybina, 2011).

Finally, we used DisCrit tenets four and seven (Annamma et al., 2013b) to reveal how the focal participants engaged in resistance to defend their integrity. Conversely, this resistance, characterized as repositioning, can also be met with perceptions of deviance and punishment (Petersen, 2009). Therefore, we reject this deficit position of disabled girls of color and instead situate them as knowledge generators (Delgado Bernal, 2002).

METHOD

This chapter discusses a subset of findings from a study examining educational opportunities for disabled girls of color in one middle school and one high school in a large Midwestern school district (Miller, 2019). Similar to the larger study, we used a critical, qualitative multiple case study design (Merriam & Tisdell, 2015).

Participants

Student participants were included in this analysis if (1) they used varied modes of expression and communicative mediums (e.g., eye gaze, facial expressions) in school; (2) their home language was a language other than English and/or paired with English; and (3) they, along with their families, described having limited to no access to preferred communication supports at school (i.e., sign language, voice output device). At the time of the study, Meena[2] was 14-years-old and in 8th grade. She had immigrated to the United States with her family from Afghanistan in the middle of the prior school year. She had a physical disability and did not use verbal speech. Jimena was 19-years-old and in her first year of the postsecondary program at the high school where she had recently graduated. Jimena's family had moved to their current school district from a neighboring state when Jimena was in middle school. Jimena had cerebral palsy and blindness. Despite their gap in ages, Meena and Jimena both experienced few communication and learning supports, which motivated us to explore how they navigated their schooling experiences.

Five teachers were secondary participants. Ms. Taub and Ms. Snow were Meena's special education teachers. Ms. Parker was Jimena's special education teacher. These three teachers identified as white and female. Mr. Armstrong, Jimena's choir teacher, and Mr. Fenn, Meena's theater teacher, were general education teachers and identified as white and male.

Table 3.1. Data Sources Across Cases

Data Source	Meena	Jimena	Total
Observations and Recordings—General Education	2 (Theater)	2 (Choir)	4
Observations and Recordings—Special Education	3 (Literacy)	2 (Literacy)	5
Detailed Field Notes—General Education	2	2	4
Detailed Field Notes—Special Education	2	2	4
Student Interviews	3	3	6
Student Focus Groups	1	1	2
Teacher Interviews	4	2	6

Data Sources

The first author conducted observations focused on Meena and Jimena and their teachers, including audio/video recordings and detailed field notes[3] in general and special education classrooms (see Table 3.1). Each student participated in three interviews (Latz, 2017; Seidman, 2013) and one focus group (Wang & Burris, 1997). Four teachers were observed by the first author and participated in the first interview. Ms. Taub and Ms. Parker participated in a second interview. Mr. Armstrong was observed but did not participate in the interview component due to scheduling constraints. See Figure 3.1 for data collection phases.

Data Preparation

First, we turned the audio/video recordings into content logs. Key moments of classroom discourse focused on interactions between focal participants and their teachers. We then transcribed those discursive practices. Next, we watched and listened for truncated or interrupted speech and laughter (Ochs, 1979). We added actions (e.g., eye gaze, facial expressions, gestures) to the transcripts (Norris, 2004). We then organized the transcripts by lines and stanzas (Gee, 2011). Afterwards, we noted turn-taking, decisionmaking, opening and closing turns, and making contributions as they related to who was exercising power in and over classroom discourse (Rogers, 2011). See Table 3.2 for transcription conventions.

Data Analysis

The team used critical multimodal discourse analysis (Kress, 2010) to develop codes of discursive practices for the two cases. To do so, we engaged in iterative data analysis entailing multiple rounds of meaning-making and

Figure 3.1. Data Collection Phases

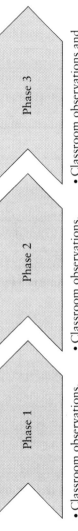

Phase 1

- Classroom observations, audio/video recordings, and detailed field notes—to observe and record discursive practices (4)
- Student interview #1—to learn about students' past and present educational experiences as well as their goals and dreams for the future (2)

Phase 2

- Classroom observations, audio/video recordings, and detailed field notes—to observe and record discursive practices (4)
- Student interview #2—to learn details about learning tools and spaces and the meaning students made of their current educational experiences using semi-structured interviewing techniques, photovoice, and cartography (2)
- Teacher interview #1—to learn concrete details about teachers' experiences with learning tools, spaces, and discursive practices (4)

Phase 3

- Classroom observations and audio/video recordings—to observe and record discursive practices (1)
- Student focus group #1—to provide opportunity to collectively make meaning of photographs and school experiences (2)
- Teacher interview #2—to learn concrete details about teachers' experiences with spaces and discursive practices (2)
- Student interview #3—to learn more details about students' educational experiences (2)

coding (Bhattacharya, 2017). Data analysis was iterative, as the team moved back and forth reading the data, looking for patterns, and turning hunches into questions. We then returned to the data with new questions to look for new patterns and emerging themes (Erickson, 1985). In addition, the team followed within- and across-case data analysis for multiple case study design (Merriam, 2001).

During within-case analysis, the team moved through two rounds of initial coding, including unitizing, categorizing, and labeling (Rodwell, 1998). We then engaged in deductive analysis wherein we used DisCrit (Annamma et al., 2013b) to look for multiple oppressions (e.g., ableism, linguicism, racism) the girls faced. For example, teachers and schooling mechanisms failed to recognize and embrace the girls' varied modes of expression and communicative mediums as strengths (Delgado Bernal, 2002).

During across-case analysis, we used axial coding (Rodwell, 1998) by placing code categories across the two cases in relationship to one another. We used checklist matrices (Miles & Huberman, 1994) to cluster and compare similarities and differences across cases. We reorganized and refocused the categories (Saldaña, 2013) as needed. Before final coding, team members coded the same transcripts and discussed inconsistencies in code application for further alignment of codes (Lincoln & Guba, 1985).

Advancing Rigor

In addition to iterative data analysis (Bhattacharya, 2017), the team advanced rigor for the subset of data discussed here through triangulation (Lincoln & Guba, 1985). For example, we used multiple data collection sources, such as fieldnotes, interviews, and transcripts of discursive practices. This enabled us to look for patterns and outliers across sources and contexts. In addition, researcher triangulation—a team of researchers interpreting the data—also contributed to increased trustworthiness. Multiple researchers coded more than one transcript of discursive practices, and allowing us to continually refine codes and interpretations (Rodwell, 1998; Saldaña, 2013). Finally, the team looked for disconfirming evidence (Erickson, 1985).

FINDINGS

Given limited space, we decided to share two themes. First, we discuss how two disabled girls of color showed their discursive ingenuity in the classroom. We then describe how the focal participants repositioned in response to marginalization.

Discursive Ingenuity Amid Limited Communication Supports

Across cases, focal participants employed discursive ingenuity in the classroom. We defined *discursive ingenuity* as disabled girls of color using resourceful discursive gifts when communicating with their teachers through varied modes of expression and communicative mediums (e.g., eye gaze, facial expressions). For example, Meena used actions during a whole class, teacher-led daily language review activity in the segregated special education classroom:

> *Ms. Taub:* Ok, good. [Look down. Picks a Popsicle stick from the tin container. Reads it. Looks up at the class.] Meena.
> *Meena:* [Looks up from her paper at Ms. Taub at the front of the room.]
> *Ms. Taub:* Do I need a comma after Sam? Bill comma Sam. Do I need a comma right here? [Points to the sentence on the worksheet projected onto the whiteboard.] Yes or no?
> *Meena:* [Picks up the green low-tech communication card from her desk. Looks at it and points to YES. Looks up at Ms. Taub and nods her head yes.]
> *Ms. Taub:* She says yes. Do you guys agree?
> *Some students give choral response:* Yes.

Ms. Taub called on Meena to help correct a sentence. In response to Ms. Taub's question, Meena showed her discursive ingenuity by using eye contact with the teacher and nodding her head while pointing to the low-tech communication tool. By using varied modes and mediums, Meena showed her knowledge *and* ensured that Ms. Taub saw and understood her. Given that disabled youth are often ignored in the classroom (Kurth et al., 2016), Meena's moves are important, as gestures are critical in language use (Jewitt, 2005) and new language acquisition (Mindel & John, 2018). We used DisCrit tenet four (Annamma et al., 2013b) to highlight the focal participants' discursive strengths, including using gestures and combining communicative mediums with low-tech communication supports (e.g., communication boards) or talk to ensure their teachers understood their ideas.

In the general education classroom, Jimena responded to Ms. Parker's questions regarding her contributions at the choir performance:

> *Ms. Parker:* Ok, so bringing a dog may not be one of the things that you did, right? Because you didn't bring a dog. So, we wouldn't list that one. But what were some of the things that you did do?
> *Jimena:* [Looking at Ms. Parker. Nods her head yes.]
> *Ms. Parker:* Give me some of those.
> *Jimena:* [Looking at Ms. Parker.] Chipper.

Ms. Parker: Chipper?

Jimena: [Looking at Ms. Parker. Nods her head yes.]

Ms. Parker: Ok. So, your chipper attitude?

Jimena: [Nods her head yes. Smiles. Quickly looks away and then back at Ms. Parker.]

Ms. Parker: Ok. [Writing Jimena's response.]

Jimena: [Bending over watching Ms. Parker write on the paper.]

In response to Ms. Parker's initial query, Jimena used talk in combination with eye contact, head nods, and smiles. Using talk paired with other modes was one way the focal participants showed their knowledge in classrooms with limited supports and where talk and English were dominant modes of expression. Moreover, Jimena's response is not centered on these dominant modes, but rather who she is as a person (Connor, 2008) and what she brings to the choir—being chipper.

Another way Meena and Jimena showed their ingenuity occurred when they were prompted for the "right" answer. Here, Meena responded to Ms. Taub's question:

Ms. Taub: "Have they throwed away the trash." Meena, what else? "Have they throwed away the trash?"

Meena: [Looks down at the table. Picks up the green low-tech communication card and turns it to the side with the symbols and words for PERIOD and QUESTION MARK.]

Ms. Taub: Have they throwed away the trash.

Meena: [Meena points to PERIOD. Looks up at Ms. Taub.]

Ms. Taub: [Looks at Meena.]

Meena: [Looks at the card and points to QUESTION MARK. Looks at Ms. Taub.]

Ms. Taub: [Looking at Meena, nods her head yes.] She's pointing to the question mark. Do you guys agree?

Some students give choral response: Yes.

When posed with a question that had two options (e.g., period or question mark, yes or no), sometimes Meena would choose one option and wait for her teacher's response. If the teacher continued to look at her, Meena knew to try the other option. If the teacher affirmed this with facial expressions, head movements, and talk, then Meena knew she was correct. This was savvy because Meena could ensure that her answer was correct by using her observation skills (Carrejo & Reinhartz, 2014) to gauge her teacher's response before settling on an answer for her classmates to also affirm.

Using DisCrit tenet one (Annamma et al., 2013b), however, we uncovered how the power-sharing between teachers and students was increasingly more inequitable for the focal participants. First, Meena and

Jimena were more disadvantaged because teachers did not honor their varied modes of expression and communicative mediums and, therefore, did not engage in deep and rich conversations with them (Lindsay & Tsybina, 2011). As such, teachers' discursive practices and ideologies positioned Meena and Jimena in disengaged roles within superficial learning opportunities. Second, the schools were not providing language services and supports consistently; bilingual educators and special education teachers were not co-teaching in Meena's and Jimena's classrooms. These findings add to existing research by illustrating how the burden of presenting themselves as knowers and doers lay almost entirely on the focal participants.

Repositioning as Resistance

Across cases, Meena and Jimena repositioned (Davies & Harré, 1990) or refused to accept marginalization. We define *repositioning* as, disabled girls of color engaging in strategic discursive and physical maneuvering in response to individual, school, or societal marginalization and expanding on Annamma et al.'s (2020) definition. For example, Jimena made a request during literacy in the special education classroom:

> *Ms. Parker:* . . . and made me squeeze the lever down. [Squeezes Jimena's hand as she reads.]
>
> *Jimena:* [Facial expression changes. Body twisted away from table. Looks toward and points to wheelchair or something in that direction, to her left with right arm and hand.]
>
> *Ms. Parker:* [Looks up from book. Points to Jimena's book. Continues reading.]
>
> *Jimena:* [Turns around and faces the other direction while her head rests on her hand, which is holding onto the back of the chair. Looking toward the ground, away from the book.]
>
> *Ms. Parker:* [Looks up briefly. Taps Jimena's upper arm. Continues reading.]

During literacy class, Ms. Parker read aloud a chapter from a popular young adult series, *Twilight*. However, the students were not afforded an opportunity to read, and Ms. Parker did not use guided reading questioning techniques. Rather, the read-aloud was a passive activity except for student predictions at the beginning and confirmations at the end. After five minutes into the chapter, Jimena repositioned physically and requested something in the direction of her wheelchair as she was sitting in a classroom chair. In response, Ms. Parker ignored her request and prompted Jimena to focus on the book. In response, Jimena repositioned physically again, ignoring her teacher and looking away from the book. Despite repeated physical repositioning, Ms. Parker prompted Jimena again while continuing to read aloud. Even though Jimena's repositioning was reoccurring, it was still brief, as her teacher continued to regain control as seen, maintaining close proximity and using multiple strategies (e.g., gestural, physical prompts). At times, the focal participants' requests were fulfilled, and at other times, they were not.

In Meena's case, she physically repositioned by honoring herself during a game in theater:

> *Mr. Fenn:* [Looking at the students.] For this game, I need you to make a position with your body, with your hands together in the middle of your body. [Motions his hands together and out in front of his body.] Prepared and ready. Every person, this is your prepared position. If you've got something in your hands, put it in your pocket.
>
> *Meena:* [Looking at Mr. Fenn, then looks in her coat pocket while holding a coloring pencil in her hands. Closes her pocket.]
>
> *Mr. Fenn:* [Looking around at the class.] If you're sitting or leaning, stand up. Join us in the circle, not behind it. Stand up. Right here in the middle. [Motions with his hands together in the middle of his body.]
>
> *Meena:* [Looking at Mr. Fenn, puts her hands together and holds the coloring pencil between her hands.]

When Mr. Fenn asked the class to put away everything in their hands and get ready for a game using their arms and hands to motion to one another, Meena held onto her coloring pencil. Mr. Fenn afforded Meena nuanced power through her actions, as he did not correct her or repeat his direction to remove everything from her hands. As such, Meena played much of the game holding the coloring pencil until she put it in her coat pocket. Honoring their own needs and wants in response to a teacher's directives was one way the focal participants could harness subtle power in the classroom.

The focal participants also repositioned in response to marginalization by attempting repairs (Macbeth, 2004) when they were misunderstood. Jimena tried to repair with Ms. Parker:

> *Ms. Parker:* [Looking at Jimena.] What are some things that maybe you think as a whole you guys could do a little better next time?
>
> *Jimena:* [Looking at Ms. Parker.] To kee-
>
> *Ms. Parker:* [Looking at Jimena.] Have cookies?
>
> *Jimena:* [Looking at Ms. Parker.] To kee-
>
> *Ms. Parker:* [Looking at Jimena.] Sing more on key?
>
> *Jimena:* [Nods her head yes, looking at Ms. Parker.]

51 seconds later

> *Ms. Parker:* [Looking at Jimena.] (HH) All right, singing more on key.
>   I'll take care of the cookies. It's fine. Alright, what else?
> *Jimena:* [Looking at Ms. Parker.] To kee-
> *Ms. Parker:* [Looking at Jimena.] Cookies? [Nods her head yes.]
> *Jimena:* [Looking at Ms. Parker. Sits up. Shakes her head no.]
> *Ms. Parker:* No, okay. [Looks down at the paper.]
> *Jimena:* I- [Raises head. Moves arm. Looking at Ms. Parker.]
> *Ms. Parker:* [Looks at Jimena.] Okay, see now, I'm just stuck on the
>   cookies. I can't help it.
> *Jimena:* (HH) [Looks over towards the class.]

Ms. Parker posed a reflection question to Jimena, but she did not know what Jimena wanted to say. In response, Ms. Parker employed a technique she often used—guessing with context clues. When her point was not understood the first time, Jimena attempted a repair less than a minute later. Jimena's attempts were unresolved, as Ms. Parker did not ask additional questions or employ low- or high-tech communication supports. Repairing was one technique the focal participants employed when they were misunderstood.

These findings are commensurate with prior research wherein youth repositioned by claiming nuanced discursive power through asking questions (Ingram & Elliot, 2014) and sharing personal information (Collins, 2011b). We used DisCrit tenet seven (Annamma et al., 2013b) to illuminate the focal participants' repositioning as creative acts of resistance. As such, this finding extends prior research illustrating how the focal participants claimed nuanced discursive power by making requests, attempting repairs, and honoring themselves, practices that others may assume they cannot do because of disability labels. This is significant because little is known about how disabled girls of color reposition in response to marginalization and how their teachers respond to them.

Using DisCrit tenet six (Annamma et al., 2013b), we uncovered how whiteness and ability as property (Harris, 1993) interacted with linguicism (Phillipson & Skutnabb-Kangas, 1996) to constrain the focal participants' discursive opportunities. While Meena and Jimena were resourceful in their communication with teachers, their access to communication supports and tools was constrained or ignored altogether. A broad range of supports to augment and enrich their communication was absent, including unaided systems (e.g., gesture dictionaries, sign language), high-tech systems (e.g., voice output or speech-generating devices), and social media (Light & McNaughton, 2014). Said differently, goodness and smartness, in tandem with communication supports and tools, were withheld from the focal participants.

DISCUSSION

This study focused on two disabled girls of color, which allowed the team to see the focal participants' individualized navigations that can go unrecognized in schools. Considering discursive ingenuity, we believe that educational systems must notice the discursive practices of disabled girls of color as underrecognized and understudied strategic abilities. The ways the two disabled girls of color in this study navigated their classrooms and learning experiences must be considered resourceful. Such an ideological and praxical shift (Erevelles, 2011) would lead to honoring and strengthening, not fixing, the discursive practices of disabled girls of color. Teachers would listen fully and respond earnestly throughout the school day. Also, this shift would place a renewed responsibility on school districts to provide the communication and learning supports suggested by disabled girls of color and their families.

In view of the focal participants' repositioning, educational systems must position disabled girls of color as knowledge holders and generators (Delgado Bernal, 2002). This shift requires teachers to give disabled girls of color more opportunities to lead their own learning, interact with peers, and engage more deeply with the content. This shift in thought and practice would create possibilities for teachers to learn from disabled girls of color, as they possess an understanding of the world that their teachers often do not (Annamma & Morrison, 2018). Moreover, teachers would notice how disabled girls of color reposition in relation to power structures and deficit thinking (Annamma et al., 2013a), the girls' responses skillful and thoughtful.

In regard to research, more scholarship rooted in the school experiences of disabled girls of color is required. Youth participatory action research is one methodology for future scholarship, as disabled girls of color are legitimate, valuable research partners (Paris & Winn, 2013). Also, teachers ought to partner with students to explore dominant norms in classrooms and schools (Annamma & Morrison, 2018). Expanding participation to family members and other school personnel (e.g., administrators, paraprofessionals, speech language pathologists) while centering student perspectives would also enrich extant scholarship.

CONCLUSION

The purpose of this study was to understand how discursive practices (e.g., talk, actions) afford or constrain academic and social opportunities for two disabled girls of color. Critical multimodal discourse analysis revealed how the focal participants employed discursive ingenuity and repositioned in response to marginalization through talk and actions (e.g., eye gaze, facial expressions, gestures), as well as how teachers positioned and responded to them. Ultimately, we hope this study illuminates the importance of centering disabled girls of color in pedagogy and scholarship.

NOTES

1. We use the term "disabled girls of color" as opposed to "girls of color with disabilities" in response to calls from the disability community to recognize disability as a political identity that cannot be separated from the person, similar to race and gender (Brown, 2011, 2017). We use the term "girls of color" instead of "young women of color" to honor the experiences, expertise, and youthfulness of the two focal participants (Annamma, 2017). While we recognize that disabled people often experience perpetual infantilization, we also want to draw attention to the fact that the two focal participants are attending K–12 schools, and childhood is often withheld from girls of color (Onyeka-Crawford et al., 2017).

2. We use pseudonyms throughout the chapter to protect participants' identities. The students chose their own pseudonyms. The first author chose pseudonyms for teacher participants.

3. The first author took detailed field notes during each audio/video recorded observation. However, field notes from one observation were missing during analysis.

REFERENCES

Annamma, S. A. (2017). *The pedagogy of pathologization: Dis/abled girls of color in the school-prison nexus*. Routledge.

Annamma, S. A., Boelé, A. L., Moore, B. A., & Klingner, J. (2013a). Challenging the ideology of normal in schools. *International Journal of Inclusive Education*, 17(12), 1278–1294.

Annamma, S. A., Connor, D., & Ferri, B. (2013b). Dis/ability critical race studies (DisCrit): Theorizing at the intersections of race and dis/ability. *Race Ethnicity and Education*, 16(1), 1–31.

Annamma, S. A., Handy, G. T., Miller, A. L., & Jackson, E. (2020). Animating discipline disparities through debilitating practices: Girls of color & withholding in the classroom. *Teachers College Record*, 122(5), 1–46.

Annamma, S. A., & Morrison, D. (2018). DisCrit classroom ecology: Using praxis to dismantle dysfunctional education ecologies. *Teaching and Teacher Education*, 73(1), 70–80.

Anzaldúa, G. (1990). *Making face, making soul/haciendo caras: Creative and critical perspectives of feminists of color*. Aunt Lute Books.

Bhattacharya, K. (2017). *Fundamentals of qualitative research: A practical guide*. Routledge.

Blanchett, W. J., Klingner, J. K., & Harry, B. (2009). The intersection of race, culture, language, and disability: Implications for urban education. *Urban Education*, 44(4), 389–409.

Bolden, G. B., & Hepburn, A. (2018). Transcription for conversation analysis. In *Oxford research encyclopedia of communication, language and social interaction*, advance online publication.

Broderick, A., & Leonardo, Z. (2016). What a good boy: The deployment and distribution of "goodness" as ideological property in schools. In D. J. Connor, B. A. Ferri, & S. A. Annamma (Eds.), *DisCrit: Disability studies and critical race theory in education* (pp. 55–67). Teachers College Press.

Brown, L. X. Z. (2011, August 4). *The significance of semantics: Person-first language: Why it matters*. Autistic Hoya. https://www.autistichoya.com/2011/08/significance-of-semantics-person-first.html

Brown, L. X. Z. (2017, July 28). *Identity and hypocrisy: A second argument against person-first language*. Autistic Hoya. https://www.autistichoya.com/2011/11/identity-and-hypocrisy-second-argument.html

Carrejo, D. J., & Reinhartz, J. (2014). Teachers fostering the co-development of science literacy and language literacy with English language learners. *Teacher Development, 18*(3), 334–348.

Causton-Theoharis, J., Theoharis, G., Orsati, F., & Cosier, M. (2011). Does self-contained special education deliver on its promises? A critical inquiry into research and practice. *Journal of Special Education Leadership, 24*(2), 61–78.

Cazden, C. B., & Beck, S. W. (2003). Classroom discourse. In A. C. Graesser & M. A. Gernsbacher (Eds.), *Handbook of discourse processes* (pp. 165–197). Lawrence Erlbaum Associates.

Collins, K. M. (2011a). Discursive positioning in a fifth-grade writing lesson: The making of a "bad, bad boy." *Urban Education, 46*(4), 741–785.

Collins, K. M. (2011b). "My mom says I'm really creative!": Dis/ability, positioning, and resistance in multimodal instructional contexts. *Language Arts, 88*(6), 409–418.

Connor, D. J. (2008). *Urban narratives: Portraits in progress, life at the intersections of learning disability, race, & social class* (Vol. 5). Peter Lang.

Cowley, D. M. (2013). *"Being grown": How adolescent girls with disabilities narrate self-determination and transitions* (Accession No. 3561437) [Doctoral dissertation, Syracuse University], ProQuest Dissertations and Theses Global.

Davies, B., & Harré, R. (1990). Positioning: The discursive production of selves. *Journal for the Theory of Social Behaviour, 20*(1), 43–63.

de Valenzuela, J. S., Copeland, S. R., Qi, C. H., & Park, M. (2006). Examining educational equity: Revisiting the disproportionate representation of minority students in special education. *Exceptional Children, 72*(4), 425–441.

Delgado Bernal, D. (2002). Critical race theory, Latino critical theory, and critical race-gendered epistemologies: Recognizing students of color as holders and creators of knowledge. *Qualitative Inquiry, 8*(1), 105–126.

Erevelles, N. (2002). (Im)material citizens: Cognitive disability, race, and the politics of citizenship. *Disability, Culture, and Education, 1*(1), 5–25.

Erevelles, N. (2011). *Disability and difference in global contexts: Enabling a transformative body politic*. Palgrave Macmillan.

Erevelles, N., Kanga, A., & Middleton, R. (2006). How does it feel to be a problem? Race, disability, and exclusion in educational policy. In E. Brantlinger (Ed.), *Who benefits from special education?* (pp. 91–114). Routledge.

Erevelles, N., & Minear, A. (2010). Unspeakable offenses: Untangling race and disability in discourses of intersectionality. *Journal of Literary & Cultural Disability Studies*, 4(2), 127–145.

Erickson, F. (1985). Qualitative methods in research on teaching. In M. C. Wittrock (Ed.), *Handbook of research on teaching* (pp. 119–162). Macmillan Publishing Company.

Foucault, M. (1972). *The archeology of knowledge and the discourse on language*. Pantheon Books.

Gee, J. (2011). *An introduction to discourse analysis: Theory and method* (3rd ed.). Routledge.

Harris, C. (1993). Whiteness as property. *Harvard Law Review*, 106(8), 1707–1791.

Hinchman, K. A., & Young, J. P. (2001). Speaking but not being heard: Two adolescents negotiate classroom talk about text. *Journal of Literacy Research*, 33(2), 243–268.

hooks, b. (1989). *Talking back: Thinking feminist, thinking Black*. South End Press.

Ingram, J., & Elliott, V. (2014). Turn taking and "wait time" in classroom interactions. *Journal of Pragmatics*, 62, 1–12.

Jewitt, C. (2005). Classrooms and the design of pedagogic discourse: A multimodal approach. *Culture & Psychology*, 11(3), 309–320.

Jewitt, C. (2008). Multimodality and literacy in school classrooms. *Review of Research in Education*, 32(1), 241–267.

Kress, G. (2010). *Multimodality: A social semiotic approach to contemporary communication*. Routledge.

Kurth, J. A., Born, K., & Love, H. (2016). Ecobehavioral characteristics of self-contained high school classrooms for students with severe cognitive disability. *Research and Practice for Persons with Severe Disabilities*, 41(4), 227–243.

Ladson-Billings, G. (1998). Just what is critical race theory and what's it doing in a nice field like education? *Qualitative Studies in Education*, 11(1), 7–24.

Latz, A. O. (2017). *Photovoice research in education and beyond: A practical guide from theory to exhibition*. Routledge.

Light, J., & McNaughton, D. (2014). Communicative competence for individuals who require augmentative and alternative communication: A new definition for a new era of communication? *Augmentative and Alternative Communication*, 30(1), 1–18.

Lincoln, Y. S., & Guba, E. G. (1985). *Naturalistic inquiry*. Sage.

Lindsay, S., & Tsybina, I. (2011). Predictors of unmet needs for communication and mobility assistive devices among youth with a disability: The role of sociocultural factors. *Disability and Rehabilitation: Assistive Technology*, 6(1), 10–21.

Macbeth, D. (2004). The relevance of repair for classroom correction. *Language in Society*, 33(5), 703–736.

Markee, N. (2015). *The handbook of classroom discourse and interaction*. John Wiley & Sons.

Merriam, S. B. (2001). *Qualitative research and case study applications in education*. Jossey-Bass.

Merriam, S. B., & Tisdell, E. J. (2015). *Qualitative research: A guide to design and implementation* (4th ed.). John Wiley & Sons.

Miles, M. B., & Huberman, A. M. (1994). *Qualitative data analysis: An expanded sourcebook*. Sage.

Miller, A. L. (2019). *Girls of color with intellectual and developmental disabilities reinventing education through an intersectional photographic lens* (Accession No. 13904326). [Doctoral dissertation, University of Kansas]. ProQuest Dissertations and Theses Global.

Mindel, M., & John, J. (2018). Bridging the school and home divide for culturally and linguistically diverse families using augmentative and alternative communication systems. *Perspectives of the ASHA Special Interest Groups, 3*(12), 154–163.

Norris, S. (2004). *Analyzing multimodal interaction: A methodological framework.* Routledge.

Ochs, E. (1979). Transcription as theory. *Developmental Pragmatics, 10*(1), 43–72.

Onyeka-Crawford, A., Patrick, K., & Chaudhry, N. (2017). *Let her learn: Stopping school pushout for girls of color.* National Women's Law Center. https://nwlc .org/wp-content/uploads/2017/04/final_nwlc_Gates_GirlsofColor.pdf

Orsati, F. T. (2015). Control, membership and consequences: Analysis of discursive practices to respond to behaviors of kindergartners with disabilities. *Classroom Discourse, 6*(2), 124–142.

Orsati, F. T., & Causton-Theoharis, J. (2013). Challenging control: Inclusive teachers' and teaching assistants' discourse on students with challenging behaviour. *International Journal of Inclusive Education, 17*(5), 507–525.

Paris, D., & Winn, M. T. (Eds.). (2013). *Humanizing research: Decolonizing qualitative inquiry with youth and communities.* Sage.

Pennington, R. C., & Courtade, G. R. (2015). An examination of teacher and student behaviors in classrooms for students with moderate and severe intellectual disability. *Preventing School Failure: Alternative Education for Children and Youth, 59*(1), 40–47.

Petersen, A. J. (2009). Shana's story: The struggles, quandaries and pitfalls surrounding self-determination. *Disability Studies Quarterly, 29*(2).

Phillipson, R., & Skutnabb-Kangas, T. (1996). English only worldwide or language ecology? *TESOL quarterly, 30*(3), 429–452.

Rodwell, M. K. (1998). *Social work constructivist research.* Routledge.

Rogers, R. (2011). *An introduction to critical discourse analysis in education* (2nd ed.). Routledge.

Saldaña, J. (2013). *The coding manual for qualitative researchers.* Sage.

Seidman, I. (2013). *Interviewing as qualitative research: A guide for researchers in education and the social sciences* (4th ed.). Teachers College Press.

Sinclair, J., Hansen, S. G., Machalicek, W., Knowles, C., Hirano, K. A., Dolata, J. K., Blakely, A. W., Seeley, J., & Murray, C. (2018). A 16-year review of participant diversity in intervention research across a selection of 12 special education journals. *Exceptional Children, 84*(3), 312–329.

Suarez, L. (2017). Restraints, seclusion, and the disabled student: The blurred lines between safety and physical punishment. *University of Miami Law Review, 71*(3), 859–894.

Wang, C., & Burris, M. A. (1997). Photovoice: Concept, methodology, and use for participatory needs assessment. *Health, Education, and Behavior, 24*(3), 369–287.

Wodak, R. (2016). Critical discourse studies: History, agenda, theory, and methodology. In R. Wodak & M. Meyer (Eds.), *Methods of critical discourse analysis studies* (pp. 1–22). Sage.

CHAPTER 4

"It Feels Like Living in a Limbo": Exploring the Limits of Inclusion for Children Living at the Global Affective Intersections of Dis/ability, Language, and Migration in Italy and the United States

Valentina Migliarini, Chelsea Stinson, & David I. Hernández-Saca

In public discourses, migration is widely treated as a controversial issue generating emotional and affective arguments hinging on perceived illegalities and outrage: transgressing political borders, stealing jobs, and subverting legal systems. Such hegemonic emotion discourses (Zembylas, 2002) are tied to affective racist and ableist ideas, constructing migrant bodies as "dangerous" and "undesirable" (Dolmage, 2018). These discourses often translate within education policies and practices. Particularly, inclusive education for first- and second-generation migrant children has failed to address the complexities of living at the global affective intersections of race, dis/ability,[1] language, and migratory status[2] (Artiles & Kozleski, 2007; Migliarini, 2017; Minow, 1991; Zembylas, 2012).

In this chapter, we draw from two case studies conducted in Italy and the United States, focusing on inclusive education for migrant students labeled with disability, in order to respond to Annamma and colleagues' invitation to reflect on how Disability Critical Race Theory (DisCrit) has grown and expanded to shift attitudes and practices in education. For this purpose, the present contribution is structured to answer the primary research question: *To what extent does DisCrit guide us in highlighting the power dynamics within emotions, discourses, and material realities of inclusive education for dis/abled migrant students?* We argue that DisCrit illuminates the limits of contemporary models of inclusive education for migrant students, especially those labeled with dis/abilities. DisCrit shows how educators, under the pressure of global neoliberal reforms, often practice forms of inclusion that replicate traditional special education models through global affective intersectional racism and ableism, and color-evasive discourses (Annamma et al., 2017).

Although we inhabit multiple and different contexts, DisCrit's mutually informing tenets guided us in exposing the power dynamics and the entrenched inequities that are often reproduced by inclusive education. Further, DisCrit's tenets helped us recognize our privileges when developing our relationship with the participants of the study presented in this chapter. The poem *Sono uno del Mediterraneo* by Italian writer and migration activist Erri De Luca (2014) reads:

> [I']m one from the Mediterranean, which is not South or North; it is not East nor West. It is the liquid stomach between Asia, Africa, and Europe. Those who are born on one of its coasts have in their blood an archipelago of people. (p. 20; translated from Italian to English by Migliarini)

Born and raised in the heart of the Mediterranean, the first author is an English language learner and multilingual in Italian, English, French, and Portuguese, and her positionality resonates with De Luca's words. However, her constructions of dis/ability, diversity, and education are tied to Western conceptualizations. As a white, able-bodied, young academic and cis woman, she holds more significant privileges than the migrant communities experiencing colonization considered here. In her research work with refugee communities, she engages with critical literature, epistemologies, theories, and methods. Furthermore, she attempts to build trust with youth by spending time with them and interviewing them multiple times, by adopting transparent research methods, by being authentic in sharing findings, and by acknowledging her own biases.

The second author approaches this work as a white, nondisabled cis woman who was born in the United States. Although she experiences forms of oppression as a survivor of domestic and sexual violence in a patriarchal, heteronormative society, she acknowledges how her positionality affords significant privileges in relation to multiply marginalized communities considered in this chapter. As a former teacher in formal and community-based migrant education settings, she aims to remain accountable to how she, like many participants in the studies presented here, has uncritically implemented policies and practices to reproduce educational inequities and harmful conceptualizations of students' identities. She is committed to cultivating and sustaining relationships with migrant students and families through transparency, reciprocity, and reflexive practice as enacted through this study.

At the age of two, the third author was an immigrant and refugee to the United States due to the civil war in El Salvador in the early 1980s. Now a naturalized citizen of the United States of six years, he is a gay, cisgender Latino of mixed ethnicity (El Salvadorean and Palestinian). As an English language learner or emergent bilingual (Martínez-Álvarez, 2019) in Spanish and English, he was assigned a special education label of auditory learning disability while in grade school that led to post-traumatic stress and psycho-emotional disableism (Thomas, 1999, 2007) due to the socially engendered, global affective intersectional ableist, racist, nativist mechanisms of control, power, and hegemony (Annamma et al., 2013; McDermott et al., 2011). Although he has experienced—and continues to navigate—master narratives that have constrained and afforded his personal narrativization (Gee, 2014; Hammack & Toolis, 2014), he is cognizant of his many significant privileges, especially in comparison to the migrant students at the focus of these studies.

We begin by delineating the empirical foundation for the chapter, situating it within a global affective intersectional research and approach. We then analyze interviewees' experiences within the education and social systems in Italy and the United States, focusing on processes that surround the assessment of language learning and special educational needs (SEN; Ministero dell'Istruzione, dell'Universita' e della Ricerca [MIUR], 2012; 2013) that underlie schools' enactment of inclusive education. We underscore the urgency to reform global inclusive policies and practices by adopting a global affective intersectional stance (Hernández-Saca & Cannon, 2019; Wetherell, 2012), which expands DisCrit to consider migrant students as subjects previously held in limbo at the affective intersections of dis/abilities, migratory status, language, and race.

RESEARCHING DIS/ABILITY, RACE, LANGUAGE, AND MIGRATORY STATUS: GLOBAL AFFECTIVE INTERSECTIONS IN ITALY AND THE UNITED STATES

This chapter offers a global affective intersectional comparative study of educators' experiences enacting inclusive education in Italy and the United States. The empirical research projects were conducted in socially and geographically separate contexts and did not focus equally on every aspect of inequality and dimensions of identities. Although the cultural, linguistic, and policy contexts are inarguably different (D'Alessio & Watkins, 2009), we see important similarities at the critical global affective intersections of dis/ability, race, language, and migratory status shared between these countries. The commonalities between the experiences of refugee students and their educators illuminate critical themes related to the global affective intersection of dis/ability, race, language, and migratory status, which, like the children at the focus of this chapter, exist and persist across political and geographic boundaries.

Global Affective Intersectionality

Intersectionality, a widely used concept in contemporary social science, originated in the work of U.S. critical race theorist Kimberlé Williams Crenshaw (1989, 1991, 1995), and its epistemological lineage is built from the perspectives of Black women and feminists such as Sojourner Truth, Anna Julia Cooper, Audre Lorde, and the Combahee River Collective (1997). In a recent interview with *Time*, Crenshaw urges against the contemporary distortion of intersectionality. As she affirms, it is not identity politics on steroids but a lens to explore how forms of inequality operate together and influence each other. Intersectionality shows how some people are subject to multiple inequalities, and their experience is *not just* the sum of its parts (Steinmetz, 2020).

Intersectionality is approached from different places, often foregrounding some identities or issues over others (Bhopal & Preston, 2012). The projects presented here began with an explicit focus on how migratory status, emotionality, and dis/ability intersect in the lives of first- and second-generation migrant children. The focus arose from the desire to address the silence and the assumptions that often shape inclusive education policy, practice, and research in Italy and the United States, where migrant students are overrepresented in special education (Artiles, 2013; Erevelles, 2014; Iniziative e Studi sulla Multietnicità [ISMU], 2016), and where teachers are not sufficiently equipped to interrupt this phenomenon (Migliarini & Stinson, 2020). By studying education professionals and migrant students (in the Italian case study), we hoped to gain a more critical understanding of the intersections of migratory status and dis/ability at the personal, interpersonal, structural, and political levels that are mediated by emotions, discourse, and materialities (Hernández-Saca et al., 2018). Global affective intersectionality not only illuminates these intersectional levels of dehumanization but also the weaponization of emotions, feelings, and affects given the legacies of colonization such as racism and ableism and the socially engendered nation-building policies and practices that have historically been undergirded by capitalism, imperialism, and nationalism. We argue that global affective intersectionality constrains the humane relationships that are possible outside of such emotion and discursive and material hegemonic realities for dis/abled migrant youth at their intersections of power and identities for what counts as inclusion (Artiles et al., 2011).

Italy and U.S. Case Study Contexts and Methods

We limited our focus to two urban contexts: one in central Italy and the other in upstate New York in the United States. These qualitative studies were conducted in 2014–2016 and 2017–2018, respectively. The Italian study was based in nine refugee service centers in the city of Rome following a constructivist grounded theory methodological approach (Charmaz, 2014). Data collection involved in-depth, semistructured interviews with 27 participants, including 17 educators, cultural mediators, and other professionals with different levels of experience in migration, and 10 migrant children from West African countries at different stages of their asylum request process.

The U.S. study developed in two phases. Phase one involved critical discourse analysis (Fairclough, 2010) of existing inclusive policies and school reforms at state and local levels, focusing on policies related to the educational label of English language learner (ELL).[3] Phase two involved qualitative semistructured interviews with 10 teachers and school-based disability-related service providers working directly with first- and second-generation migrant students in upstate New York. The participants in Italy and the United States were selected through a combination of purposive and snowballing sampling (Glaser & Strauss, 1967; Miles & Huberman, 1994).

Data analysis and comparison between Italy and the United States revealed interesting global affective intersections among dis/ability, migratory status, language, and race that we did not expect. For example, in the nine refugee centers in Rome, most of the professionals did not consider dis/ability as an issue for young West African refugees and, therefore, were unequipped to offer dis/ability-related services:

> [W]ithin these centers where asylum seekers arrive, there is neither the competence nor the tools to identify a disability and implement a suitable intervention. But instead, they are sorted into normal reception, with normal problems. [Lorenzo, Prof]

This excerpt demonstrates how intake processes for migrant youth do not consider the possibility of offering support for dis/abilities. Indeed, dis/ability is not considered for forced migrants who are cast in a hegemonic narrative that renders them functioning subjects able to contribute to the economy of the host society (Migliarini, 2017). As we discuss in the following sections of this chapter, similar intake processes in the United States preclude recognition of dis/abled identities illegible to white, Western norms. For the purpose of this chapter, several DisCrit tenets are applied to the experiences of migrant children at the affective intersections of dis/ability, migratory status, language, and race. In presenting the comparative data analysis between Italy and the United States, we highlight how excerpts speak to and expand specific tenets of DisCrit.

Lorenzo's account aligns with DisCrit tenet three, which "emphasizes the social constructions of race and ability and yet recognizes the material and psychological impacts of being labeled as raced or dis/abled, which sets one outside of the western cultural norms" (Annamma et al., 2016 p. 19). It expands tenet three by adding the migratory status social construct component to the intersection of race and dis/ability. Migrant students are labeled disabled by imposed assessments, supports, and emotionalities (Ahmed, 2000) that do not affirm their cultural, racialized, linguistic, and dis/abled experiences, thus dehumanizing them within an affective atmosphere of practice (Wetherell, 2012).

DisCrit tenet one focuses on ways that the forces of racism and ableism circulate interdependently, often in neutralized and invisible ways, to uphold notions of normalcy. Our case studies expand tenet one by exposing the intersections of racism and ableism with the normalizing forces of white European citizenship and power majority languages. Migrant students in Italy and the United States are simultaneously constructed as dis/abled and racialized upon arrival, as professionals in both studies constructed them as illiterate and intellectually different. Many professionals relied on Western expectations and assumptions about schooling:

> We have realised that the teens from Sub-Saharan Africa, which flee persecution in their country and thus they have the condition to request for asylum, they are illiterate . . . most of them, they didn't go to school, because they were facing dangerous situations back at home. [Elena, Prof_Serv 3.1]

Elena's account shows very specifically how illiteracy is a fictitious construction to mask the process of racialization of migrant children. Under the pressure of neoliberal reforms in education, emphasizing school and individualized accountability for student performance and achievement, Italian and U.S. professionals do not seem to be particularly willing to explore culturally sustaining educational strategies (e.g., Paris, 2012; Paris & Alim, 2014), that embrace migrant youth culture and historicity. On the contrary, they reproduce a deficit approach to education, taking migrant youth out of the educational endeavor. Such an attitude is in line with the tendency of labeling migrant children as having special educational needs because of their cultural, social, and linguistic disadvantage (Migliarini et al., 2019). Such labeling has emotive and affective consequences on youth's human agency (Ahearn, 2001), given how special education labels have also been empirically documented within the literature as creating an additional stigma on the well-being of historically multiply marginalized youth (Hernández-Saca & Cannon, 2019).

ASSESSMENT OF LANGUAGE AND SPECIAL EDUCATIONAL NEEDS

The provision of education and services for migrant youth in Italy and the United States emphasizes processes of assessment of language proficiency, which do not necessarily result in adequate or sustained support for the perceived deficits these assessments aim to identify. This contributes to the construction of a binary between being labeled a migrant student who is deserving of inclusive educational supports, services, and spaces or a migrant student with a disability who is only deserving of special education-related supports, services, and spaces. While most education professionals interviewed in both studies were ill equipped to offer inclusive supports and services, they were poised to enact and affirm bureaucratic evaluation processes that yielded these deficit-based labels related to disability, illiteracy in the dominant language, and special education placement (Artiles, 2013; Valencia, 2010).

Italian Context

The complex relationship between race and special educational needs is well known within the Black and immigrant communities in the United States (Erevelles, 2000; Ferri & Connor, 2006; Harry & Klingner, 2014), but it only recently became clear in the Italian context following policy reform regarding the identification and assessment of students in the macro-category of special educational needs (SEN; MIUR, 2012; 2013).[4] Although these policies were introduced to bring equity for all learners experiencing failure due to lack of educational support, they tend to focus on the individual deficit rather than on rendering the educational system—its context and methods—inclusive (Migliarini et al., 2018). Following the implementation of these policies, an increasing number of migrant and refugee students attending public schools have been labeled as SEN (ISMU, 2016). Like the teachers in the U.S. study, Italian educators label migrants as disabled due to their lack of training and knowledge about students' backgrounds. They refer migrant students to professionals for standardized certification of dis/abilities. In both contexts, the construction of migrant children dis/abilities by education professionals serves as a dog whistle for enacting racism, ableism, and, in turn, exclusion and dehumanization.

Most participants in the Italian study allude to "the culture of referral" (Harry & Klingner, 2014, p. 103), which can be defined as the attitude toward and beliefs about certain children who were not doing well in the general education or social programs, as well as beliefs about special education:

> I'm thinking of the boy from Cameroon [. . .]; he was here with us, he had some psychological issues, I think depression. After he left our organization, he was referred to the ASL then to a psychiatric center, I don't know what was the diagnosis but then they put him in a foster care specialized for mental diseases. [Paolo, Prof_Serv 3.1]

As Paolo emphasizes, only the migrant youth with significant symptoms (e.g., depression) are referred to local mental health facilities. In this process, race and dis/ability are used to justify the labeling of migrants as at-risk and the weaponization of their emotions, feelings, and affects through the biomedical establishment (Mills, 2014). As stated in DisCrit's tenet one, the intertwining forces of institutional racism and ableism in place during the process of labeling reinforce the norms of white supremacy and signal those students deemed incapable in body and mind (Annamma et al., 2013; Beratan, 2008). This predicament indicates DisCrit tenet three, since the social constructions of both race and ability are structuring the lived experiences of these migrant students in both the Italian and U.S. contexts. Contrary to what Lorenzo affirmed in relation to the lack of support for disability diagnosis within refugee reception centers, Paolo shows how for the boy from Cameroon assistance was put in place to address his mental health issue. The referral of this Black asylum-seeking youth out of the mainstream reception center links and expands DisCrit tenet six. Whiteness and ability are properties, and gains for people at the intersections of dis/ability, race, migratory status, and language are made as a result of interest convergence of white European middle-class citizens.

U.S. Context

Assessment of language and dis/ability was a primary focus for many of the educators in both studies, as participants who taught migrant students expressed concern about teaching English to migrant students with unrecognized dis/abilities in addition to ELL status. In the United States, first- and second-generation migrant youth are subjected to comprehensive evaluation processes upon enrollment in public school in New York State. One major component of these processes, the New York State Identification Test for English Language Learners (NYSITELL), is administered in English and limits the implementation of testing accommodations to students who already have qualifying Individualized Education Programs (IEPs), 504 plans, or "incur an injury (e.g., broken arm) or experience the onset of either a short- or long-term disability (either cognitive or physical) within 30 days prior to test administration" based on administrative discretion (NYSDE, 2018). As such, education professionals are poised to construct students through a binary grounded in the prevailing hegemonic narrative of ability and function. This narrative extends beyond the initial language proficiency assessment processes to schools, where students are placed in specialized programs or spaces depending on the determination of their status as learners—reifying an ethos of a medical–racist–psychological model of disability rooted within students.

As an example, Kelly, a white, monolingual English teacher, describes her school specifically created for newly arrived migrant students who are labeled English language learners (ELLs) based on their scores on the NYSITELL. The mission of this special school is to provide targeted instruction and support across subject areas while maintaining respect for the cultural backgrounds and values of the students.

> . . . We're not really supposed to have any kids with disabilities because we really just want to get the kids that know nothing to really be set to be put back into the mainstream schools. But, in other schools in [CITY], there's plenty with IEPs. (Teacher_ Kelly)

Here, Kelly conceptualizes dis/ability status as exclusively constitutive from migrant status. That is, dis/ability is something singular and separate from migrant status. As such, the international center, with its specialized structures to support language acquisition and development, was intended for students assigned a narrow conceptualization of migrant status. At the same time, they are considered kids that know nothing, which is why they are in need of a segregated, specialized program to prepare them for inclusion.

Conversely, students with disabilities cannot claim the same status and, therefore, belong in other schools. Following DisCrit tenet one, which emphasizes how racism and ableism circulate interdependently in neutralized ways to uphold notions of normalcy, this exclusionary assessment process highlights how the targeted instruction and supports disabled migrant students deserve is yet unaddressed by policy and practice in U.S. and Italian school systems. Further, the development of a segregated learning space for migrant students to provide targeted instruction in a culturally sustaining setting demonstrates an approach to inclusion through individualization (Migliarini et al., 2019), which reinforces singular notions of identity. In other words, disability status trumps migrant or ELL status (Kangas, 2014), and only migrant or ELL status calls for targeted, culturally sustaining instruction in school environments.

Many educators interviewed in both studies expressed frustration with the dis/ability and language proficiency identification processes in their schools after students were enrolled, often citing beliefs that their students demonstrated deficits beyond what they typically expected of migrant students. These teachers pointed to individual students for whom they were advocating for a disability diagnosis. Teachers often seek to rework students' identities so that they align with a framework for schooling informed by Western cultural norms. For example, Maureen, a white monolingual second-grade teacher in a classroom for ELL students, asks during her interview,

> *Interviewer:* . . . How many students with [a] disability [do] you have in your class?
> *Maureen:* Um, with a labeled disability, or, uh, a disability I'm trying to get them labeled with? [Teacher_ Maureen]

This incident relates to DisCrit tenets one and two, which are connected in a dialogic process. DisCrit tenet one, which emphasizes the interdependent circulation of racism and ableism to uphold hegemonic notions of normalcy, highlights how teachers like Maureen use labeling as a tool for upholding their understanding of normalcy in their classrooms. In other words, when students do not appear to be making growth or progress as a result of teachers' general education practices, the students' abilities are targeted as the site of deviance—again illuminating the institutionalization of the medical–psychological model of disability. This is exacerbated for migrant students, who often enter the school with an educational label that predisposes them to individualized support and surveillance from their classroom teachers. As such, when these students do not appear to make adequate progress, they are fast-tracked into the migrant ELL/dis/abled migrant binary construction following DisCrit tenet two. Students' lack of progress can be attributed to either migrant status or underlying dis/ability. However, the teachers in both studies, rather than adjust their instruction to support students' needs more comprehensively, turn to clinical models of intervention, disability, and referral to remediate students. These models are rooted in historical racist and ableist notions of backwardness (Franklin, 1980), a label used by educators at the turn of the 20th century to identify students who, due to "poor home environment, the inability to speak English, and poor school attendance" (p. 11), did not perform as expected in schools.

In these schooling contexts, disability and race are co-constructed through assessment and identification processes to uphold affective hegemonic notions of mythical order and normalcy rooted in historical concepts of backwardness in children (Franklin, 1980). In other words, bureaucratic mechanisms facilitate segregation and control under the guise of benevolence and educational appropriateness. To U.S. teachers, the way that non-disabled migrant students know nothing—that is, the deficit-based view of these students' capacity upon arrival to the United States—is conceptually different from how disabled students might know nothing. This is connected to the interviews with professionals in the Italian context, who conceptualize migrant students' identities as inherently culturally, socially, and linguistically disadvantaged. The disabled migrant context of knowing nothing is distinct from the language learner context of knowing nothing because the first one is fixed and extricated from racial–linguistic identity, whereas the second is solely attributed to racial–linguistic identity, starting with language proficiency assessment upon enrollment in school. The findings within this section are not decoupled from the role of emotion, feelings, and affect as it relates to language learning and how affect structures our human relationships within global educational contexts (Benesch, 2013; Prior, 2015).

CONCLUSION: DISCRIT AND MIGRANT STUDENTS

Across migration and inclusive education policy contexts, migrants and teachers are positioned as objects of policy, rather than agents of their own social, emotional, and political futures (Turner & Mangual Figueroa, 2019).

In this chapter, we offered a comparative global affective intersectional analysis of qualitative case studies conducted in Italy and the United States focused on the limits of inclusive education of dis/abled migrant students. Although inclusive education is conceptualized differently internationally, the category of migrant student exists within and across social, emotional, affective, political, and geographic boundaries—often through multiple journeys and returns. It is crucial that inclusive education researchers seek to understand migrant students' experiences and voices in comparison and in contrast. As the findings presented in this chapter demonstrate, existing migration policies function in tandem with hegemonic language- and disability-related education policies and practices at state and local levels to reproduce and reverberate the negative racist and ableist conceptualization of migrant identities. However, because the social, affective, and political category of migrant student intersects with a variety of marginalized social identities, migrant students are often relegated to a position of precarity in education practice and research. As such, we argue that global affective intersectional approaches to inclusive education research through expanding Disability Critical Race Theory (DisCrit) can address the emotive, feelings, and affective intersecting oppressions impacting dis/abled migrant students. Global affective intersectional approaches help move toward counterhegemonic inclusive education policies and practices that can lead to new critical emotion praxis. This praxis implies the coupling of critical thinking, reflection, and feeling before all educational agents act within global educational contexts with first- and second-generation migrant students at their intersections of power and identities (Artiles & Kozleski, 2007; Zembylas, 2012).

The authors came together to analyze data from Italy and the United States to forge a new educational equity research practice based on the practical and theoretical expansion of DisCrit. As such, we aim to personally take DisCrit through a global affective intersectional approach, which counters the legacy of social science positivism and scientism hegemony in special education and migration. This is evident in our sense-making of the medical professionals' experiences of the Italian and American participants, whose work often functions to dehumanize and devalue bodyminds within the hegemonic order of inclusive education for migrant students. The dehumanization of the migrant students in both countries occurred through not only the personal, interpersonal, structural, and political dimensions of their intersectionality but also emotionally, discursively, and materially. Crucially, DisCrit, with its lineage centered within the African diaspora in resisting the violence of global colonization, is expanded in this chapter to account for migrants as global affective intersectional subjects whose oppression is normalized by the policies and the practices of whiteness and ableism in special education across both countries. In this way, the emotional, material, and discursive realities engendered by global affective intersectionality constrains the human agency (Ahearn, 2001) of migrant students through moment-to-moment interactions with education professionals. Without expanding DisCrit to address global affective intersectionality, migrant subjects at the intersection of emotions, feelings, affects, dis/ability, language, and race are held in endless limbo.

Lastly, through this chapter we envision a superordinate meta-affective and metacognitive model of critical emotional praxis (Artiles & Kozleski, 2007; Zembylas, 2012) for teachers and school professionals working with migrant students. This model is informed by the critical affective turn within the social sciences (Athanasiou et al., 2009; Clough & Halley, 2007). We argue that DisCrit can be expanded to contribute to the study of emotions, feelings, and affects from an explicitly historical, social, cultural, and political lens to account for the emotive in the lives of students with multidimensional identities and lives in local and global contexts against global affective hegemony. Through this expanded framework, knowledge, feelings, emotions, and affect enter a reciprocal relationship with teaching practice (Hernández-Saca, 2019; Valle & Connor, 2019). Our expansion of DisCrit toward global affective intersectionality helps teachers to understand *and feel* how migrants have been pathologized and perceived as maladjusted in the host society (King, 1968). We argue that teachers and education professionals must engage in personal and interpersonal, structural and political critical emotion praxis toward professional-, program-, and systems-level renewal for continuous improvement and teacher learning (Artiles & Kozleski, 2007; Zembylas, 2012). Such meta-affective and metacognitive critical emotion praxis can engender a transformative praxis and counter affective-hegemonic actions and choices, internally and externally, to enable a self, other, and world relationship that proactively co-creates critical affective practices (Wetherell, 2012) when engaging migrant students and their families toward transformative justice and humanization for the common good (Annamma & Handy, 2019).

NOTES

1. By dis/ability, we mean the social and emotional construction of both disability and ability mediated by feelings, affects, and political, relational, cultural, and social factors that both afford and constrain people and students with impairments' agency and their material and psychological well-being (Annamma et al., 2013; Thomas, 1999, 2007).

2. In light of the tenets of DisCrit, we are very conscious about the language used to describe the migrant communities that we focus on in this chapter. As Benhabib (2000) and Rumbaut (1991) highlight, the motives for migration determine whether a subject is called a migrant or forced migrant because they are fleeing because of fear of persecution (political motives), or a migrant because they are traveling because they are motivated by the aspiration of better material opportunities. In this chapter, we explicitly use migratory status as the general term indicating all different reasons

determining migration. We believe that the different classifications between migrant/immigrant/refugees do not do justice to the history and the pathway of a person at their intersections of power, emotionality, and identities. Importantly, we reckon that the state-imposed definitions of refugee or im-migrant (and conversely illegal or undocumented im-migrant) have social, political, economic, emotional, and educational impacts on the life of people at their intersections of power and identities.

3. The term "English language learner" is the student classification used in the New York State policy context. We worked directly with New York State policy documents and teachers who used variations of the term ELL, which refers to first- and second-generation migrant students and other bilingual or multilingual students whose primary language is not English. When referring to U.S. data and specific policy documents, we use the term ELL, but otherwise use the term migrant students or first- and second-generation migrant students to facilitate continuity across data, findings, and discussion sections in this chapter.

4. Since the 1970s, Italy has been considered an inclusive educational system. Following a significant increase in the number of migrant students in Italian classrooms, the Italian Ministry of Public Education (MIUR) introduced in 2012 the macro-category of special educational needs (SEN) through a three-tiered categorization system that focuses on different types of provisions for learners. The first subcategory includes children with severe physical or intellectual impairments; the second and third subcategories comprise children with learning difficulties certified by public or private clinical diagnosis, and students with cultural, linguistic, and socioeconomic disadvantage without certified medical diagnosis but still requiring support (D'Alessio & Watkins, 2009).

REFERENCES

Ahearn, L. M. (2001). Language and agency. *Annual Review of Anthropology, 30*(1), 109–137.

Ahmed, S. (2000). *Strange encounters: Embodied others in post-coloniality.* Routledge.

Annamma, S. A., Boelé, A. L., Moore, B. A., & Klingner, J. (2013). Challenging the ideology of normal in schools. *International Journal of Inclusive Education, 17*(12), 1278–1294. https://doi.org/10.1080/13603116.2013.802379

Annamma, S. A., Connor, D., & Ferri, B. (2013). Dis/ability critical race studies (DisCrit): Theorizing at the intersections of race and dis/ability. *Race Ethnicity and Education, 16*(1), 1–31. https://doi.org/10.1080/13613324.2012.730511

Annamma, S. A., & Handy, T. (2019). DisCrit solidarity as curriculum studies and transformative praxis. *Curriculum Inquiry, 49*(4), 442–463.

Annamma, S. A., Jackson, D. D., & Morrison, D. (2017). Conceptualizing color-evasiveness: Using dis/ability critical race theory to expand a color-blind racial ideology in education and society. *Race Ethnicity and Education, 20*(2), 147–162. https://doi.org/10.1080/13613324.2016.1248837

Artiles, A. J. (2013). Untangling the racialization of disabilities: An intersectionality critique across disability models. *Du Bois Review: Social Science Research on Race, 10*(2), 329–347. https://doi.org/10.1017/S1742058X13000271

Artiles, A. J., & Kozleski, E. B. (2007). Beyond convictions: Interrogating culture, history, and power in inclusive education. *Language Arts*, *84*(4), 351–358.

Artiles, A. J., Kozleski, E. B., & Gonzalez, T. (2011). Beyond the allure of inclusive education in the United States: Facing power, pursuing a cultural-historical agenda. *Revista Teias*, *12*(24), 285–308.

Athanasiou, A., Hantzaroula, P., & Yannakopoulos, K. (2009). Towards a new epistemology: The affective turn. *Historein*, *8*, 5–16.

Benesch, S. (2013). *Considering emotions in critical English language teaching: Theories and praxis*. Routledge.

Benhabib, S. (2000). *The rights of others: Aliens, residence, citizens*. Cambridge University Press.

Beratan, G. D. (2008). The song remains the same: Transposition and the disproportionate representation of minority students in special education. *Race Ethnicity and Education*, *11*(4), 337–354. https://doi.org/10.1080/13613320802478820

Bhopal, K., & Preston, J. (Eds.). (2012). *Intersectionality and "race" in education* (Vol. 64). Routledge.

Charmaz, K. (2014). *Constructing grounded theory* (2nd ed.). Sage.

Clough, P. T., & Halley, J. (2007). *The affective turn: Theorizing the social*. Duke University Press.

Combahee River Collective. (1977). A black feminist statement. In J. James & T. D. Sharpley-Whiting (Eds.), *The black feminist reader* (pp. 261–270). Blackwell Publishers Ltd.

Connor, D., Cavendish, W., Gonzalez, T., & Jean-Pierre, P. (2019). Is a bridge even possible over troubled waters? The field of special education negates the overrepresentation of minority students: A DisCrit analysis. *Race Ethnicity and Education*, *22*(6), 723–745. https://doi.org/10.1080/13613324.2019.1599343

Crenshaw, K. (1989). Demarginalizing the intersection of race and sex: A black feminist critique of antidiscrimination doctrine, feminist theory and antiracist politics. *University of Chicago Legal Forum*, *1989*(1), 139–167. https://chicagounbound.uchicago.edu/uclf/vol1989/iss1/8

Crenshaw, K. (1991). Mapping the margins: Intersectionality, identity politics, and violence against women of color. *Stanford Law Review*, *43*(6), 1241–1299. https://doi.org/10.2307/1229039

Crenshaw, K., Gotanda, N., Peller, G., & Thomas, K. (1995). *Critical race theory: The key writings that formed the movement*. The New Press.

D'Alessio, S., & Watkins, A. (2009). International comparisons of inclusive policy and practice: Are we talking about the same thing? *Research in Comparative and International Education*, *4*(3), 233–249. https://doi.org/10.2304%2Frcie.2009.4.3.233

De Luca, E. (2014). Sono uno del Mediterraneo. In *La Musica Provata*. Cambridge University Press.

Dolmage, J. T. (2018). *Disabled upon arrival: Eugenics, immigration, and the construction of race and disability*. Ohio State University Press.

Erevelles, N. (2000). Educating unruly bodies: Critical pedagogy, disability studies, and the politics of schooling. *Educational Theory*, *50*(1), 25–47. https://doi.org/10.1111/j.1741-5446.2000.00025.x

Erevelles, N. (2014). Crippin' Jim Crow: Disability, dis-location, and the school-to-prison pipeline. In L. Ben-Moshe, C. Chapman., & A.C. Carey (Eds.), *Disability incarcerated* (pp. 81–99). Palgrave Macmillan.

Fairclough, N. (2010). *Critical discourse analysis: The critical study of language* (2nd ed.). Routledge.

Ferri, B. A., & Connor, D. J. (2006). *Reading resistance: Discourses of exclusion in desegregation & inclusion debates* (Vol. 1). Peter Lang.

Franklin, B. M. (1980). From backwardness to LD: Behaviorism, systems theory, and the learning disabilities field historically reconsidered. *Journal of Education, 162*(4), 5–22. https://doi.org/10.1177%2F002205748016200403

Gee, J. P. (2014). *An introduction to discourse analysis: Theory and method.* Routledge.

Glaser, B. G., & Strauss, A. L. (1967). *The discovery of grounded theory: Strategies for qualitative research.* Aldine de Gruyter.

Hammack, P. L., & Toolis, E. (2014). Narrative and the social construction of adulthood. In B. Schiff (Ed.), *Rereading personal narrative and life course: New directions in child and adolescent development* (pp. 43–56). John Wiley & Sons.

Harry, B., & Klingner, J. K. (2014). *Why are so many minority students in special education?: Understanding race & disability in schools* (2nd ed.). Teachers College Press.

Hernández-Saca, D. (2019). Youth at the intersections of dis/ability, other markers of identity and emotionality: Toward a critical pedagogy of student knowledge, emotion, feeling, affect and being. *Teachers College Record, 121*(13), 1–16.

Hernández-Saca, D., & Cannon, M. A. (2019). Interrogating disability epistemologies: Towards collective dis/ability intersectional emotional, affective and spiritual autoethnographies for healing. *International Journal of Qualitative Studies in Education, 32*(3), 243–262.

Hernández-Saca, D. I., Gutmann Kahn, L., & Cannon, M. A. (2018). Intersectional dis/ability research: How dis/ability research in education engages intersectionality to uncover the multidimensional construction of dis/abled experiences. *Review of Research in Education, 42*(1), 286–311.

Iniziative e Studi sulla Multietnicità (ISMU). (2016). *Alunni con cittadinanza non Italiana. La scuola multiculturale nei contesti locali. Rapporto nazionale A.S. 2014/2015.* Fondazione ISMU.

Kangas, S. E. (2014). When special education trumps ESL: An investigation of service delivery for ELLs with disabilities. *Critical Inquiry in Language Studies, 11*(4), 273–306. https://doi.org/10.1080/15427587.2014.968070

King Jr., M. L. (1968). The role of the behavioral scientist in the civil rights movement. *American Psychologist, 23*(3), 180–186.

Martínez-Álvarez, P. (2019). Dis/ability labels and emergent bilingual children: Current research and new possibilities to grow as bilingual and biliterate learners. *Race Ethnicity and Education, 22*(2), 174–193. https://doi.org/10.1080/13613324.2018.1538120

McDermott, R., Edgar, B., & Scarloss, B. (2011). Global norming. In A. J. Artiles, E. B. Kozleski, & F. R. Waitoller (Eds.). *Inclusive education: Examining equity on five continents* (pp. 223–235). Harvard Education Press.

Migliarini, V. (2017). Subjectivation, agency and the schooling of raced and dis/abled asylum-seeking children in the Italian context. *Intercultural Education, 28*(2), 182–195. https://doi.org/10.1080/14675986.2017.1297091

Migliarini, V. (2018). "Colour-evasiveness" and racism without race: The disablement of asylum-seeking children at the edge of fortress Europe. *Race Ethnicity and Education*, *21*(4), 438–457. https://doi.org/10.1080/13613324.2017.1417252

Migliarini, V., D'Alessio, S., & Bocci, F. (2018). SEN policies and migrant children in Italian schools: Micro-exclusions through discourses of equality. *Discourse: Studies in the Cultural Politics of Education*, *41*(6), 887–900. https://doi.org/10.1080/01596306.2018.1558176

Migliarini, V., & Stinson, C. (2020). Inclusive education in the (new) era of anti-immigration policy: Enacting equity for disabled English language learners. *International Journal of Qualitative Studies in Education*, *34*(1), 72–88. https://doi.org/10.1080/09518398.2020.1735563

Migliarini, V., Stinson, C., & D'Alessio, S. (2019). "SENitizing" migrant children in inclusive settings: Exploring the impact of the Salamanca statement thinking in Italy and the United States. *International Journal of Inclusive Education*, *23*(7–8), 754–767. https://doi.org/10.1080/13603116.2019.1622804

Miles, M. B., & Huberman, A. M. (1994). *Qualitative data analysis: An expanded sourcebook* (2nd ed.). Sage.

Mills, C. (2014). *Decolonizing global mental health: The psychiatrization of the majority world*. Routledge.

Ministero dell' Istruzione, dell' Università e della Ricerca (MIUR). (2012). *Strumenti d'intervento pera alunni con bisogni educativi speciali e organizzazione territoriale per l'inclusione scolastica*. http://www.marche.istruzione.it/dsa/allegati/dir271212.pdf

Ministero dell' Istruzione, dell' Università e della Ricerca (MIUR). (2013). *Circolare n°8, strumenti d'intervento per gli alunni con i bisogni educativi speciali*. http://www.flcgil.it/leggi-normative/documenti/circolari-ministeriali/circolare-ministeriale-8-del-6-marzo-2013-strumenti-di-intervento-per-gli-alunni-con-bisogni-educativi-speciali-bes.flc.

Minow, M. (1991). *Making all the differences: Inclusion, exclusion, and the American law*. Cornell University Press.

New York State Department of Education (NYSDE). (2018). *NYSITELL: Guide to the NYSITELL* [Assessment Administration Manual]. http://www.p12.nysed.gov/assessment/nysitell/2018/nysitellguide18rev.pdf

Paris, D. (2012). Culturally sustaining pedagogy: A needed change in stance, terminology, and practice. *Educational Researcher*, *41*(3), 93–97.

Paris, D., & Alim, H. S. (2014). What are we seeking to sustain through culturally sustaining pedagogy? A loving critique forward. *Harvard Educational Review*, *84*(1), 85–100.

Prior, M. T. (2015). *Emotion and discourse in L2 narrative research*. Multilingual Matters.

Rumbaut, R. G. (1991). The agony of exile: A study of the migration and adaptation of Indochinese refugee adults and children. In F. L. Ahearn & J. L. Athey (Eds.). *Refugee children: Theory, research, and services* (pp. 53–91). Johns Hopkins University Press.

Steinmetz, K. (2020, February 20). *She coined the term "intersectionality" over 30 years ago. Here's what it means to her today*. Time. https://time.com/5786710/kimberle-crenshaw-intersectionality/

Thomas, C. (1999). *Female forms: Experiencing and understanding disability*. Open University Press.

Thomas, C. (2007). *Sociologies of disability and illness: Contested ideas in disability studies and medical sociology.* Palgrave Macmillan.

Turner, E. O., & Mangual Figueroa, A. (2019). Immigration policy and education in lived reality: A framework for researchers and educators. *Educational Researcher, 48*(8), 549–557. https://doi.org/10.3102%2F0013189X19872496

Valencia, R. R. (2010). *Dismantling contemporary deficit thinking: Educational thought and practice.* Routledge.

Valle, J. W., & Connor, D. J. (2019). *Rethinking disability: A disability studies approach to inclusive practices* (2nd ed.). Routledge.

Wetherell, M. (2012). *Affect and emotion: A new social science understanding.* Sage. http://dx.doi.org/10.4135/9781446250945

Zembylas, M. (2002). "Structures of feeling" in curriculum and teaching: Theorizing the emotional rules. *Educational theory, 52*(2), 187–208.

Zembylas, M. (2012). Critical emotional praxis for reconciliation education: Emerging evidence and pedagogical implications. *Irish Educational Studies, 31*(1), 19–33.

Part II

INWARD INQUIRIES

CHAPTER 5

Does DisCrit Travel? The Global South and Excess Theoretical Baggage Fees

Tanushree Sarkar, Carlyn Mueller, & Anjali Forber-Pratt

India has the highest number of disabled children between the ages of 10–18 in the world, yet disabled people are "one of the most disenfranchised groups in India" (Hiranandani & Sonpal, 2010, p. 1). The current policies around inclusive education are "largely exclusive of children with a disability" (Grills et al., 2019, p. 1756). Thus, children with disabilities in India are less likely to be in school and more likely to drop out (Bakhshi et al., 2017). However, exclusion from educational opportunities is not limited to disabled children—historical inequities toward the poor, Dalits,[1] Adivasis,[2] and Muslims continue to be features of the educational landscape in India. The exclusionary aspects of the Indian education system are in part a lineage of the colonial education system, devised to create a class of Indians who were "English in tastes, in opinions, in morals, and in intellect" (Macaulay, 1835, as cited in Kalyanpur, 2018, p. 400). Furthermore, disabled children from specific disability categories and genders are affected disproportionately; children with autism and cerebral palsy are least likely to be enrolled in schools (Singal et al., 2017), and girls with disabilities are also less likely to be enrolled in schools (Bakhshi et al., 2017; Singal et al., 2017). Limited but growing research exists showcasing the strengths and the resiliency of multiply minoritized disabled students in India (Forber-Pratt & Lyew, 2019).

India's government enacted several policies to create a more inclusive education system. Historically, these policies and programs were and are influenced and funded by international agencies and organizations such as the United Nations Educational, Scientific and Cultural Organization (UNESCO), the United Nations Children's Fund (UNICEF), and the World Bank (Naraian, 2016; Singal, 2006b). However, scholars argue that international agencies have not always attended to the needs of children with disabilities in India (Kalyanpur, 2008; Singal, 2005, 2006b). The critiques of Northern inclusive education led Indian scholars to call for indigenous and culturally relevant understandings of inclusion (Hodkinson & Devarakonda, 2011; Johansson, 2014). One critical missing element toward the goal of a culturally relevant inclusive education is a theoretical foundation that appreciates culturally held values and local knowledge while addressing intersecting forms of exclusion and inequity in the Indian context.

In the United States, DisCrit emerged as a powerful framework to reimagine schools as sites of resistance by acknowledging intersectional oppressions in the curriculum, pedagogy, and classroom relationships (Annamma & Morrison, 2018). DisCrit examines and "exposes how ability is distributed and withheld based on race through policies and practices," through the recognition of marginalizing processes that shape and impact multiple dimensions of identity simultaneously (Annamma & Morrison, 2018, p. 72). What affordances might this theory hold in an Indian context? In this chapter, we focus our deeper analysis on tenets two and three, focusing on identity and the material and social impacts of disability in India while highlighting broader application to other tenets throughout.

Both DisCrit and inclusive education scholars in India seek to trouble the "unmarked norms of white, middle class and able-bodied population" (Singal, 2019, p. 836) that are at the center of educational systems in the United States and India. Stienstra and Nyerere (2016) note the importance of coloniality and globalization in the intersections of race, ethnicity, and disability in the Global South; we extend this thinking toward inclusive education in India. This chapter addresses the consequences of traveling with DisCrit in our baggage and offers a glimpse into what DisCrit's journey to India might look like: How will DisCrit be received at customs? Do we need to repack our theoretical backpacks? What other luggage do we need to take with us, and what do we bring back?

THE NEED TO GET AWAY: PROBLEMS IN NORTHERN INCLUSIVE EDUCATION

First-generation countries such as Norway, Sweden, the United States, the United Kingdom, and Canada are considered "pioneers in inclusive education," which often relied on established financial and political institutions (Artiles et al., 2011, p. 3). As a result, inclusive education became a traveling theory in contemporary education policy (Naraian, 2016; Slee, 2008): the policies and practices of inclusive education have been diffused, borrowed, and imposed across the globe, particularly in the Global South. However, it was not just inclusive education policy that traveled from the North to the South; the problems embedded within Northern theory traveled with it. This chapter discusses three of these problems: inequity in inclusive education and misapplied principles from special education; overreliance on the social model of disability; and the tensions between neoliberal policy and social justice.

While related, special educational principles are intertwined with and potentially misapplied to inclusive education in confusing ways. First, the connections between special and inclusive education are embedded within the 1994 Salamanca Statement and the 1990 Jomtien Education for All conference (Florian, 2019). While connected, the two terms are also distinct. Special education responds to difference through individually targeted interventions, while inclusive education is a rights-based approach toward children who are marginalized and excluded from education systems (Florian, 2019; Schuelka et al., 2019). Specifically, inclusive education scholars critique special education for its excessive focus on deficit-oriented, individualistic explanations of children's behaviors and outcomes to treat and identify disability through segregation (Naraian, 2016).

Under Article 24 of the United Nations Convention on the Rights of Persons with Disabilities (UNCRPD), inclusive education is considered an integral right of people with disabilities. The goal of inclusive education is to promote democratic public education with an agenda of justice by emphasizing how human differences can facilitate learning (Artiles et al., 2011). For some, the special education origins of inclusive education are at odds with the social justice goals of inclusive education (Artiles et al., 2011; Schuelka et al., 2019). There is a concern that inclusive education became the "new iteration of special education" (Schuelka et al., 2019, p. xxxvii), which led to increasing equity concerns (Waitoller & Artiles, 2013).

The problem of inequity is further complicated by a second issue: Special education practices are largely situated within the medical model of disability. The medical model focuses primarily on assessment, identification, and treatment of problems thought to reside within the individual. Inclusive education, on the other hand, broadly aligns itself with a social model of disability (Naraian, 2016). Broadly, there is a consensus among proponents of the social model that learning challenges experienced by disabled children in schools result from socially constructed barriers such as rigid curricula, discriminatory classroom practices, and inaccessible infrastructure (Schuelka et al., 2019). Theorizing disability as *either* an entirely medicalized problem of individuals' bodies *or* an entirely social problem of barriers draws hard boundaries around disability itself. These boundaries make it difficult for inclusive education as a field to theorize exclusion in a way that can address social justice concerns in education for all marginalized groups.

The third problem is the tension between values underlying widescale testing and ranking regimes and the transformational goals of inclusive education (Kozleski, Artiles, & Waitoller, 2014; Slee, 2013). The tension between the two is related to the impact of neoliberal economic policies on discourses of equity and inclusion in the Global North. In Sweden, standardization and competition had a detrimental impact on equity, such that students failing to meet standardized norms were considered to require special education, giving rise to school segregation and overrepresentation of immigrant children in special education (Berhanu, 2011). Moreover, much of the tension between neoliberalism and inclusion falls on teachers, who are viewed as individual change agents and held accountable for conflicting policy demands (Done & Murphy, 2018). Thus, first-generation inclusive education countries struggle to balance neoliberal values of efficiency and individualism with democratic ideals.

DisCrit emerged as a critical framework that seeks to push back against such pressures on inclusive education in the Global North. DisCrit's framing of racism and ableism as multidimensional, interrelated forces allows for new ways of understanding thorny Northern educational issues such as school choice (Waitoller & Super, 2017), the school-to-prison pipeline (Annamma, 2015), and education debts (Thorius & Tan, 2015). The foundations of DisCrit offer a nuanced critique of how inclusive education is diffused, borrowed, and transferred from the Global North to the Global South.

PLANNING THE TRIP, BOOKING OUR TICKETS: CONTESTATIONS AROUND INCLUSIVE EDUCATION AND DISABILITY IN INDIA

A collective lack of resources and expertise to successfully implement Northern models and standards of inclusive education led to parallel systems perpetuating the same issues presented earlier throughout the Global South (Duke et al., 2016; Kalyanpur, 2018). In Samoa, for example, there are both special, segregated schools and inclusive schools for children with disabilities but no direct translation for the term inclusion in the local language or parallel concept in Samoan culture. Kalyanpur (2016) finds that Northern inclusive education can "become distorted versions of the original intention" (p. 20) when applied without adequate consideration of local contexts of disability and education by international agencies.

The global move toward inclusive education was largely uncritically adopted in the Indian context, such that the change in terminology led to minimal changes in policy or teacher practices (Singal, 2006a). The uncritical import of Northern standards seems to have led to detrimental effects not only on the theoretical and conceptual development of inclusive education but also on the educational needs of children with disabilities in India (Kalyanpur, 2008; Singal, 2005, 2006b). As such, disability scholars argue for a conceptual and methodological model that is "more sensitive to diverse cultural contexts" (Anand, 2016, p. 37). There is a need to develop or expand existing theories and methods that are attuned to Indian cultural norms, beliefs, and practices. Thus, a burgeoning focus on embracing local, culturally relevant, indigenous understandings of disability and inclusion in India became increasingly important (Elton-Chalcraft et al., 2016; Hodkinson & Devarakonda, 2011; Johansson, 2014).

Overall, southern countries like India face dual pressures that may hinder engagement with local knowledge and practices for successful inclusion. The first is Northern epistemic dominance, that is, the pressure to adopt Northern ideals and practices of inclusive education. The second is the global rise of neoliberal policies in education (Apple, 2017), which contributed to inequities in inclusive education in the North.

PACKING DISCRIT IN OUR LUGGAGE: TROUBLING LOCAL, INDIGENOUS INCLUSIVE EDUCATION

The notion of the local is complicated by exclusionary beliefs about disability and difference in local knowledge practices. For example, the conceptualization of karma (Ghai, 2015), which stigmatizes disability as a personal sin or caste-based segregation, is embedded within Hindu politics and practices (Quigley, 2003). In India, *Vasudhaiva kutumbakam*[3] co-exists with casteism, gender discrimination, and disability exclusion. Traditional knowledge in the popular imagination is often synonymous with what is Hindu, Brahmanical, and in the Hindi language—excluding diverse local knowledges (Sundar, 2002). Thus, with the overlay of DisCrit, it is important to interrogate and expand the notion of indigenous, local, or culturally grounded inclusive education.

In the African context, efforts to decolonize inclusive education embraced Africanist philosophies of *ubuntu, botho* (humanity), and *kagisano* (social harmony). However, scholars caution against their uncritical adoption because exclusion and oppression of individuals with disabilities persist within these philosophical traditions (Muthukrishna & Engelbrecht, 2018), and community-based values can be equally oppressive and discriminatory (Walton, 2018). Without consultation and engagement with local contexts, a process of adopting Africanist values that is led by elites can disempower the very people it seeks to include (Walton, 2018). An explicit critical, social justice agenda—as espoused by DisCrit—can equip teachers to be vigilant toward exclusionary tendencies within local and global inclusive education practices (Muthukrishna & Engelbrecht, 2018).

There are different perspectives about how to create or honor local, indigenous, traditional, or cultural knowledge based on the context. For one, embracing local knowledge is not only complicated by its exclusionary tendencies but also by internalized extraversion or Western orientation (Khoja-Moolji, 2017), that is, the postcolonial denigration of local knowledge practices with an eye of embracing Western ways of being. Thus, will DisCrit, as a U.S. import to India, overshadow theories and ideas stemming from India? It is also important to recognize that local knowledge is not static and is in conversation with global networks. Conceptualizing inclusive education through local knowledge in India is a parallel exercise: of critiquing exclusionary tendencies within local knowledge while examining how colonialism may have contributed to the exclusionary tendencies of local knowledges and at the same time engaging with transnational knowledge networks while acknowledging the geopolitical inequalities in these networks (Canagarajah, 2002).

The tenets within DisCrit can serve as a template through which we can explore how local or indigenous conceptualizations of inclusive education in India address multiple identities, intersect oppressive systems, privilege marginalized voices, and support resistance. DisCrit can be viewed as a means to engage with, critique, and expand upon local knowledges toward inclusive education. DisCrit can offer support as a critical friend (Khoja-Moolji, 2017), written from a "subaltern epistemic location" (p. S153) in the North, that uncovers how racism and ableism work together to disempower and marginalize students of color in the United States. At the same time, we must make tentative (Singal & Muthukrishna, 2014) what DisCrit offers in order to focus on the strengths and the capacities of local and indigenous communities.

CUSTOMS AND IMMIGRATION: ENTERING THE SOUTH

In this section, we extend the argument that colonialism and globalization reinforce the complex intersections between race, ethnicity, and disability in the Global South (Stienstra & Nyerere, 2016) to address the role DisCrit can play in envisioning a contextually relevant inclusive education in India. In particular, what must DisCrit confront at customs if it travels to India? The answer to this question lies in the critiques of hegemonic Northern disability studies and inclusive education research, which address the neglect of historical, cultural, political, discursive, and material realities of disabled people in the Global South (Grech & Soldatic, 2015; Nguyen, 2019). We address aspects of this critique and its relevance to extending DisCrit into inclusive education in India, re-examining binary notions of identity and disrupting the distinction between medical and social models.

Multiple and Intersectional Identities

Scholars interrogate the use of singular and binary identity categories in postcolonial contexts (Ghai, 2012; Grech & Soldatic, 2015). They argue that the centrality of coloniality and colonial violence in the South ties together the experiences of different identities, such that identity categories in the South are understood as fluid and intersectional. In particular, Western discourses produce binary perspectives around self/other, disabled/able-bodied, and Black/white, which preclude nuanced, fluid, and complex understandings of the lives of people with disabilities in India (Ghai, 2012).

DisCrit attends to the fluidity and the multidimensionality of identities in tenet two and relates to Southern theory, which argues that "we cannot meaningfully separate the racialized subaltern from the disabled subaltern in the process of colonization" (Meekosha, 2011, p. 673).

However, DisCrit can go further to explicitly engage with how coloniality, as an aspect of white supremacy (Patel, 2014), ties together racism and ableism within (Imada, 2017) and beyond the United States. The interaction and fluidity between disability, caste, gender, and race in the Indian context are not just based on colonial logics but also based on existing religious and philosophical beliefs, leading to solidarity, contestation, and competitions between and within marginalized groups (Ghai, 2012; Parekh, 2007). Grech (2015), who writes about disability in the Global South, echoes DisCrit's claims of the paradox between race and disability. Expanding on the notion of neocolonized bodies, he demonstrates how colonialism rendered racialized bodies as both physically strong and intellectually inferior. Racialized bodies were disabled through violence, labor, disease, and punishment, and the disabled bodies were then considered unfit for labor and in need of intervention through healing by Christian missionaries (Grech, 2015).

In India, DisCrit must confront the interplay between disability and caste, considering long-standing debates on theorizing caste itself. As a system of hierarchical stratification, caste is described based on religious scripture, as an artifact of traditional society, and as a dynamically evolving phenomenon. It attempts to uphold upper-caste supremacy by regulating knowledge, land, labor, and other sociocultural and economic resources (Subramanian, 2019). As a form of systemic oppression, it is deeply entangled with other systems of oppression, including class, race, gender, religion, and disability.

While caste is not easily analogous to race (see Goodnight, 2017; Slate, 2011), scholars describe the racialization of caste that resulted from the colonial encounter (Subramanian, 2019). The racialization of caste loosened the linkages of caste with codes of practice. Instead, caste became associated solely with birth and heredity. The idea of caste purity and race tied caste categorizations to innate characteristics and eugenics-based ideologies; for example, Brahmins[4] came to be associated with inherent intelligence and leadership. Subramanian (2019) draws on a comparison between whiteness and uppercasteness such that merit, achievement, and ability become property of upper castes (tenet six).

However, critical questions remain. Goodnight (2017) evaluates CRT, DisCrit's parent theory, in the Indian context: "Does India's population—not characterized by a white majority with racial minorities—shift foundational concepts within CRT? How does CRT methodology allow for the complexity and uniqueness of India?" (p. 2). That is, DisCrit must account for the complex interplay between caste, language, gender, disability, religion, and class, in addition to the impacts of white supremacy underlying colonialism. The emphasis on marginalized voices within DisCrit (tenet four) allows us to incorporate experiences of marginalization and discrimination faced by Dalit communities into global understandings of oppression and support transnational social justice movements (Goodnight, 2017).

Overall, decolonial, postcolonial, and Southern scholarship emphasizes the need to acknowledge intersecting systems of oppression that are tied together through the coloniality of power (Reed-Sandoval & Sirvent, 2019). By critically examining coloniality, DisCrit's intersectional approach on material and social conditions of being labeled as raced and disabled can address the conditions that lead to intersecting forms of oppression crucial for the social justice and democratic agenda of inclusive education in the Global South (Artiles & Kozleski, 2016; Nguyen, 2019; Slee, 2008).

MODELS OF DISABILITY

As discussed previously, the medical versus social model of disability is a well-worn theoretical debate within Northern inclusive and special education. For some Southern theorists, the binary between the medical and social model rests on a false distinction between the body and society and, therefore, between impairment and disability (Connell, 2011). The distinction between disability and impairment conceives of disability as a social or political concept, while impairment is construed as a bodily, medical, or natural issue. This distinction seems to ignore the production of impairment through state and geopolitical violence, which Soldatic (2013) refers to as the "bio-politics of geopolitical power" (p. 747). Contemporary examples of geopolitical violence such as the Bhopal gas tragedy in India, wherein impairment was a consequence of geopolitical power, highlight the limits of understanding impairment as neutral.

In addition to geopolitics, clear distinctions between disability models are tenuous in the South, as they do not always capture cultural complexities. For example, the vast history of medical practices such as Ayurveda and Siddha in India makes it difficult to determine what might be a medical model of disability in the Indian context (Anand, 2016). The knowledge systems within Ayurveda and Siddha view disease in the context of the individual's social circumstances, obfuscating the clear distinctions between impairment and disability that are common to Euro-American disability models. While the practices are often labeled as the charity or moral model of disability, Anand (2016) argues that attaching such labels tends to reinscribe hierarchies—placing Western medicine as a more evolved, modern form of practice.

Relatedly, although there is pushback against the medicalization of disability in the global disability movement, in the Global South, the medical model serves as a helpful tool for empowerment and mobilizing for access to services (Meekosha, 2011). However, conversations about preventing impairment in the North are often met with the need to consider disability as a unique identity. This duality is typified in tenets two and three of DisCrit theory, which emphasize multidimensional identities while recognizing the impact of marginalizing labels (Annamma et al., 2013). On the other hand, Meekosha (2011) suggests that in the Southern context of colonial violence and poverty, the prevention of impairment is an aspect of disability advocacy for equitable access to health and educational services. Thus, between the North and South is an "intellectual and political tension between pride, celebration, and prevention" (Meekosha, 2011, p. 677).

Altogether, the unsteady dualism between the medical and the social models in the Global South (Nguyen, 2019) requires us to nuance the view of inclusive education as a critique of the medical model. Within the Indian context, lack of access to health care, immunization, and sanitation in rural areas and among the urban poor is a primary cause of impairment (Kalyanpur, 2008). In 2018, 42% of those classified as disabled listed disease as the cause of impairment. Enrollment figures might indicate a picture of inclusive education—only 2.4% of disabled people between the ages of 3 and 35 were ever enrolled in special schools. In urban areas, this figure is 9.2%, and in rural areas, it is 2.4% (Ministry of Statistics and Programme Implementation, 2019), which co-exists with the characterization of India's inclusive education as "exclusive of children with disabilities" (Grills et al., 2019). The low enrollment in special schools is not indicative of inclusive education but of a shortage of special schools for disabled children in rural areas (Rao et al., 2020). These complexities in the underrepresentation of disabled children from special and inclusive education and its relationship to economic and healthcare inequities do not indicate a labeling problem that DisCrit highlights. Instead, there are structural factors that underlie the interplay between bodies and society.

Power structures often play out within international conventions and human rights treaties around disability. India ratified the UNCRPD in 2007 (Narayan et al., 2011). The United States is a signatory to the UNCRPD but has yet to ratify it (Kanter, 2019). The UNCRPD highlights the importance of effective participation and inclusion in society and advocates for autonomy and dignity of disabled people. For many, the UNCRPD was a critical development for the movement, as it shifted the discussion from a charity or medical model to a global rights-based model. Successful examples of disability rights led by grassroots organizations for inclusive education in India (Forber-Pratt & Lyew, 2019) set the precedent for state actors to guarantee the educational rights of disabled children (Rao et al., 2020). However, other scholars from the South critique the rights-based approach because of its tendency to universalize disability language and experience (Meekosha & Soldatic, 2011; Rao & Kalyanpur, 2020; Soldatic, 2013) and the top-down nature of its implementation (Tikly, 2011)—highlighting the importance of local meanings, movements, and contexts. It seems that there is a missed opportunity for greater collaboration among grassroots disability activists, policymakers, and implementers to address issues typified in tenets five[5] and seven.[6] DisCrit could provide the missing framework to critique intersecting oppressions enacted through policy, privilege activism, and resistance of marginalized communities and focus on how these can help forge solidarities between grassroots disability rights movements and activism across India and the United States.

WE'RE ALL TRAVELING COACH: SOLIDARITIES AND THE SOUTH

In this chapter, we outlined the need to challenge Northern dominance within inclusive education and put forth DisCrit as a means to expand and appraise efforts toward an intersectional, culturally relevant, and contextually grounded conceptualization of inclusive education in India.

However, what may appear to be a natural alliance (Elder & Migliarini, 2020) must be interrogated so that DisCrit does not become yet another theoretical framework that travels uncritically from the North to the South. What will it take for DisCrit to be a helpful framework in the Global South? How can theory and practice from the South push our understanding of race and disability in the North? This line of thinking does not hinder but strengthens the opportunities for coalition and solidarity—it provides theoretical tools to dismantle the power of white, able-bodied middle-class norms embedded within educational systems that exclude and marginalize Black and Brown disabled children (Annamma et al., 2018; Singal, 2019).

DisCrit in India must address the complex intersections among caste, language, gender, disability, religion, and class. Much of this work, particularly in the Global South, requires a lens critical of coloniality and transnationalism. Indeed, even if CRT and DisCrit are yet to travel to India, the recent lawsuit citing caste discrimination against a Dalit employee at a California-based organization indicates that caste has traveled to the United States (Dutt, 2020). Following the #BlackLivesMatter protests in the United States, several Indian academics and activists based in the United States have been calling for a #DalitLivesMatter movement and a revival of Black–Dalit solidarity (West & Yengde, 2017; Yengde, 2020). The support for activism and resistance embedded within DisCrit (tenet seven) can perhaps serve as a basis for solidarity toward a transnational, intersectional inclusive education (Nguyen, 2019; Schuelka et al., 2019). Thus, if DisCrit were to travel to the Global South, it must not only require activism and support all forms of resistance (tenet seven), but it must also further global and transnational solidarities. Global alliances and frameworks can help develop, unpack, and critique interventions and policies aimed at socially just, inclusive education.

What does our analysis hold for tenets within DisCrit in the Indian context? It depends. DisCrit's journey to India depends on the positionality and the theoretical inclination of the one carrying this suitcase and their final destination. The history, language, and politics of oppression vary widely. The conflict over sovereignty in Kashmir is different from the lives of migrant workers in New Delhi, which is different from the embodiment of caste in the lived experiences of disabled girls in Kolkata. We are hesitant to rewrite the tenets of DisCrit within the Indian context until future empirical work can be done in these diverse Indian contexts to deepen the analyses presented here. The authors feel there is grave risk in prematurely editing the tenets, inadvertently perpetuating the very colonizing acts we are calling out. Ultimately, the voices and the experiences of people who have been pushed to the margins of existing theoretical frameworks are the ones left with the excess theoretical baggage fees. It is incumbent on the theories and the theorists that describe these experiences to forge an agenda that harnesses advocacy, activism, and action against oppression.

NOTES

1. *Dalit* refers to marginalized caste groups.
2. *Adivasi* refers to tribal and indigenous communities.
3. "The world is one family."
4. Brahmins are considered the highest group in the caste hierarchy.
5. DisCrit considers legal and historical aspects of dis/ability and race and how both have been used separately and together to deny the rights of some citizens.
6. DisCrit requires activism and supports all forms of resistance.

REFERENCES

Anand, S. (2016). The models approach in disability scholarship: An assessment of its failings. In N. Ghosh (Ed.), *Interrogating Disability in India* (pp. 23–38). Springer.

Annamma, S. A. (2015). Disrupting the school-to-prison pipeline through disability critical race theory. In L. D. Drakeford (Ed.), *The race controversy in American education* (Vol. 1, pp. 191–211). Praeger.

Annamma, S. A., Connor, D., & Ferri, B. (2013). Dis/ability critical race studies (DisCrit): Theorizing at the intersections of race and dis/ability. *Race Ethnicity and Education*, 16(1), 1–31. https://doi.org/10.1080/13613324.2012.730511

Annamma, S. A., Ferri, B. A., & Connor, D. J. (2018). Disability critical race theory: Exploring the intersectional lineage, emergence, and potential futures of DisCrit in education. *Review of Research in Education*, 42(1), 46–71. https://doi.org/10.3102/0091732X18759041

Annamma, S., & Morrison, D. (2018). DisCrit classroom ecology: Using praxis to dismantle dysfunctional education ecologies. *Teaching and Teacher Education*, 73, 70–80. https://doi.org/10.1016/j.tate.2018.03.008

Apple, M. W. (2017). What is present and absent in critical analyses of neoliberalism in education. *Peabody Journal of Education*, *92*(1), 148–153. https://doi.org/10.1080/0161956X.2016.1265344

Artiles, A. J., & Kozleski, E. B. (2016). Inclusive education's promises and trajectories: Critical notes about future research on a venerable idea. *Education Policy Analysis Archives/Archivos Analíticos de Políticas Educativas*, *24*, 1–29.

Artiles, A. J., Kozleski, E. B., & Waitoller, F. R. (Eds.). (2011). *Inclusive education: Examining equity on five continents*. Harvard Education Press.

Bakhshi, P., Babulal, G. M., & Trani, J. F. (2017). Education of children with disabilities in New Delhi: When does exclusion occur? *PLoS ONE*, *12*(9), 1–15. https://doi.org/10.1371/journal.pone.0183885

Berhanu, G. (2011). Inclusive education in Sweden: Responses, challenges, and prospects. *International Journal of Special Education*, *26*(2), 128–148.

Canagarajah, S. (2002). Reconstructing local knowledge. *Journal of Language, Identity & Education*, *1*(4), 243–259. https://doi.org/10.1207/S15327701JLIE0104_1

Connell, R. (2011). Southern bodies and disability: Re-thinking concepts. *Third World Quarterly*, *32*(8), 1369–1381. https://doi.org/10.1080/01436597.2011.614799

Done, E. J., & Murphy, M. (2018). The responsibilisation of teachers: A neoliberal solution to the problem of inclusion. *Discourse: Studies in the Cultural Politics of Education*, *39*(1), 142–155.

Duke, J., Pillay, H., Tones, M., Nickerson, J., Carrington, S., & Ioelu, A. (2016). A case for rethinking inclusive education policy creation in developing countries. *Compare: A Journal of Comparative and International Education*, *46*(6), 906–928. https://doi.org/10.1080/03057925.2016.1204226

Dutt, Y. (2020, July 14). *The specter of caste in Silicon Valley*. New York Times. https://www.nytimes.com/2020/07/14/opinion/caste-cisco-indian-americans-discrimination.html

Elder, B., & Migliarini, V. (2020). Decolonizing inclusive education: A collection of practical inclusive CDS- and DisCrit-informed teaching practices implemented in the Global South. *Disability and the Global South*, *7*(1), 1852–1872.

Elton-Chalcraft, S., Cammack, P., & Harrison, L. (2016). Segregation, integration, inclusion and effective provision: A case study of perspectives from special educational needs children, parents and teachers in Bangalore India. *International Journal of Special Education*, *31*(1), 2–9.

Florian, L. (2019). On the necessary co-existence of special and inclusive education. *International Journal of Inclusive Education*, *23*(7–8), 691–704. https://doi.org/10.1080/13603116.2019.1622801

Forber-Pratt, A. J., & Lyew, D. A. (2019). A model case: Specialized group home for girls with disabilities in India. *Child and Adolescent Social Work Journal*, *37*(3), 315–327. https://doi.org/10.1007/s10560-019-00633-8

Ghai, A. (2012). Engaging with disability with postcolonial theory. In D. Goodley, B. Hughes, & L. Davis (Eds.), *Disability and social theory: New developments and directions* (pp. 270–286). Palgrave Macmillan.

Ghai, A. (2015). *Rethinking disability in India*. Routledge.

Goodnight, M. R. (2017). Critical race theory in India: Theory translation and the analysis of social identities and discrimination in Indian schooling. *Compare: A*

Journal of Comparative and International Education, 47(5), 665–683. https:// doi.org/10.1080/03057925.2016.1266926

Grech, S. (2015). Decolonising eurocentric disability studies: Why colonialism matters in the disability and Global South debate. *Social Identities, 21*(1), 6–21. https://doi.org/10.1080/13504630.2014.995347

Grech, S., & Soldatic, K. (2015). Disability and colonialism: (Dis)encounters and anxious intersectionalities. *Social Identities, 21*(1), 1–5. https://doi.org/10.1080 /13504630.2014.995394

Grills, N., Devabhaktula, J., Butcher, N., Arokiaraj, S., Das, P., & Anderson, P. (2019). Inclusive education in India largely exclusive of children with a disability. *Disability and the Global South, 6*(2), 1756–1771.

Hiranandani, V., & Sonpal, D. (2010). Disability, economic globalization and privatization: A case study of India. *Disability Studies Quarterly, 30*(3–4) 1–21.

Hodkinson, A., & Devarakonda, C. (2011). Conceptions of inclusion and inclusive education: A critical examination of the perspectives and practices of teachers in India. *Research in Education, 82*(1), 85–99. https://educationstudies.org.uk /wp-content/uploads/2013/11/alan_4.pdf

Imada, A. L. (2017). A decolonial disability studies? *Disability Studies Quarterly, 37*(3), 1–3. https://doi.org/10.18061/dsq.v37i3.5984

Johansson, S. T. (2014). A critical and contextual approach to inclusive education: Perspectives from an Indian context. *International Journal of Inclusive Education, 18*(12), 1219–1236. https://doi.org/10.1080/13603116.2014.885594

Kalyanpur, M. (2008). Equality, quality and quantity: Challenges in inclusive education policy and service provision in India. *International Journal of Inclusive Education, 12*(3), 243–262. https://doi.org/10.1080/13603110601103162

Kalyanpur, M. (2016). Inclusive education policies and practices in the context of international development: Lessons from Cambodia. *ZEP: Zeitschrift Für Internationale Bildungsforschung Und Entwicklungspädagogik, 39*(3), 16–21.

Kalyanpur, M. (2018). Using indigenous knowledge to provide educational services for children with disabilities. *Journal of Early Childhood Studies, 2*(2), 397–413. http://dx.doi.org/10.24130/eccd-jecs.196720182273

Kanter, A. S. (2019). Let's try again: Why the United States should ratify the United Nations convention of the rights of people with disabilities. *Touro Law Review, 35*(1).

Khoja-Moolji, S. (2017). Pedagogical (re)encounters: Enacting a decolonial praxis in teacher professional development in Pakistan. *Comparative Education Review, 61*(S1), S146–S170. https://doi.org/10.1086/690298

Kozleski, E., Artiles, A., & Waitoller, F. (2014). Equity in inclusive education: A cultural historical comparative perspective. *The SAGE Handbook of Special Education: Two Volume Set, 1*, 231–250. https://doi.org/10.4135/9781446282236.n16

Meekosha, H. (2011). Decolonising disability: Thinking and acting globally. *Disability & Society, 26*(6), 667–682. https://doi.org/10.1080/09687599.2011.602860

Meekosha, H., & Soldatic, K. (2011). Human rights and the Global South. *Third World Quarterly, 32*(8), 1383–1398. https://doi.org/10.1080/01436597.2011 .614800

Ministry of Statistics and Programme Implementation (2019). *Persons with disabilities in India: NSS 76th round.* Government of India.

Muthukrishna, N., & Engelbrecht, P. (2018). Decolonising inclusive education in lower income, Southern African educational contexts. *South African Journal of Education, 38*(4), 1–11. https://doi.org/10.15700/saje.v38n4a1701

Naraian, S. (2016). Inclusive education complexly defined for teacher preparation: The significance and uses of error. *International Journal of Inclusive Education, 20*(9), 946–961. https://doi.org/10.1080/13603116.2015.1134682

Narayan, C. L., Narayan, M., & Shikha, D. (2011). The ongoing process of amendments in MHA-87 and PWD Act-95 and their implications on mental health care. *Indian Journal of Psychiatry, 53*(4), 343–350.

Nguyen, X. T. (2019). Unsettling "inclusion" in the Global South: A post-colonial and intersectional approach to disability, gender, and education. In M. J. Schuelka, C. J. Johnstone, G. Thomas, & A. J. Artiles (Eds.), *The SAGE handbook of inclusion and diversity in education* (pp. 28–40). Sage.

Parekh, P. N. (2007). Gender, disability and the postcolonial nexus. *Wagadu, 4,* 142–161.

Patel, L. (2014). Countering coloniality in educational research: From ownership to answerability. *Educational Studies, 50*(4), 357–377.

Quigley, D. (2003). On the relationship between caste and Hinduism. In G. Flood (Ed.). *The Blackwell companion to Hinduism* (pp. 495–508). John Wiley & Sons.

Rao, P., Shrivastava, S., & Sarkar, T. (2020, May 1). *Towards an inclusive education framework for India.* Vidhi Centre for Legal Policy. https://vidhilegalpolicy.in/2020/05/01/how-can-children-with-disabilities-be-meaningfully-included-in-indias-education-framework/

Rao, S., & Kalyanpur, M. (2020). Universal notions of development and disability: Towards whose imagined vision? *Disability and the Global South, 7*(1), 1830–1851.

Reed-Sandoval, A., & Sirvent, R. (2019). Disability and the decolonial turn: Perspectives from the Americas. *Disability and the Global South, 6*(1), 1553–1561.

Schuelka, M., Johnstone, C., Thomas, G., & Artiles, A. (2019). Diversity and inclusion in education: Inclusive education scholarship in the twenty-first century. In M. J. Schuelka, C. J. Johnstone, G. Thomas, & A. J. Artiles (Eds.), *The SAGE handbook of inclusion and diversity in education* (pp. xxxi–xliii). Sage.

Singal, N. (2005). Mapping the field of inclusive education: A review of the Indian literature. *International Journal of Inclusive Education, 9*(4), 331–350. https://doi.org/10.1080/13603110500138277

Singal, N. (2006a). An ecosystemic approach for understanding inclusive education: An Indian case study inclusive education. *European Journal of Psychology of Education, 21*(3), 239–252.

Singal, N. (2006b). Inclusive education in India: International concept, national interpretation. *International Journal of Disability, Development and Education, 53*(3), 351–369. https://doi.org/10.1080/10349120600847797

Singal, N. (2019). Challenges and opportunities in efforts towards inclusive education: Reflections from India. *International Journal of Inclusive Education, 23*(7–8), 827–840. https://doi.org/10.1080/13603116.2019.1624845

Singal, N., & Muthukrishna, N. (2014). Education, childhood and disability in countries of the South—Re-positioning the debates. *Childhood, 21*(3), 293–307. https://doi.org/10.1177/0907568214529600

Singal, N., Ware, H., & Bhutani, S. K. (2017, November). *Inclusive quality education for children with disabilities*. https://doi.org/10.13140/RG.2.2.14016.23045

Slate, N. (2011). Translating race and caste. *Journal of Historical Sociology, 24*(1), 62–79. https://doi.org/10.1111/j.1467-6443.2011.01389.x

Slee, R. (2008). Beyond special and regular schooling? An inclusive education reform agenda. *International Studies in Sociology of Education, 18*(2), 99–116. https://doi.org/10.1080/09620210802351342

Slee, R. (2013). Meeting some challenges of inclusive education in an age of exclusion. *Asian Journal of Inclusive Education, 1*(2), 3–17.

Soldatic, K. (2013). The transnational sphere of justice: Disability praxis and the politics of impairment. *Disability & Society, 28*(6), 744–755. https://doi.org/10.1080/09687599.2013.802218

Stienstra, D., & Nyerere, L. (2016). Race, ethnicity and disability: Charting complex and intersectional terrains. In S. Grech & K. Soldatic (Eds.), *Disability in the Global South* (pp. 255–268). Springer.

Subramanian, A. (2019). *The caste of merit: Engineering education in India*. Harvard University Press.

Sundar, N. (2002). "Indigenise, nationalise and spiritualise"—an agenda for education? *International Social Science Journal, 54*(173), 373–383.

Tikly, L. (2011). Towards a framework for researching the quality of education in low-income countries. *Comparative Education, 47*(1), 1–23.

Thorius, K. A. K., & Tan, P. (2015). Expanding analysis of educational debt: Considering intersections of race and ability. In D. J. Connor, B. A. Ferri, & S. A. Annamma (Eds.), *DisCrit: Disability studies and critical race theory in education* (pp. 87–97). Teachers College Press.

Waitoller, F. R., & Artiles, A. J. (2013). A decade of professional development research for inclusive education: A critical review and notes for a research program. *Review of Educational Research, 83*(3), 319–356. https://doi.org/10.3102/0034654313483905

Waitoller, F. R., & Super, G. (2017). School choice or the politics of desperation? Black and Latinx parents of students with dis/abilities selecting charter schools in Chicago. *Education Policy Analysis Archives, 25*(55), 1–42. https://doi.org/10.14507/epaa.25.2636

Walton, E. (2018). Decolonising (through) inclusive education? *Educational Research for Social Change, 7*(SPE), 31–45.

West, C., & Yengde, S. (2017, June 12). *A shared history of struggle should unite India's Dalits and African Americans in the fight for equality*. The Root. https://www.theroot.com/a-shared-history-of-struggle-should-unite-india-s-dalit-1795973401

Yengde, S. (2020, July). *The harvest of casteism*. Caravan Magazine. https://caravanmagazine.in/magazine/2020/07

Identity Politics: Exploring DisCrit's Potential to Empower Activism and Collective Resistance

Joy Banks, Phillandra Smith, & D'Arcee Charington Neal

> An identity would seem to be arrived at by the way in which a person faces and uses his experiences.
> —James Baldwin (1985), *The Price of the Ticket*

> If I didn't define myself for myself, I would be crunched into other people's fantasies for me and eaten alive.
> —Audre Lorde (1982), *Learning from the 60s*

What exactly encompasses a disability identity? How might I, as a disabled person, begin to conceptualize it? Is my identity constructed from the limited understandings I might have of myself due to socially constructed narratives that I have internalized? Might it be crafted from conversations with members of special-interest groups found across digital media in the age of the Internet or in deliberately sculpted classrooms, schools, or academic institutions? How might I begin to think about disability in the absence of socially constructed narratives about dis/abled bodies? Would stigmatizing assumptions about disability continue to exist in the absence of hegemonic notions about able-bodied normality? Questions about the ways in which one constructs a disability identity become increasingly complicated when one considers the multifaceted intersection of multiple identities—gender, race/ethnicity, socioeconomic status, regionality, language—that contribute to the construction of personal identities of individuals who are multiply marginalized. Erevelles and Minear (2010) purport that the challenge of asserting an intersecting identity in Western society is complicated because it is often believed that a "single characteristic that is foregrounded (e.g., female or Black) is expected to explain all of the other life experiences of the individual or group" (p. 383). Moreover, establishing a self-affirming, intersecting identity can prove to be complicated when sociocultural narratives about a group consist of a history perceived of pain and deficiency. To move forward in understanding marginalized identities, we argue that Disability Critical Race Theory (DisCrit) must unearth the sociocultural processes that are applied as individuals from multiply marginalized backgrounds construct oppositional identities, which are cultural identities that are absent of hegemonic notions of difference. An examination of the construction of an oppositional intersecting identity might be achieved by bringing in line elements of DisCrit with cultural psychology for persons from minoritized backgrounds.

It is in this spirit that we propose an expansion of DisCrit to include an analysis of the inward cultural transformations and paradigm shifts that are influenced by sociocultural psychology and situated at the core of identity politics. Although the main focus of DisCrit is to transform societal structures by challenging Westernized considerations of gender, race, disability, and socioeconomic status, there is an absence of literature that explicitly connects DisCrit with cultural identity development. Also absent is literature that connects DisCrit to epistemologies of self-empowerment or modes of social psychology that inform the development of a politicized identity and its consequent responses concerning interconnecting structural oppressions. Patricia Hill Collins (1989) contends, "one key reason that standpoints of oppressed groups are discredited and suppressed by the more powerful is that self-defined standpoints can stimulate oppressed groups to resist their domination" (p. 749). Collins's assertion underscores the importance of employing theoretical frameworks that foster the development of oppositional knowledge. Therefore, the purpose of this chapter is to highlight how both racial/ethnic and disability identity development function to subvert hegemonic notions of corporal difference. We also aim to provide insight into the way racial/ethnic and disability identity development may inoculate individuals living at the intersection of marginalized identities with a self-definition that rejects dominant notions of difference while embracing perceptions of intersectionality. In this chapter, we ask how does one's identity contribute to the development of a cultural consciousness, and how might Disability Critical Race Theory be used as a theoretical framework and pedagogical instrument to empower those living at the intersection of disability and race/ethnicity to apply tools of resistance?

DISABILITY CRITICAL RACE THEORY

Critical theorists propose that race and disability are not biological markers but are instead socially constructed categories. Each socially constructed identity is entangled in the histories of racism and ableism in which difference is perceived as a deficit deviation from a white, middle-class, able-bodied ideology of normalcy. Annamma and colleagues (2013) further propose that DisCrit "rejects the understanding of both race and disability as primarily biological facts and recognize the social construction of both as society's response to 'differences' from the norm" (p. 12). DisCrit theorists likewise recognize that race and disability are socially constructed identity markers that have substantial psychological and tangible impacts (tenet three) on those who are labeled with marginalized identities that are outside of Western cultural norms. Further, social perceptions of race and disability often inform educators' perceptions about the abilities of those who are labeled as persons of color and individuals identified with a disability, yet what is often missing from the dialogue about socially constructed identity markers is the way individuals from marginalized backgrounds construct a self-image that is free of deleterious, hegemonic, cultural perceptions of difference and, alternatively, construct a self-identity that is grounded in cultural agency and cultural awareness.

We recommend that DisCrit should continue to center the experiences of multiply marginalized voices (tenet four), while also emphasizing the ways in which individuals navigate and name oppressive structural barriers. Additionally, researchers who employ DisCrit as a theoretical framework must also begin to unearth the empowering psychological practices that allow students to become agents of their own life experiences. We contend that DisCrit and other critical literacies would benefit from an exploration of the ideological beliefs and processes applied by individuals from marginalized backgrounds as they develop self-affirming identities that are embedded in an emancipatory narrative of cultural agency. The absence of research that includes conversations that examine the act of constructing positive cultural identities may cause DisCrit researchers to inadvertently focus solely on documenting a series of tragic counternarratives, which recount reactionary responses to whiteness and able-bodied ideologies. Consequently, we, as critical theorists, may risk reifying the belief that Blackness and disability exist only as a response to whiteness.

In order to counter the deleterious psychological impact of deficit notions, it is necessary to privilege the insider voice of those who live at the intersection of socially constructed narratives related to racial/ethnic and disability identities. Annamma et al. (2013) recommend listening to counternarratives in order to assist in "learn[ing] how individuals from marginalized backgrounds respond to injustice, not through passive acceptance, but through tactics such as strategic maneuvering" (p. 13). We agree with the suppositions of DisCrit researchers that counternarratives are important in undermining institutionalized oppressions. However, we offer a cautionary warning, and we maintain that it is important for researchers to acknowledge the ways in which individuals might make use of racial and disability identities and histories (tenet five) to reimagine their cultural identities and also establish decolonized identities. The question that remains unanswered is, what are the processes that one engages in to resist internalizing pejorative, dominant narratives that shape the complex intersection among racial, gender, disability, and economic histories within our communities?

Researchers who apply DisCrit as a theoretical framework must, therefore, examine the ways in which specific contextualized realities and epistemologies of historically marginalized communities intersect with disability identities to contribute to emancipatory outcomes for people of color with disabilities. Moreover, an exploration of the psychological and material consequences of developing an emancipatory identity may provide insight into how historically marginalized individuals with disabilities willfully resist cultural obscurity by constructing a self-narrative, independent of pejorative dominant narratives. The ability to highlight processes applied in the construction of a cultural identity has the potential to inform our understandings of psychological strategies adopted by multiply marginalized individuals as they engage in actions to resist internalization of dominant narratives that shape the complex intersection among racial, gender, and economic histories. Teachers and researchers may also learn about the individual emotional and psychological resilience that is required of minoritized persons prior to engaging in broad social movements (tenet seven) that challenge structural oppression within our schools and communities. Teachers and researchers who have knowledge of the cultural strategies that are employed in the everyday lives of those who are multiply marginalized can transform instructional pedagogy to include practices that can empower students to resist hegemonic beliefs while also developing strategies for self-definition and community transformation. Therefore, there is a need for DisCrit to expand its vision of becoming an emancipatory theory by examining the ways in which inward cultural transformations and paradigm shifts assist in the construction of a self-narrative independent of the pejorative dominant narratives.

HISTORICAL EXPERIENCES RELATED TO BLACK
AND DISABLED INTERSECTIONALITY

African Americans in the United States have historically negotiated the significance of race/ethnicity and disability identities and the meanings they attribute to intersecting identities in their everyday lives. Historian Dea Boster (2013) reminds us of the ways in which enslaved Africans with disabilities were often devalued and considered useless in the antebellum South. As a consequence of their economic devaluation, enslaved individuals with disabilities were used for medical research, as learning tools for medical students, sold in order to free owners from debt, and sometimes murdered, yet enslaved Africans found ways to passively refuse socioeconomic narratives related to notions of disability. Instead, enslaved Africans challenged capitalist notions of economic devaluation by exploiting disability as a tool of resistance. Boster (2013) notes that disabled enslaved Africans would highlight their ailments and defects to avoid being sold away from children and family members. This, of course, was a careful negotiation between self-representation and realities of their everyday context, given that the pronouncement of a disability could also render them useless in the eyes of the slave owner and lead to death.

We also see the complexity of intersectional identities within the historical representations of Sojourner Truth and Harriet Tubman. Sojourner Truth is known within American popular culture as a major contributor to the abolition and women's rights movements. Established as a heroine and a strong Black woman, Truth's own self-representation demonstrates the complexity of living within a Black and disabled body. Self-portraits of Sojourner Truth drew attention away from her injured hand and often attempted to correct for it by showing her hand performing tasks such as knitting. Minister (2012) acknowledged the way in which Sojourner Truth "used her body to confront social norms and construct new ways of existing in her nineteenth century context." During her unforgettable speech, "Ain't I a Woman?" which took place at the 1851 Ohio Women's Rights Convention, Sojourner Truth exposed her shoulder and forearm in order to emphasize her strength as a woman who is able to carry out work that is equal to that of a man. Her Black identity needed less formal disclosure, but her disabled identity remained suppressed from public discourse and other forms of historical representation (Al-Mohamed, 2015). Another notable presence in African American history is that of Harriet Tubman. Hypervisible as a legend and public figure, Harriet Tubman is well known as the conductor of the Underground Railroad, a women's suffragist, and a Civil War hero. However, similar to Sojourner Truth, Harriet Tubman's disabled identity as a woman with epilepsy remains invisible within her historical legacy (Hobson, 2019).

The contextualized experiences of Sojourner Truth and Harriet Tubman demonstrate the ways in which African Americans with disabilities have been required to distance themselves from disabled identities. Simultaneously, we see how the need to preserve the integrity of one's racial identity causes the stigma attached to disabled identity to be left uninterrupted (Minister, 2012). Admittedly, we must acknowledge that the development of an affirmative intersectional identity may not be easily achieved in the context of a society that devalues both Black and disabled bodies. The historical legacies of Sojourner Truth and Harriet Tubman allow us to recognize and memorialize their Black identities, but what would it mean for history to have them claim their identity as disabled women? In considering this question, we should also ask ourselves how might these women have experienced life if they were provided the opportunity to embrace their disability identities? In our current era of modern civil rights movements, scholars note that there is focus on "values, lifestyles and self-actualization, or what some would call identity politics" (Peters et al., 2009, p. x). We argue that in the current era of social movements the development of a cultural consciousness that empowers individuals to bring their whole self to the context to resist structural oppression is also essential.

SHIFTING THE PARADIGM ABOUT RACIAL AND DISABILITY IDENTITIES

As an overly complex and historically contextualized psychosocial system of beliefs, one's notion about their own racial and disability identity does not remain static. Racial identity emerges out of the cumulative context of specific experiences that impact the individual as they engage with the environment over time. The construct of racial identity in psychological disciplines is explained as the importance an individual ascribes to being a member of their racial group (Thompson et al., 2000). Central to the theories of racial identity are the consequences of social, political, legal, and economic inequities and the protective coping strategies that develop as a result of experiencing these inequities (Carter et al., 2017). Sellers et al. (1998), therefore, defined four elements of racial status: *identity salience, centrality, regard,* and *ideology. Racial identity salience* refers to the relevance of race as a significant part of the individual's self-concept at a specific moment in time. *Race centrality* is the extent to which an individual normatively regards racial membership as primary to their self-definition. In this element, race is relatively stable across time. *Racial regard* refers to positive or negative evaluative judgments regarding one's racial group. *Racial ideology* is the individual's set of beliefs and opinions about how members of their racial group should behave. Previous research has demonstrated that individuals require an appreciation of one's racial group in order to maintain a sense of personal identity and self-concept that is absent of deleterious notions of cultural deficit (Sellers et al., 1998). A growing body of literature about youth from marginalized backgrounds also demonstrates that racial identity has protective measures that result in increased academic resilience (higher academic achievement, school engagement, and self-esteem) (Rivas-Drake et al., 2014) and enhanced future career expectations (Moses et al., 2020) and promotes psychosocial mental health. The beneficial psychological outcomes related to racial centrality may be an indication that a politicized racial/ethnic identity may be a prerequisite for academic and personal achievement and mental health in oppressive Western societies.

Early research on racial identity development for African Americans focused on their response to oppression (Cross, 1985; Helms, 1990; Parham, 1989). Early approaches to understanding racial identity assumed that self-hatred and lower self-esteem were inextricably intertwined with characteristics of racial identity for those who are members of historically marginalized backgrounds. However, we must also consider that racial identity does not begin solely with a response to oppression. Sellers et al. (1998) argued that an alternative way to view racial oppression is as institutionalized faulty beliefs about racialized groups that cause an associated affective response within those who are being oppressed. The individual assumes greater personal agency when the problem of racial discrimination is externalized and identified as being outside of one's personal characterizations. The ability to constructively evaluate marginalization as institutionalized faulty beliefs with associated affective response results in increased positive protective measures for individuals from intersecting, historically marginalized identities. In this sense, the alternative of affirming cultural self-knowledge that rejects faulty notions regarding racialized groups becomes a tool of resistance against white, able-bodied oppression.

When thinking about the interdependence of racism and ableism, there is historical evidence to demonstrate the ways in which both racial and disability status have resulted in segregation and exclusion in Western societies (Annamma et al., 2013; Ferri, 2010). The influence of uninterrupted historical social inequities related to racial identity suggests that the presence of a disability may further complicate the growth cycle toward cultural agency and personal identity. Similar to racial identity, disability identity is a socially constructed identity marker that is the result of environmental barriers that deny daily life access to citizenship as well as physical establishments (Gill, 1997; Linton, 1998). Dunn and Burcaw (2013) further define disability identity as a "sense of self that includes one's disability and feelings of connection to, or solidarity with the disability community" (p. 148). Forber-Pratt et al. (2017) developed a 37-item survey to identify preliminary characteristics of disability identity. The exploratory analysis resulted in four factors: personal beliefs about disability and the disability community, emotional responses to experiences that emerge as a result to disability, internalizing disability community values, and active engagement in and contribution to the disability community. Drawing parallels between racial and disability identity frameworks highlights the importance of having a cultural identity. A positive sense of identity can assist individuals to navigate the social stresses and day-to-day hassles related to disability identities (Dunn & Burcaw, 2013). For example, within disability identity literature, there is evidence that an individual's disability identity and disability efficacy status have a positive significant impact on satisfaction in life (Bogart, 2014; Mueller, 2019).

Intersectionality, Identity, and Adolescent Development

The importance of examining intersecting racial and disability identity becomes more pronounced given the developmental transitions experienced during adolescence. Adolescents with racialized and disability characterizations must construct culturally self-affirming identities while simultaneously confronting and traversing stigmatizing dominant narratives about their race/ethnicity and disability labels. In this sense, the development of intersecting racial and disability identities during adolescence invites the opportunity for the application of DisCrit to be applied as a theoretical framework to assist students in shifting deleterious perceptions related to minoritized identities. Students whose identity exists at the intersection of race and disability can strengthen their psychological resistance to oppression by appropriately viewing dominant forms of oppression as institutionalized faulty beliefs held by the dominant society. In turn, this framing prevents students from internalizing self-doubt. As students reconstruct personal and collective truths about their intersecting identities, they can construct affirming racial and disability identities that deconstruct notions of white and able-bodied superiority. Take, for example, a statement from an African American college student as he reflects upon his high school experiences:

> In my educational career [because I was] an African American male and had ADHD, [high school] teachers put me in two boxes—disabled and African American. Then with me being above 6 feet tall, they expected me to be aggressive. [Teachers] have had to check themselves, but after I talk to them about my learning style, they would see me in a whole different light. . . . It got harder at times. I used to wish I didn't have to deal with it . . . all of the negative labels and assumptions from students, from instructors. I [also] had to deal with white male instructor issues. So, I realized [to be more successful] I can adjust my actions, and that's what I did, I adjusted myself, and it got easier. I deal with [stereotypes] a lot, but I'm ready to address those issues. Luckily, I didn't disengage. [Banks, 2017, pp. 103–104]

The student affirms his multiple intersecting identities as they relate to gender, disability, and race/ethnicity. The student also rejects dominant pejorative narratives related to his intersecting identities and, essentially, characterizes his high school teachers' bias as a result of institutionalized faulty beliefs about minoritized groups. The student also acknowledges that his affective response to oppression might have caused him to disengage from the schooling experience. Derived from one of the primary tenets of DisCrit, the student's experience or voice becomes the criterion for exploring the *truth* of racial and disability identities within the context of schooling. In this way, teachers can apply components of critical theory to assist students in acknowledging that there are multiple ways to knowing the truth (Frank, 2013; Mills, 2007). In this regard, socially constructed narratives or perceived *truths* that are constructed by any society are subjective. Successively, teachers may apply the vision of DisCrit as an emancipatory theoretical framework, thus empowering students to free themselves from existing stigmatizing narratives that can result in self-constructed definitions of race/ethnicity and disability. By examining racism as a historical event that remains entrenched in today's society, teachers may assist students in the development of oppositional knowledge, which allows students to recognize the experience of marginalization as an institutionalized fixture in dominant society. Students then can begin to acknowledge that the challenges of racism and ableism should not be internalized as a cultural deficit. Students also learn the importance of producing, centering, and consuming personal knowledge in the development of intersecting identities. Finally, DisCrit may be applied to build collective and personal response to injustice, thus allowing the student to shift their understandings of dominant narratives about race and disability and also enter a transformed psychological space that is emancipatory.

Patricia Hill Collins (2000) discusses this psychological concept as the "conscious sphere of freedom," whereby individuals whose lives exist at the intersection of multiple identities are able to shift their thinking from one of self-disparaging notions of difference that are conferred by dominant narratives to one where they are able to enact the power to control their own reality—where they are able to construct empowering self-constructed identities that lead to personal freedom. Collins (2000) refers to the process of self-definition as the politics of empowerment. It is the process in which an individual from a historically marginalized background develops oppositional knowledge (Collins, 2016). Further, individuals cannot be fully empowered until intersecting oppressions themselves are deconstructed and eliminated (Collins, 2000; Frank, 2013). We contend that the ability to acknowledge an intersecting identity is an insufficient strategy for undermining stigmatizing societal notions of difference. We propose that the conceptualization of identity also requires an emancipatory, politicized racial and disability identity or development of an oppositional identity, which we believe is a prerequisite for activism and resistance that disrupt structural oppression.

SHAPING ACTIVISM THROUGH INTERSECTIONAL KNOWLEDGE

Engaging in activism often does not lead to sustained participation without individuals first interrogating the technology of self that is encompassed by the "matrix of language, practice, body effects, dispositions and aspirations" (Peters et al., 2009, p. 544) that the individual possesses. We acknowledge that the development of identity is complex and nuanced, and so too is the selection of strategies of resistance. We also recognize that an individual's ability to develop an oppositional identity is the first action toward activism and diverse forms of resistance (Annamma et al., 2013). An oppositional identity is the ability of multiply marginalized individuals to construct narratives that highlight the strengths, power, and potential of themselves and their communities. Drawing from adolescent development, disability identity, and Black civil rights movement literature, we believe that youth who exist at the intersection of racial, disabled, gendered, and classed identities should be encouraged to embrace tools of resistance in order to undermine structural systems of oppression. We propose that tools of resistance are the protective measures one takes to combat the psychological and material consequences of day-to-day oppressions.

Take, for example, the findings of Darlin and Heckert (2010), who have written about participatory and observational disability engagement. Older participants with disabilities were more likely to reject the belief that disability is a socially constructed identity marker. Instead, older participants adopted the medical model of disability, while younger participants embraced notions of identity being constructed through dominant master narratives. The findings of Darlin and Heckert (2010) emphasize the importance of engaging youth in the resistance struggle against intersectional oppression by viewing themselves as knowledge producers. It is also likely, then, that individuals with disabilities often traverse various ideological modes of resistance. Thus, selecting one's strategies for resistance or tools of resistance becomes personal and fluid. As individuals continue to develop their identity, facilitated through their connection with others, we expect that strategies may shift, experience renewal, be revitalized, and be released. We understand, then, that racial and disability identity are highly personal, in which "small decisions concerning oppositional practice may matter just as much as visible actions of broad-based social movements" (Collins, 2016, p. 136).

We argue that within the current context of identity politics, social justice, and resistance DisCrit may serve as a theoretical framework to usher multiply marginalized youth into an arena of self-definition and toward a conscious sphere of freedom. DisCrit can be used as an emancipatory framework to demonstrate that our response to domination should and will vary, based on our historical, contextual, and corporeal differences (Annamma et al., 2013; Collins, 2016). We propose four types of diverse tools of resistance: traditional resistance, solidary resistance, corporeal resistance, and conforming resistance. *Traditional resistance* can be thought of as marches and sit-ins, which Annamma et al. (2013) indicate may not offer accessibility for those with corporeal differences. *Solidary resistance* requires the coalescing of nondisabled and disabled persons in the building of an alliance related to social justice issues connected to disability. *Corporeal resistance* is more problematic in that it requires the individual to understand the dominant narratives about their identities and disabilities while also capitalizing upon (or manipulating) a situation to provoke pity or shame in order to expose the absurdity of the underlying beliefs within the dominant narrative. *Conforming resistance* is the willingness of an individual to confront discriminatory policies in school environments as well as the workplace. We believe that by examining our four categories of inclusive tools for resistance multiply marginalized youth can more readily and intentionally claim and discover tools of resistance that can add to their sense of empowerment. These categories also transform able-bodied perceptions about strategies of resistance and diversify the ways individuals participate in activism.

The act of resistance, regardless of the tool of resistance, should capture the complexity of intersecting power relations that subvert or marginalize one's intersecting racial and disability identities. Intersectional resistance also addresses the structural barriers that impede equity in schools and communities, as well as promote issues of social justice. Intersectional resistance, as we propose, additionally addresses the intracultural biases that exist simultaneously in racially/ethnically diverse communities as well as the disability community. Therefore, engagement in activism becomes more complex for multiply marginalized youth. Racially/ethnically diverse youth with disabilities must address issues of ableism that may exist within the racial/ethnic group (see Banks, 2015), while simultaneously addressing racism that may exist with the disability community. Therefore, the most effective intersectional tools of resistance are those that undermine institutionalized beliefs, while also allowing for the opportunity for multiply marginalized persons to construct self-affirming narratives that are free of deleterious hegemonic cultural perceptions of difference.

IMPLEMENTATION OF DISCRIT IN THE CLASSROOM TO EMPOWER INTERSECTIONAL IDENTITIES

Researchers and educators who employ DisCrit as a theoretical framework may also begin to apply the framework as a pedagogical tool, which allows multiply marginalized individuals to see themselves through a lens of empowerment and encourages youth to construct oppositional identities. We believe the tenets of DisCrit can be used to transform U.S. schools into sites of liberation for students who experience life at the intersection of disability and marginalized identities.

Participatory Action Research

While research established within critical theory is often associated with the expansion of theoretical inquiry, DisCrit can extend the foundations of critical pedagogies to prioritize students' voices and personal experiences of intersectionality. The implementation of participatory action research, when combined with DisCrit as a theoretical framework and pedagogical tool, can be used to center the historical and contemporary experiences of students who are racially/ethnically diverse and identified with disabilities. Participatory action research encourages participants to seek to acknowledge institutional structures and attempt to collaboratively transform existing societal barriers to equity and inclusion. Thus, students who are racially/ethnically diverse and identified with disabilities can be centered as subjects in their own research with the intention to develop literacies of power. Further, Black disabled students can actively participate in their emancipation through participant action research where they can engage in a collective investigation of issues in their immediate communities and rely on their personal knowledge to understand problems that are of greatest concern related to the intersection of race/ethnicity and disability. Collective action becomes a part of the process to address concerns in schools and community and within peer relations. Individuals living at the intersection of multiple identities can then be guided through inquiry to develop their own solutions that may subvert negative portrayals of themselves and their communities.

Examining Historical Intersectional Figures and Building Solidarity Alliances

Lorraine O'Grady (2003), whose work explores the cultural construction of identity, stated, "to name ourselves rather than be named, we must first see ourselves. For some of us, this will not be easy. So long unmirrored, we may have forgotten how we look. Nevertheless, we can't theorize in a void; we must have evidence" (p. 176). The evidence that Black adolescents with disabilities require in order to adopt oppositional knowledge that challenges hegemonic deficit framings of both Blackness and disability can be found in African American history. For example, the presentation of racialized historical figures such as Harriet Tubman and Sojourner Truth should be complicated by highlighting their human diversity, which includes their experiences as individuals with disabilities. Further, researchers and educators should also begin to feature narratives about contemporary African American figures who have experienced life at the intersection of race and disability. Positioning students as researchers in the investigation of their own histories allows for self-discovery through exploration and allows students to construct images of Black and disability identities that are more representative of the human variance that exists in our communities. It is here that students can examine history at the intersections of Blackness and disability for themselves and unearth the strategies of oppression used against racialized, classed, gendered, and disabled communities. Students can practice self-definition and validate their own truths related to race and disability, adopt oppositional knowledge that they construct from historical investigations, and challenge existing social hierarchies. The experience of constructing self-affirming personal knowledge is also developed as students build their collective and personal responses to injustice.

The examination of historical intersectional alliances presents the opportunity for students to identify and cultivate cultural spaces with their peers that foster their Black and disabled identities in a way reminiscent of the Black Panther Party's investment in the disability rights movement. This coalition, fostered by disabled members of the Black Panther Party such as Dennis Billups, a young African American man from San Francisco with a visual impairment, who compelled Black people with disabilities to join the disability rights movement and "framed the audience for the 504 demonstration as one composed of black disabled people" (Schweik, 2011, n.p.), testifies to the legacy of brilliant and empowered Black and disabled identities. Narratives that highlight intersectionality and solidarity between marginalized groups are often absent from school curricula but are essential if we are to transgress pejorative descriptions of oppressed people and communities. Students can establish an authentic collective experience and identify themselves as an extension of history by identifying the history of activism and racism and exploring these events through historic and present-day interviews with former activists from cultural spaces.

Bidirectional Activism for Teachers and Students

The implementation of DisCrit pedagogical frameworks that foster the construction of oppositional knowledge within students may be difficult to fathom, given that public schools are composed of a predominantly white teacher workforce and, as hooks (2003) noted, "teachers are often among the group most reluctant to acknowledge the extent to which white-supremacist thinking informs every aspect of our culture including the way we learn, the content of what we learn, and the manner in which we are taught" (p. 25). To this end, we view the previously identified tenets of DisCrit as tools teachers can use to interrogate their personal beliefs about racism, ableism, and how institutionalized faulty notions about difference circulate interdependently and in invisible ways in their own pedagogies, practice, and school systems (Annamma et al., 2013). By attending to the tenets of DisCrit, education professionals are directed to confront personal ideals misidentified as universal truths, which often become structures that inhibit the development of diverse identities and push students to conform to hegemonic ways of being. Once confronted through reflexive practice that is steeped in the tenets of DisCrit, we believe teachers will identify the need to engage in cultural reciprocity with their students and emphasize the importance of participating in structural transformation. We also assert that teachers should begin to share with students how the construction of a self-defined identity, which is created independent of whiteness and ableism, can be liberating and emancipatory for those who are multiply marginalized.

CONCLUSION

As Black academics of various ages, nationalities, and dis/abilities, we can attest that the ability to establish politicized intersectional, self-defined identities that are free of dominant notions of difference is a multifaceted process that requires significant reflection about notions of difference related to minoritized groups. We propose that the development of an intersecting oppositional identity is a beginning point for engaging in resistance and can, therefore, be used to amend socially constructed narratives to ensure that new socially constructed narratives originate from the voices of those who experience race and disability in their everyday lives. We demonstrate that the historical representations of enslaved African Americans with disabilities explain a historical context in which African Americans with disabilities were disallowed, for reasons of safety and well-being, from embracing multidimensional intersectional identities. However, we acknowledge that the ability to represent historic figures in ways that emphasize their intersecting identities offers the occasion for multiply marginalized youth to reimagine the continuum of human diversity and begin to proudly embrace a disabled identity that incorporates both racialized and disabled identities. We conclude that the formation of a politicized, intersecting identity is always established through the negotiation of dueling societal narratives and requires the courage to navigate through corresponding affective responses that result from confronting racism and ableism. Until we engage in the process of intersecting oppositional identity development, we cannot fully address the challenges of institutionalized structural racism and ableism. Therefore, researchers who utilize DisCrit as a theoretical framework must begin to highlight the cultural psychological inward inquiries that are necessary to lead to a more liberated identity and a more empowering educational curriculum.

REFERENCES

Al-Mohamed, D. (2015). True inclusion: Museums need more disability narratives. *Museum*, September/October, 22–25.

Annamma, S. A., Connor, D., & Ferri, B. (2013). Dis/ability critical race studies (DisCrit): Theorizing at the intersections of race and dis/ability. *Race Ethnicity and Education*, 16(1), 1–31.

Baldwin, J. (1985). *The price of the ticket: Collected nonfiction, 1945–1985.* St. Martin's Press.

Banks, J. (2015). Gangsters and wheelchairs: Urban teachers' perceptions of disability, race, and gender. *Disability & Society*, 30(4), 569–582.

Banks, J. (2017). "These people are never going to stop labeling me": Educational experiences of African American male students labeled with learning disabilities. *Equity & Excellence in Education*, 50(1), 96–107.

Bogart, K. R. (2014). The role of disability self-concept in adaptation to congenital and acquired disability. *Rehabilitation Psychology*, *59*(1), 107–115.

Boster, D. H. (2013). *African American slavery and disability: Bodies, property, and power in the antebellum South, 1800–1860*. Routledge.

Carter, R., Seaton, E. K., & Rivas-Drake, D. (2017). Racial identity in the context of pubertal development: Implications for adjustment. *Developmental Psychology*, *53*(11), 2170–2181.

Collins, P. H. (1989). The social construction of Black feminist thought. *Signs: Journal of Women in Culture and Society*, *14*(41), 745–773.

Collins, P. H. (2000). Gender, black feminism, and black political economy. *The Annals of the American Academy of Political and Social Science*, *568*(1), 41–53.

Collins, P. H. (2016). Black feminist thought as oppositional knowledge. *Departures in Critical Qualitative Research*, *5*(3), 133–144.

Cross Jr., W. E. (1985). Black identity: Rediscovering the distinction between personal identity and reference group orientation. In M. B. Spencer, G. K. Brookins, & W. R. Allen (Eds.), *Child psychology: Beginnings: The social and affective development of Black children* (pp. 155–171). Lawrence Erlbaum Associates.

Darlin, R. B., & Heckert, D. A. (2010). Orientations toward disability: Differences over the lifecourse. *International Journal of Disability, Development and Education*, *57*(2), 131–143.

Dunn, D. S., & Burcaw, S. (2013). Disability identity: Exploring narrative accounts of disability. *Rehabilitation Psychology*, *58*(2), 148–157.

Erevelles, N., & Minear, A. (2010). Unspeakable offenses: Untangling race and disability in discourses of intersectionality. *Journal of Literary and Cultural Disability Studies*, *4*(2), 127–145.

Ferri, B. (2010). A dialogue we have yet to have: Race and disability. In C. Dudley-Marling & A. Gurn (Eds.), *The myth of the normal curve* (pp. 139–150). Peter Lang.

Forber-Pratt, A. J., Merrin, G. J., Mueller, C. O., Price, L. R., & Kettrey, H. H. (2017). Initial factor exploration of disability identity. *Rehabilitation Psychology*, *65*(1), 1–10.

Frank, J. (2013). Mitigating against epistemic injustice in educational research. *Educational Researcher*, *42*(7), 363–370.

Gill, C. J. (1997). Four types of integration in disability identity development. *Journal of Vocational Rehabilitation*, *9*(1), 39–46.

Helms, J. E. (1990). *Black and white racial identity: Theory, research, and practice*. Greenwood Press.

Hobson, J. (2019). Of "sound" and "unsound" body and mind: Reconfiguring the heroic portrait of Harriet Tubman. *Frontiers: A Journal of Women Studies*, *40*(2), 193–218.

Linton, S. (1998). *Claiming disability: Knowledge and identity*. NYU Press.

Lorde, A. (2007). Learning from the 60s. *Sister outsider: Essays and speeches*. Crossing Press.

Mills, C. (2007). White ignorance. In S. Sullivan & N. Tuana (Eds.), *Race and epistemologies of ignorance* (pp. 26–31). SUNY Press.

Minister, M. (2012). Female, black, and able: Representations of Sojourner Truth and theories of embodiment. *Disability Studies Quarterly*, *32*(1). http://dx.doi.org/10.18061/dsq.v32i1.3030

Moses, J. O., Villodas, M. T., & Villodas, F. (2020). Black and proud: The role of ethnic-racial identity in the development of future expectations among at-risk adolescents. *Cultural Diversity and Ethnic Minority Psychology*, 26(1), 112–123.

Mueller, C. (2019). Adolescent understandings of disability labels and social stigma in school. *International Journal of Qualitative Studies in Education*, 32(3), 263–281.

O'Grady, L. (2003). Olympia's maid: Reclaiming black female subjectivity. In A. Jones (Ed.), *The feminism and visual culture reader* (pp. 174–187). Routledge.

Parham, T. A. (1989). Cycles of psychological nigrescence. *The Counseling Psychologist*, 17(2), 187–226.

Peters, S., Gabel, S., & Symeonidou, S. (2009). Resistance, transformation and the politics of hope: Imagining a way forward for the disabled people's movement. *Disability & Society*, 24(5), 543–556.

Rivas-Drake, D., Seaton, E. K., Markstrom, C., Quintana, S., Syed, M., Lee, R. M., Schwartz, S. J., Umaña- Taylor, A. J., French, S., & Yip, T. (2014). The ethnic and racial identity in the 21st century study group. Ethnic and racial identity in adolescence: Implications for psychosocial, academic, and health outcomes. *Child Development*, 85(1), 40–57.

Schweik, S. (2011). Lomax's matrix: Disability, solidarity, and the black power of 504. *Disability Studies Quarterly*, 31(1). http://dsq-sds.org/article/view/1371/1539

Sellers, R. M., Smith, M. A., Shelton, J. N., Rowley, S. A, & Chavous, T. M. (1998). Multidimensional model of racial identity: A reconceptualization of African American racial identity. *Personality and Social Psychology Review*, 2(1), 18–39.

Thompson, C. P., Anderson, L. P., & Bakeman, R. A. (2000). Effects of racial socialization and racial identity on acculturative stress in African American college students. *Cultural Diversity and Ethnic Minority Psychology*, 6(2), 196–210.

CHAPTER 7

A DisCrit Call for the Abolition of School Police

Christina Payne-Tsoupros & Najma Johnson

ABSTRACT

Risk and harm that uniformed police officers stationed in schools, typically called school resource officers or SROs, pose to Black children, especially Black children with disabilities, is well documented. This chapter argues that as a moral and policy position, the threat and harm that SROs pose to Black children makes the presence of school police unacceptable. This chapter uses Disability Critical Race Theory (DisCrit) a theoretical framework developed by Annamma et al. (2013), to illustrate why these particular groups of children are especially vulnerable to school police and why traditional reform methods are insufficient. This chapter, therefore, rejects traditional reform measures and argues that the path forward must be the removal of police in schools.

A DISCRIT CALL FOR ABOLITION OF SCHOOL POLICE

When an officer is present, I lose my peace of mind. I automatically start watching my back and making sure that I don't stick out for any reason. All of this arises from the fear that many other Black youth and I share: a fear of being harassed, a fear of being targeted, of being shot and killed.
　　—Jonathan "JaJa" Janvier, age 17, Advancement Project & Alliance for Educational Justice, 2019, (p. 32).

The disparities in school discipline for Black children, particularly Black children who have disabilities, are well documented. Black children with disabilities experience harsher levels of discipline and punishment, including interactions with school police, than white students. While Black students represented 15% of nationwide public school enrollment for the 2015–2016 school year (the most recent year for which such data is available), Black students comprised 31% of students who were arrested or referred to law enforcement (U.S. Department of Education, Office for Civil Rights, 2018). Students of all races with disabilities are disciplined more harshly than students without disabilities. Within the disabled student population, Black students with disabilities, despite representing 19% of students with disabilities, comprised 36% of the students with disabilities who were arrested or referred to law enforcement (U.S. Government Accountability Office, 2018).

This chapter uses the DisCrit framework developed by Annamma et al. (2013) to show why these children are exceptionally vulnerable to abuse by school police and why traditional reform measures are insufficient. This chapter adds to the growing body of literature calling for the abolition of school police. In doing so, we hope to support Black and Brown youth fighting for the removal of police in schools.

We begin with a brief history of school policing in the United States. We then use the DisCrit framework to illustrate why particular groups of children—specifically, Black children—are especially vulnerable to abuse by school police. Building on that analysis, we then use DisCrit to illustrate why traditional reform methods are insufficient and why abolition is the path forward that children deserve.

In this chapter, we focus predominantly on the dangers of school police to Black children. Many of these same concerns may also apply to Indigenous and Latinx children as well (see Redfield & Nance, 2016). We conclude the chapter by identifying some of the areas that warrant additional study, including considering effects of school police on other marginalized and multiply marginalized groups of children, including Indigenous, Latinx, lesbian, gay, bisexual, trans, queer+, and/or gender-nonconforming (LGBTQ+ GNC) children, as well as the impact of overpolicing on Black girls. This chapter also suggests research into the effects of school police on families from multiply marginalized groups.

With respect to language, in this chapter we use "person-first" (i.e., "children with disabilities" or "child of color") and "identity-first" (i.e., "disabled children") language interchangeably in an effort to be the most inclusive of the multitudes of children affected by school police and their preferences.

OVERVIEW OF SCHOOL POLICING IN THE UNITED STATES

This section provides a brief overview of school policing in the United States. For a comprehensive report on school policing across the nation, a recommended source is *We Came to Learn: A Call to Action for Police-Free Schools*, published in 2019 by the Advancement Project and the Alliance for Educational Justice (AEJ), two racial justice organizations. As a companion to the *We Came to Learn* report, the organizations host an interactive website, wecametolearn.com, and maintain #AssaultAt Map, which attempts to track all of the incidents of student assaults by police in schools.

A Brief History of School Policing

Today, the sight of uniformed police officers stationed in schools is common in elementary, middle, and high schools across the United States. A survey by the National Center for Education Statistics (2017) found that 47.7% of K–12 schools had a sworn law enforcement officer[1] during the 2015–2016 school year, the most recent year for which data are available. While high-profile school shootings, such as those in Columbine, Colorado; Newtown, Connecticut; and Parkland, Florida, were often an impetus for increased police presence in schools, police have been regularly assigned to schools since the 1940s (Advancement Project & AEJ, 2019). These officers are typically called school resource officers or SROs (Advancement Project & AEJ, 2019; Nance, 2016b; see also 34 U.S.C. § 10389(4), 2020).[2]

While police have been installed in schools for decades, the current SRO movement can be traced to the three strikes laws of the 1980s (the Anti-Drug Abuse Act of 1986, 21 U.S.C. § 801 et seq., as amended, part of the war on drugs) that led to the zero tolerance regimes in schools in the 1990s, which we still see today. President Bill Clinton signed into law the Gun Free Schools Act of 1994. This federal law had a profound impact on schools, including school discipline. Reflecting the political climate pressuring Democratic politicians to appear tough on crime, Congress modeled these juvenile offender laws after the adult offender laws (Advancement Project & AEJ, 2019; Nance, 2016a).

Against this federal landscape, state and local legislatures passed laws requiring schools to adopt these zero tolerance policies and mandating referrals to police (Nance, 2016a). As a result, the laws required automatic expulsion as well as automatic long-term suspensions for certain offenses, without principal or teacher discretion. Some states also passed laws criminalizing certain student behavior (Advancement Project & AEJ, 2019).

State laws created additional involvement and interaction with school police, which was also facilitated by the federal government's creation of the Office of Community Oriented Policing Services (COPS). Created as part of the Violent Crime Control and Law Enforcement Act of 1994 (P.L. 103-322; U.S. Department of Justice, Community Oriented Policing Services, n.d.), the COPS program is significant in the context of school policing. After the 1999 mass school shooting at Columbine High School, the COPS program created COPS in Schools grants, which dramatically increased the number of police in schools (Advancement Project & AEJ, 2019). As the first mass school shooting filmed on camera, Columbine "forever alter[ed] society's view of school policing" (Advancement Project & AEJ, 2019, p. 22). In the wake of the ever-increasing list of high-profile mass school shootings, public outcry for more school safety measures has manifested itself in increased police presence in schools, the brunt of which has been borne disproportion-ately by low-income communities of color.

Roles and Functions of School Police Officers

School police officers can serve a variety of roles. They are often framed as using the triad model, in which the SRO serves three primary roles: educa-tor, counselor, and law enforcement officer (National Association of School Resource Officers, 2015). Under this framing, the SRO acts as an educator by guest lecturing, as a counselor by assisting in bullying or other student conflict issues, and as a law enforcement officer by taking on "school-related matters that police traditionally would have handled, including off-campus activities that involve students, making arrests or issuing citations on cam-pus for particular conduct, and taking action against unauthorized persons on school grounds" (James & McCallion, 2013, p. 2).

With respect to the triad model, researchers have found that SROs spend most of their time engaged in law enforcement activities (Shaver & Decker, 2017), compared to educating or counseling: "Although there is consider-able diversity . . . most spent at least half their time in law enforcement" (Raymond, 2010, p. 6). Against the federal landscape of zero tolerance and COPS in Schools grants, SROs are installed in schools under different structures, depending on state and local law and school board policy. Many SROs are installed in schools pursuant to a memorandum of understanding (MOU) between the law enforcement agency and the school district, which sets forth the roles and duties of the SRO.

Variations in the structure of school policing contribute to challenges in addressing problems with school police, including, as the Advancement Project and AEJ note, a lack of transparency regarding school policing data and funding and a lack of police accountability (Advancement Project & AEJ, 2019, p. 48). Moreover, even the number of school police is not trans-parent. The National Association of School Resource Officers (NASRO) es-timates there are 14,000–20,000 SROs installed in schools (NASRO, n.d.). Data from the National Center for Education Statistics (Jackson et al., n.d.) show at least 52,100 SROs (full- and part-time) in public schools in 2016.

The remainder of this chapter explores how the system of school polic-ing, operating within larger society, makes certain groups of children par-ticularly vulnerable to harm.

DISCRIT ANALYSIS OF SCHOOL POLICING

Black children, especially Black children with disabilities, receive harsher dis-cipline across all levels, including interactions with SROs. "National, state, and local data *across all settings and at all school levels* clearly demonstrate that school administrators and teachers discipline minority students, particularly African American students, more harshly and more frequently than similarly situated white students" (Nance, 2016a, p. 318, emphasis added).

Disability Critical Race Theory (DisCrit) is an intersectional theoretical framework developed by Annamma et al. (2013) that highlights both why particular groups of children are especially vulnerable to abuse by school police and why traditional reform methods are insufficient. In using DisCrit to analyze *why* these children are particularly vulnerable, DisCrit also shows why traditional reform methods are unacceptable.

DisCrit Shows Why Particular Groups of Children Are Especially Vulnerable to School Police

Annamma et al. (2013) set forth seven tenets of DisCrit "to operationalize what kinds of specific questions and issues can be illuminated from a DisCrit approach" (pp. 11–18). While the DisCrit tenets necessarily work together, this section specifically highlights tenets one, three, five, and six to analyze the relationships between vulnerable children and school police.

> Tenet one: "DisCrit focuses on ways that the forces of racism and ableism circulate interdependently, often in neutralized and invisible ways, to uphold notions of normalcy."
> Tenet three: "DisCrit emphasizes the social constructions of race and ability and yet recognizes the material and psychological impacts of being labeled as raced or dis/abled, which sets one outside of the western cultural norms."
> Tenet five: "DisCrit considers legal and historical aspects of dis/ability and race and how both have been used separately and together to deny the rights of some citizens."
> Tenet six: "DisCrit recognizes Whiteness and Ability as Property and that gains for people labeled with dis/abilities have largely been made as the result of interest convergence of White, middle-class citizens" (p. 11).

DisCrit Recognizes that Racism and Ableism Place Black Children at Greatest Risk

The first tenet of DisCrit is crucial to understanding how Black children with disabilities are situated differently than their white peers. Law professor Jason Nance, among others, has written extensively about how strict security measures in schools disproportionately impact Black children. Black children are more likely than white children to attend schools that are overpoliced and underresourced (Nance, 2016a). Black children are more likely than white children to be arrested by school police (Redfield

& Nance, 2016). Nance (2017) found that the percentage of enrollment of children of color predicts the use of strict security measures, including SROs, in place at schools. DisCrit illustrates that the factor of being Black positions children differently and makes them more vulnerable to school police. Due to Black students being more likely to attend overpoliced schools, they are at greater risk of harm by SROs.

The third tenet of DisCrit is intimately linked with tenet one. Because of the interconnection of racism and ableism, the social constructions of racial and ability identities "hold profound significance in people's lives, both in the present and historically" (Annamma et al., 2013, p. 13). Schools assign disability differently for Black children and white children. For example, as has been frequently discussed in the literature, Black children are disproportionately identified with the special education label "emotionally disturbed (ED)" (Adams & Erevelles, 2016; see also 34 C.F.R. § 300.8.(c)(4)[3]). Nanda, describes emotional disturbance as a "catchall category used when no other label fits" (2019, p. 310), noting that the ED designation is particularly prone to abuse because it "turns largely on the subjective assessment of teachers and administrators. White children, by contrast, are more likely to receive specific medical diagnoses of autism, attention deficit hyperactivity disorder, or others" (Adams & Erevelles, 2016). Thus, Black students with disabilities face compounded levels of risk (Nanda, 2019).

Black students, as well as Indigenous and Latinx students, are also overrepresented in other discretionary categories in special education that involve subjective determinations by teachers, clinicians, or administrators, including the categories of "intellectual disability," "specific learning disability," and "linguistically disabled" (Adams & Erevelles, 2016; Redfield & Nance, 2016).

As explained by Nelson (2018), these differences in disability labels position Black children to be criminalized by their disability and white children to receive treatment and resources. Nanda (2019) argues that this contributes to at least a double level of bias facing Black children, in that certain disabilities are stigmatized, and these particularly stigmatizing disabilities are more likely to be ascribed to Black children. Adams and Erevelles (2016) characterize this phenomenon as an example of the construction of disability as a structural problem whereby disability is a mechanism by which Black students are sorted and criminalized, thereby ensuring ongoing continuing educational segregation.

Critically, the more stigmatized labels also rely heavily on teacher discretion. Nanda refers to the special identification process as a "playground for [teachers'] implicit biases," as teacher discretion "allows for bias to influence each step of the multilayered process from start to finish" (2019, pp. 296, 298). Thus, the special education identification and the treatment and resource options that follow are different for Black and non-Black children. Black children are more likely to be overrepresented in stigmatized disability categories and attend overpoliced schools.

DisCrit Recognizes the Power Structures Placing Black Children at Greatest Risk

The fifth tenet of DisCrit reinforces that the current climate of school policing needs to be situated within its broader legal and historical context. The power structures that have segregated Black students in education throughout history have continued through the disproportionate overpolicing in majority Black schools and the differences in how disability is ascribed to Black and non-Black students.

School overpolicing of Black children is part of the greater historical and cultural landscape where Black adults with disabilities have been targeted, imprisoned, subject to police brutality, and murdered. Fenton (2016) traces eugenics laws to their racist origins following the passage of Amendment XIII: "Once the 13th Amendment changed the status of Blacks from property to legal personhood, the social agenda transformed from the reproduction of property to a eugenic one of reduction and elimination" (p. 208). Fenton (2016) explains that those who were forcibly sterilized for feeblemindedness under eugenics laws "were sometimes disabled but often just poor, Black, and/or female" (p. 208).

Drawing on the work of Burch and Joyner, Erevelles and Minear use the story of Junius Wilson's life and the horrific abuse he endured at the hands of the state as an example of "how eugenic practices continue to reconstitute social hierarchies in contemporary contexts via the deployment of hegemonic ideology of disability that have real material effects on people located at the intersections of difference" (Erevelles & Minear, 2010, pp. 133–134).

Junius Wilson, a Black Deaf man born in 1908, attended the North Carolina School for the Colored Blind and Deaf, a segregated school for the Deaf in Raleigh, where he learned Raleigh signs, which were specific to that particular Black Deaf school community. While hearing Black people communicated in spoken English and white Deaf people communicated in American Sign Language, Wilson had access to neither language. Accused of assault and attempted rape in 1925, Wilson was unable to communicate with anyone in court and was therefore judged to be feebleminded. Seventeen-year-old Wilson was committed to the North Carolina State Hospital for the Colored Insane where he was subsequently surgically castrated. Wilson remained institutionalized for 76 years. He was never found guilty of any crime.

As Erevelles and Minear (2010) stated, "being black and deaf located him at the lowest rungs of the social hierarchy of the time" (p. 140). As a Black Deaf man, Junius Wilson was marginalized and excluded from the white Deaf community because he was Black. He was marginalized and excluded from the hearing Black community because he was Deaf. Wilson was Black in the Jim Crow South and Deaf in a phonocentrist system where access to spoken language is dominant and assumed. The legal, medical, and cultural system used Wilson's Deafness and race—individually and together—to institutionalize him, to castrate him, to extract forced labor from him, and to keep him institutionalized for more than seven decades.

Our laws, past and present, including the Violent Crime Control and Law Enforcement Act,[4] that encourage, incentivize, and require police in schools have racist origins and underpinnings, reflecting and reinforcing the legal and cultural structure of larger society. These laws encourage, incentivize, and require schools to accept the funds and the racist terms that accompany them. Thus, the laws themselves contribute to student vulnerability to school police. In addition, public perception of the need to increase school safety can create additional pressures on school and public officials, particularly following widely publicized school shootings.

Related to the fifth tenet, the sixth tenet of DisCrit maintains that "the political interests of oppressed groups have often been gained only through interest convergence" (Annamma et al., 2013, p. 17). Annamma et al. (2013) quote the work of Derrick Bell (1980): Interest convergence means that "the interests of Blacks in receiving racial equality will be accommodated only when it converges with the interests of Whites" (p. 17). In the context of school policing, this tenet helps highlight that the particular harm faced by Black children is different than that faced by white children. Tenet six explains why SRO policies continue to put Black children at risk despite the known and undisputed disparities. White middle-class children do not face these same dangers.

DisCrit Shows Why Traditional Reforms Are Insufficient

Scholars and advocates have recommended a variety of reforms for school resource officers. These reforms include more comprehensive training for SROs, clarity about the specific role of the SRO, and making a grievance procedure available to students and families (Archerd, 2017; Nance, 2016a; Shaver & Decker, 2017). Reforms often demand an MOU between the law enforcement agency and the school district, setting forth the roles and duties of the SRO. Such MOUs typically (1) require that all SROs be carefully selected and receive specialized training; (2) clearly define the role of the SRO to include those of law enforcement officer, teacher, and informal counselor (the triad model); and (3) prohibit SROs from involvement in formal school discipline situations that are the responsibility of school administrators. NASRO considers such an MOU a best practice (NASRO, 2015). As DisCrit highlights why school police are especially harmful to certain groups of children, it also illustrates why traditional calls for reform are insufficient: Reform efforts are ineffective at dismantling the larger legal and historical structure of school police.

This section highlights some of the work of Black and Brown youth-led organizations across the nation in their pursuit of police-free schools. In the the wake of police killing a Black man named George Floyd in spring 2020, protests in support of Black Lives Matter erupted across the nation, with widespread calls to defund the police. The police-free-schools movement, which organizers have been working on for years, was put into the national spotlight, with local efforts gaining attention and momentum.

One of the longest-running groups in this effort is the Black Organizing Project (BOP) in Oakland, California. BOP launched its Bettering Our School System (BOSS) campaign in the wake of the 2011 murder of Raheim Brown, a 20-year-old Black man who was murdered on school property by an Oakland school police officer (Advancement Project & AEJ, 2019; BOP, 2019). As part of its BOSS campaign, BOP pressured the Oakland Unified School District (OUSD) to enter into an MOU with the Oakland School Police Department. OUSD maintains its own police department, separate from the Oakland Police Department. In addition to the MOU, BOP also fought for and won a school district–wide complaint system (Advancement Project & AEJ, 2019).

At the same time as advocating for and winning the reforms of the MOU and complaint system, BOP was also seeking the longer-term abolitionist solution of the complete removal of police from OUSD. In its case study of BOP, the Advancement Project and AEJ explained that "[BOP's] position was radical: at the time, traditional allies in the education advocacy field were focused on addressing the harms of school policing through trainings and policy change" (Advancement Project & AEJ, 2019, p. 34). On June 10, 2020, the Board of Education of OUSD approved Resolution No. 1920-0260—George Floyd Resolution to Eliminate the Oakland School Police Department. The resolution eliminates the school police department and directs the superintendent "to reallocate the school police funds to student support positions" (BOP, 2020). This is a huge win for BOP on behalf of students and the community. BOP's demands include barring future contracts with law enforcement, to prevent OUSD from engaging with another law enforcement agency (such as the Oakland Police Department) to provide the same policing services as the Oakland School Police Department did (BOP, 2019, p. 3).

In the District of Columbia during the 2018–2019 school year, Black children represented 66% of the student population (District of Columbia, Office of the State Superintendent, 2019), yet in the nation's capital, Black children comprised 92% of school-based arrests (Washington Lawyers' Committee for Civil Rights and Urban Affairs, 2020). Black girls are arrested at a rate of more than *30 times* that of white children in the District of Columbia (Vafa et al., 2018).

Black Swan Academy is a youth-focused organization that has been leading the call for police-free schools in Washington, DC. In July 2020, Black Swan Academy earned two small but important wins in the fight against school policing. The Council of the District of Columbia voted to move the public schools' security contract from under the control of the Metropolitan Police Department to the control of the District of Columbia Public Schools (Black Swan Academy, n.d.-a.). In addition, the District of Columbia's State Board of Education, which is an independent agency that provides advocacy and policy guidance to the District of Columbia Public Schools, passed resolution SR20-10, State Board of Education Resolution to Recognize the Importance of Removing All Police from D.C. Public and Charter Schools (DC.gov, State Board of Education, 2020, n.d.).

These examples from Oakland and Washington, DC, illustrate some of the extent of the policing in schools and some of the challenges of reform. In addition to these recent wins in Oakland and Washington, DC, youth-led organizations across the nation have won hard-fought gains in the struggle to remove police from schools.[5] The list continues to grow during this national movement. While these are hard-fought wins, these reforms often fall short of organizers' demands, as the reforms leave intact the policing infrastructure. Reform efforts fail because they do not challenge this foundational architecture, which is built on racist and ableist laws and practices. Their architecture does not consider how certain populations of children are particularly vulnerable to school police.

Analyzing the assault by an SRO on a high school student in Spring Valley, South Carolina—and the reform efforts in its aftermath—may be instructive on this point. The assault led to the Advancement Project and AEJ's development of the #AssaultAt campaign, starting with #AssaultAtSpringValley (Advancement Project & AEJ, 2019). When a 16-year-old Black high school student Shakara refused to put away her cell phone in response to her math teacher's directive, the teacher called a school administrator, who then called an SRO. When Shakara again refused to put away her phone, the SRO violently assaulted her. Shakara was "placed in a headlock, flipped over in her desk, then dragged and thrown across her classroom" (Advancement Project & AEJ, 2019, p. 55). A classmate, Niya Kenny, objected, and the SRO arrested both girls. As a result of sustained pressure from AEJ and other youth organizers, the charges against Shakara and Niya were dropped, yet no criminal charges were brought against the SRO.

In researching the Spring Valley assault, Gupta-Kagan (2017) used it as an example of how an incident of student misbehavior led to an arrest and prosecution rather than a school-based intervention. The #AssaultAtSpringValley was, as Gutpa-Kagan (2017) stated, "a product of a series of choices: by educators who asked an SRO to become involved in a classroom management situation, and by the SRO who agreed to do so and who chose to make two arrests" (p. 85). Gupta-Kagan (2017) notes that these choices did not happen in isolation—instead, they are the product of the laws, policies, and practices "that create the legal architecture of the school-to-prison pipeline" (p. 85). These choices in schools—where policies and culture mean teachers conceive of calling police on students and where there are systems in place to facilitate this—reflect and further the legal and historical structure of overpolicing Black adults and children.

The same reasons why certain populations of students are especially vulnerable to abuse by SROs are the same reasons why traditional reforms fail. This risk of harm to Black children is impermissible and also virtually unavoidable in the current structure of school policing.

CALL FOR THE ABOLITION OF SCHOOL POLICE

The abolition of school police is the path forward that children deserve. Abolition is consistent with DisCrit principles (Annamma et al., 2013). In addition to recognizing tenets one, three, five, and six discussed previously, it is consistent with DisCrit principles four and seven. Most importantly, abolition is what Black and Brown youth are demanding.

> Tenet four: "DisCrit privileges voices of marginalized populations, traditionally not acknowledged within research."
> Tenet seven: "DisCrit requires activism and supports of all forms of resistance" (p. 11).

Police-free schools is expressly rooted in abolition (AEJ, 2020). Police-free schools means "dismantling school policing infrastructure, culture, and practice; ending school militarization and surveillance; and building a new liberatory education system" (AEJ, 2020). This collective definition was developed by youth organizers in partnership with AEJ and is widely used across the movement. This definition moves beyond the removal of officers from school grounds. This push for abolition is consistent with Ben-Moshe's theory of dis-epistemology of abolition. Ben-Moshe (2018) defines carceral locales as:

> referring to more than prisons to encompass a variety of enclosures such as psychiatric hospitals, detention centers and residential institutions for people with disabilities, to name a few. By "carceral" I am also referring to not only physical spaces but to particular logics and discourses that abolition (penal/prison/carceral) opposes. (p. 342)

Ben-Moshe then explores how the conception of carceral expands beyond criminalization and imprisonment. The police-free schools movement uses a similar abolitionist rationale. In viewing schools as a carceral locale, the police-free schools movement seeks to move beyond the removal of school police by changing the culture of policing with the goal of "building a new liberatory education system" (AEJ, 2020).

As calls to defund police and remove police from schools become more widely adopted, organizers have worked to clarify that the demand to defund the police is much more comprehensive than reducing a percentage of dollars allocated to the budget of the local police department. In Washington, DC, for example, organizers behind the Defund MPD movement define defunding the police as follows:

> In DC, defunding the police means intentionally removing funding from the metropolitan police department (MPD). By removing funding, we decrease MPD ability to harass, arrest, incarcerate, and surveil Black people in the district.
>
> Divesting from the police is part of an abolitionist strategy. Abolition is a political vision with the goal of eliminating imprisonment, policing, and surveillance while creating lasting alternatives to punishment and incarceration.
>
> Defunding is the strategy, but a police-free world where everyone has the resources needed to thrive is the goal. We call for divestment from the police in order to support investment in health care, mental health care, housing, education, public transportation, food, and good jobs for our community. (Defund MPD, n.d.)

Black and Brown youth-led groups have been organizing and demanding change nationwide, pushing for and leading the call for the removal of school police. As the Advancement Project and AEJ (2019) commented about BOP, "[m]oving with community who were ready to demand a radical shift in policing, *even when advocates and organizations did not want to* [emphasis added], allowed BOP to have a strong, powerful base supporting the campaign" (p. 35). In acting with and by the community, BOP practices the DisCrit tenets of privileging the perspectives of marginalized populations as well as requiring and supporting various forms of activism. BOP has set forth movement building in solidarity principles aimed at its potential and current allies. BOP seeks to adhere to the principles to build "an overall collective understanding that following the leadership of those who have done the work and who will be impacted by the solutions, is the way to liberation" (BOP, n.d.). As the Advancement Project and AEJ report, from the outset, AEJ members focused on supporting the two students who were arrested in the #AssaultAtSpringValley, as AEJ members recognized that "it was important to not only organize to end the criminalization and abuse of youth of color in schools, but to also show up and support those young people who experienced violence first hand" (AEJ, 2019, p. 56). AEJ's actions demonstrate privileging voices of marginalized communities and supporting activism in all its forms.

In BOP's 2019 *The People's Plan for Police-Free Schools*, BOP outlines specific implementation proposals to dismantle school police in 2020. The comprehensive plan contains four parts: (1) divesting from school police; (2) reorganizing the campus safety and security program; (3) reinvesting the police budget into mental and behavioral health and special education; and (4) establishing a community oversight committee (BOP, 2019). The Black Swan Academy's petition to remove police from District of Columbia schools featured explicit demands both to remove police from District of Columbia schools and reinvest in mental health services, social–emotional learning, and transformative justice (Black Swan Academy, n.d.-b.).

Consistent with DisCrit tenets four and seven, Black and Brown youth are imagining and creating a different future—"a noncarceral present and future" (Ben-Moshe, 2018, p. 344) that goes beyond removing police officers. These plans and demands set forth by BOP and Black Swan Academy, as well as the plans and demands set forth by other local groups across the country, represent immediate and tangible steps that we can take now.

CONCLUSION

There are other issues related to school policing that warrant further study under a DisCrit analysis, including analyzing the impact of school police on children of different genders. A study published by the Gay-Straight Alliance Network and Crossroads Collaborative found that gender-nonconforming children (GNC) are disproportionately subject to harsh school discipline practices compared to non-GNC peers (Burdge et al., 2014). The African American Policy Forum and the Center for Intersectionality and Social Policy Studies issued a report in 2015, *Black Girls Matter: Pushed Out, Overpoliced and Underprotected*, calling attention to the lack of attention around the racial disparities in school discipline experienced by Black girls (Crenshaw et al., 2015). As noted earlier, in 2015 in the District of Columbia, Black girls were arrested at a rate over *30 times* that of white peers (Vafa et al., 2018, p. 29). The effects of school police on disabled Indigenous and Latinx children, immigrant children, undocumented children, and poor children, as well as the effects of school police on families from multiply marginalized groups, also merit study.

A critique of SROs is that there is no evidence that SROs make schools safer (Redfield & Nance, 2016). This chapter offers a different critique. The school safety framing makes the safety of Black children negotiable. According to 14-year-old Tamika, a District of Columbia student involved with the Black Swan Academy, "Instead of maintaining a good environment for kids, [police] make us scared and escalate situations. Students spend so much of their time in school; they deserve to be comfortable and not afraid" (Gomez, 2020). We know school police are not safe for Black children.

DisCrit leads us to the premise that SROs are unacceptable from a moral and policy position and allows us to imagine possibilities for safe schools for all our children.

NOTES

1. "School resource officers (SROs) include all career sworn law enforcement officers with arrest authority who have specialized training and are assigned to work in collaboration with school organizations. Under 'Any sworn law enforcement officers,' schools that reported having both SROs and other sworn law enforcement officers were counted only once." (National Center for Education Statistics, 2017).

2. "'School resource officer' means a career law enforcement officer, with sworn authority, deployed in community-oriented policing, and assigned by the employing police department or agency to work in collaboration with schools and community-based organizations—

   (A) to address crime and disorder problems, gangs, and drug activities affecting or occurring in or around an elementary or secondary school,
   (B) to develop or expand crime prevention efforts for students,
   (C) to educate likely school-age victims in crime prevention and safety,
   (D) to develop or expand community justice initiatives for students,
   (E) to train students in conflict resolution, restorative justice, and crime awareness,
   (F) to assist in the identification of physical changes in the environment that may reduce crime in or around the school, and
   (G) to assist in developing school policy that addresses crime and to recommend procedural changes."

   34 U.S.C. § 10389(4)

3. (4)(i) "Emotional disturbance means a condition exhibiting one or more of the following characteristics over a long period of time and to a marked degree that adversely affects a child's educational performance:

   (A) An inability to learn that cannot be explained by intellectual, sensory, or health factors.
   (B) An inability to build or maintain satisfactory interpersonal relationships with peers and teachers.
   (C) Inappropriate types of behavior or feelings under normal circumstances.
   (D) A general pervasive mood of unhappiness or depression.
   (E) A tendency to develop physical symptoms or fears associated with personal or school problems.
   (ii) Emotional disturbance includes schizophrenia. The term does not apply to children who are socially maladjusted, unless it is determined that they have an emotional disturbance under paragraph (c)(4)(i) of this section."

   34 C.F.R. § 300.8.(c)(4)

4. As stated by the Advancement Project and AEJ, First Lady Hillary Clinton rallied support for the bill's passage by making her now-infamous statement calling children superpredators with no conscience and no empathy (Advancement Project & AEJ, 2019, p. 22).

5. Dignity in Schools, a national coalition of advocacy groups working to end school pushout and dismantle the school-to-prison pipeline, chronicled several recent wins of local advocacy groups in their challenge to remove police from schools, including Minneapolis, Minnesota (on June 2, 2020, the school board voted to terminate its contract with the police department); Portland, Oregon (on June 4, 2020, the public school superintendent announced the removal of SROs from Portland's high schools and investment into social workers, counselors, and culturally responsive programming); St. Paul, Minnesota (on July 23, 2020, the school board voted to stop contract negotiations and terminate its MOU with the police department); San Francisco, California (same); and Madison, Wisconsin (on July 29, 2020, the school board voted to remove police from its schools) (Dignity in Schools, 2020).

REFERENCES

Adams, D. L., & Erevelles, N. (2016). Shadow play: DisCrit, dis/respectability, and carceral logics. In S. A. Annamma, D. Connor, & B. Ferri (Eds.), *DisCrit: Disability studies and critical race theory in education* (pp. 131–144). Teachers College Press.

Advancement Project & Alliance for Educational Justice. (2019). *We came to learn: A call to action for police-free schools.* www.wecametolearn.com

Alliance for Educational Justice [@4EdJustice]. (2020, May 30). *What's #Police-FreeSchools you ask? We got you. Here is our collective definition: Dismantling school policing infrastructure, culture, and practice* [Image attached] [Tweet]. Twitter. https://twitter.com/4EdJustice/status/1266732552678670336

Annamma, S. A., Connor, D., & Ferri, B. (2013). Dis/ability critical race studies (DisCrit): Theorizing at the intersections of race and dis/ability. *Journal of Race Ethnicity and Education, 16*(1), 1–31.

Anti-Drug Abuse Act of 1986, 21 U.S.C. § 801 et seq. https://www.govinfo.gov /content/pkg/STATUTE-100/pdf/STATUTE-100-Pg3207.pdf

Archerd, E. R. (2017). Restoring justice in schools. *University of Cincinnati Law Review, 85*(1), 761–814.

Ben-Moshe, L. (2018). Dis-epistemologies of abolition. *Critical Criminology, 26*(3), 341–355.

Black Organizing Project. (n.d.). *Movement building in solidarity.* http://blackorganizingproject.org/movement-building-in-solidarity-pledge/

Black Organizing Project. (2019). *The people's plan for police-free schools.* http:// blackorganizingproject.org/bops-peoples-plan/

Black Organizing Project. (2020, June 10). *The George Floyd resolution.* http:// blackorganizingproject.org/the-george-floyd-resolution/

Black Swan Academy. (n.d.-a.). *D.C. police free schools toolkit.* https://docs.google .com/document/d/1W3HODYeAJ65V5r_xswX8B5S-3w72uElW_FRJql5UuUc /edit

Black Swan Academy. (n.d.-b.). *Police-free schools.* https://www.blackswanacademy .org/policefree-schools

Burdge, H., Hyemingway, Z. T., & Licona, A. C. (2014). *Gender nonconforming youth: Discipline disparities, school push-out, and the school-to-prison pipeline.* Gay-Straight Alliance Network and Crossroads Collaborative. https://

www.njjn.org/uploads/digital-library/GSA-Network_LGBTQ_brief_FINAL
-web_Oct-2014.pdf

Crenshaw, K. W., Ocen, P., & Nanda, J. (2015). *Black girls matter: Pushed out,
overpoliced and underprotected*. Center for Intersectionality and Social Policy
Studies.

DC.gov, State Board of Education. (n.d.). *About SBOE*. https://sboe.dc.gov/page/roles

DC.gov, State Board of Education. (2020). *State board of education resolution to
recognize the importance of removing all police from D.C. public and charter schools, SR20-10*. https://simbli.eboardsolutions.com/Meetings/Attachment
.aspx?S=9000&AID=180499&MID=6006

Defund MPD. (n.d.). *FAQs*. https://www.mpd150.com/faq/

Dignity in Schools. (2020, June 30). *Organizers in Madison, Oakland and other
cities celebrate historic victories as communities ask #WhoGotNext for #Po-
liceFreeSchools across the nation*. http://dignityinschools.org/organizers-in
-madison-oakland-and-other-cities-celebrate-historic-victories-as-communities
-ask-whogotnext-for-policefreeschools-across-the-nation/

District of Columbia, Office of the State Superintendent of Education. (2019). *State
of discipline: 2018–2019 school year*. https://osse.dc.gov/sites/default/files
/dc/sites/osse/page_content/attachments/Discipline%20Report%20OSSE
%202018-19%20School%20Year.pdf

Erevelles, N., & Minear A. (2010). Unspeakable offenses: Untangling race and disability in discourses of intersectionality. *Journal of Literary & Cultural Disability Studies, 4*(2), 127–145.

Fenton, Z. E. (2016). Disability does not discriminate: Toward a theory of multiple
identity through coalition. In S. A. Annamma, D. Connor, & B. Ferri (Eds.),
DisCrit: Disability studies and critical race theory in education (pp. 203–212).
Teachers College Press.

Gomez, A. M. (2020, June 18). Black activists reimagine public safety in essays and poetry. *Washington City Paper*. https://www.washingtoncitypaper
.com/news/city-desk/article/21137647/activists-explain-defund-the-police-and
-reimagine-public-safety

Gun Free Schools Act of 1994, 20 U.S.C. § 7151 et seq.

Gupta-Kagan, J. (2017). The school-to-prison pipeline's legal architecture: Lessons
from the Spring Valley incident and its aftermath. *Fordham Urban Law Journal, 45*(1), 83–147.

Jackson, M., Diliberti, M., Kemp, J., Hummel, S., Cox, C., Gbondo-Tugbawa, K.,
Simon. D., & Hansen R. (n.d.). *Multi-year Table 1. Number of school resource
officers, number of public schools, and the number of public schools with school
resource officers, by full- and part-time school resource officer status: 2003–
04 through 2015–16*. National Center for Education Statistics. nces.ed.gov
/surveys/ssocs/tables/tab_my01_2016_all.asp

James, N., & McCallion G. (2013). *School resource officers: Law enforcement officers in schools*. Congressional Research Service. https://sgp.fas.org/crs/misc
/R43126.pdf

Nance, J. P. (2016a). Dismantling the school-to-prison pipeline: Tools for change.
Arizona State Law Journal, 48, 313–372.

Nance, J. P. (2016b). Students, police, and the school-to-prison pipeline. *Washington
University Law Review, 93*(4), 919–987.

Nance, J. P. (2017). Student surveillance, racial inequalities, and implicit racial bias. *Emory Law Journal*, 66(4), 765–837.

Nanda, J. (2019). The construction and criminalization of disability in school incarceration. *Columbia Journal of Race and Law*, 9(2), 265–321.

National Association of School Resource Officers. (n.d.). *Frequently asked questions*. https://www.nasro.org/faq/

National Association of School Resource Officers. (2015, April 14). *Position statement on police involvement in school discipline*. https://www.nasro.org/news/2015/04/14/news-releases/nasro-position-statement-on-police-involvement-in-student-discipline

National Center for Education Statistics. (2017). *Table 233.70b. Percentage of public schools with security staff present at least once a week, by type of security staff, school level, and selected characteristics: 2005–06, 2009–10, and 2015–16.* https://nces.ed.gov/programs/digest/d18/tables/dt18_233.70b.asp

Nelson, S. L. (2018). Special education, overrepresentation, and end-running education federalism: Theorizing toward a federally protected right to education for black students. *Loyola Journal of Public Interest Law*, 20(2), 205–240.

Raymond, B. (2010). *Assigning police officers to schools*. U.S. Department of Justice Office of Community Oriented Policing Services. https://rems.ed.gov/docs/DOJ_AssigningPoliceOfficers.pdf

Redfield, S. E., & Nance, J. P. (2016). American Bar Association: Joint task force on reversing the school-to-prison pipeline. *University of Memphis Law Review*, 47(1), 1–180.

Shaver, E. A., & Decker, J. R. (2017). Handcuffing a third grader? Interactions between school resource officers and students with disabilities. *Utah Law Review*, 2017(2), 229–282.

U.S. Department of Education, Office for Civil Rights. (2018). *2015–2016 Civil rights data collection: School climate and safety*. https://www2.ed.gov/about/offices/list/ocr/docs/school-climate-and-safety.pdf

U.S. Department of Justice, Community Oriented Policing Services. (n.d.). *About*. https://cops.usdoj.gov

U.S. Government Accountability Office. (2018). *K–12 education: Discipline disparities for black students, boys, and students with disabilities*. https://www.gao.gov/products/GAO-18-258

Vafa, Y., Ferrer, E., Kaleem, M., Hopkins, C., & Feldhake, E. (2018). *Beyond the walls: A look at girls in DC's juvenile justice system*. Rights4Girls & the Georgetown Juvenile Justice Initiative.

Violent Crime Control and Law Enforcement Act of 1994, P.L. 103-322.

Washington Lawyers' Committee for Civil Rights and Urban Affairs. (2020, June 16). *Testimony of the Washington lawyers' committee for civil rights and Urban Affairs Budget Oversight hearing of the Committee on Education and the Committee of the Whole of the Council of the District of Columbia*. https://www.washlaw.org/wp-content/uploads/2020/06/WLC-Education-Budget-Testimony-June-2020.pdf

CHAPTER 8

Perfect or *Mocha*: Language Policing and Pathologization

Jennifer Phuong & María Cioè-Peña

The subject of policing, particularly the policing of bodies in schools, is prevalent in the minds of educators and parents (Mallett, 2017), yet there continues to be a form of policing that is situated in both the body and the mind that garners few critiques: language policing. Like other forms of regulation, the practices expounded in schools are reflective of larger systemic structures and trickle into the home. Language policing in schools manifests in many ways, such as teachers telling students to use certain words or prioritizing one language variety over another, typically regional standard English in the United States. Language policing is often depicted as care grounded in elevating students' linguistic practices, academic performance, and economic opportunities (Delpit & Dowdy, 2008). However, it is buoyed by the pathologization of language practices based on educational structures rooted in ableism and racism.

The introduction of Dis/ability Critical Race Theory (DisCrit) reframed discussions of disability and race. Integrating core principles from intersectionality (Crenshaw, 1989), Critical Race Theory (Solórzano & Yosso, 2001), and disability studies (Danforth & Gabel, 2016), DisCrit brought forth an understanding of "why the location of being both a person of color *and* a person labeled with a dis/ability is qualitatively different for students of color than white students with a dis/ability" (Annamma et al., 2013, p. 5, emphasis in original). Despite naming language as an additional construction of difference, DisCrit did not explicitly explore how language is used both to pathologize minoritized communities and to celebrate the intellectual and cultural capacity of majoritized communities.

Similarly, when Flores and Rosa (2015) introduced the concept of raciolinguistic ideologies, they:

> highlight[ed] the racializing language ideologies through which different racialized bodies come to be constructed as engaging in appropriately academic linguistic practices. Specifically, [they] argue[d] that the ideological construction

and value of standardized language practices are anchored in what [they] term[ed] raciolinguistic ideologies that conflate certain racialized bodies with linguistic deficiency unrelated to any objective linguistic practices. That is, raciolinguistic ideologies produce racialized speaking subjects who are constructed as linguistically deviant even when engaging in linguistic practices positioned as normative or innovative when produced by privileged white subjects. (p. 150)

The framing of the co-construction of language and race to uphold values entrenched in white supremacy remains critical to this day. Yet, in focusing on the white gaze rather than the white normative gaze, Flores and Rosa missed an opportunity to explore how the focus on what is (and what is not) normal makes the categorization of deviant even possible.

In this chapter, we show how categorizations of students based on language are informed by ableism and racism, ultimately serving as a policing mechanism. Language thus becomes a color-evasive tool in so-called objectively assessing and labeling students, as well as surveilling and policing populations in schools, such as students from immigrant families. We examine language policing in educational policy and practice and how a mixed-status family navigates such language policing. In doing so, we present the need to use frameworks that explicitly address the intersection of race, disability, and language.

THEORETICAL FRAMEWORK

Cioè-Peña (2021) brings together central tenets of DisCrit with key components of a raciolinguistic perspective to propose a Critical Disabilities Raciolinguistic (CDR) perspective to address the particular needs of linguistically minoritized students of color with disabilities[1] and to counter the white normative gaze. Borrowing from DisCrit, a CDR perspective argues that people are not only racialized but also pathologized on account of their linguistic practices. Borrowing from raciolinguistic perspectives, a CDR perspective acknowledges that this pathologization happens not on the basis of an individual or community's language practices but instead on others' perceptions, who, regardless of their own identity, enforce the values and the perspectives under a white normative gaze. We especially draw attention to the fact that just as raciolinguistic perspectives need stronger theorization around disability, DisCrit needs stronger theorization around how languages and language practices are co-opted for the promotion and enforcement of ableism, particularly within immigrant communities. To extend Cioè-Peña's (2021) theoretical explorations, we focus on four DisCrit tenets that we believe are the most apt for reimagining.

Tenet one can be expanded to consider issues of not just language but also immigration status; this tenet "focuses on ways that the forces of racism and ableism circulate interdependently, often in neutralized and invisible ways, to uphold notions of normalcy" (Annamma et al., 2013, p. 11). As mentioned, discussions about normalcy must also encompass ideals around language possession, language practice, and immigration status. While these ideals are encompassed by racism, it is important to parse out how language becomes a proxy for both race and ability, thus allowing policymakers and educators to make choices about a student's ability by perceiving a student's so-called deviant linguistic practice as a *racially neutral* assessment of ability. Thus, even when interlocutors share overlapping language practices, the racialization of the speaker mediates the assessment of the validity of their linguistic practices, the outcome of which is used to *neutrally* enforce a pathology. Therefore, the linguistic practices of emergent bilinguals labeled as disabled (EBLADs) are often discounted (e.g., bilingual education is often described as confusing for these students) regardless of their actual linguistic practices (Cioè-Peña, 2020). Similarly, ideas around normalcy are also tied to immigration status—enacting labels as ways to create in-group distinctions, establishing legitimacy by decreeing right and wrong ways of immigrating and right and wrong places to immigrate from. Thus, discussions about immigrants as public charges are not just about racism and ability but also classism and linguicism—with linguistic practices and linguistic ability often being used as markers for citizenship and belongingness.

Considerations around language and immigration status also fit with tenet two: "DisCrit values multidimensional identities and troubles singular notions of identity such as race or dis/ability or class or gender or sexuality, and so on" (Annamma et al., 2013, p. 11). While this tenet is meant to be expansive, we believe the current nationalistic and monoglossic[2] political context demands that language and immigration status be explicitly named. Rather than these being categorizations possessed by the subject, they are imposed by structural systems that bolster the white normative gaze, like disability and race. As such, they triangulate into a multidimensional source of oppression in which each categorization works to uphold the other. Tenet four additionally demands the explicit naming of marginalization at the nexus of multiple axes of oppression to intentionally privilege the "voices of marginalized populations, traditionally not acknowledged within research" (Annamma et al., 2013, p. 11); this must then include those who are users of minoritized languages as well as those who are deemed to be (un)documented immigrants. These communities are often excluded from even the most niche narratives.

Finally, tenet five, which "considers legal and historical aspects of dis/ability and race and how both have been used separately and together to deny the rights of some citizens," could be expanded to reflect a more inclusive meaning of *citizen* (Annamma, et al., 2013, p. 11). While the neutral definition of citizen relates to an inhabitant or resident, given the resurgence of white nationalism around the world, most laypeople often associate citizenship, alongside linguistic practice, with concepts of nativeness and belonging (Banks, 2017; Cioè-Peña, 2015). It is thus critical to make explicit how ableism and racism are used to deny citizens of rights *and* to deny citizenship and humanity to certain populations. Linguistically minoritized people of color with disabilities are often discounted as rightful citizens, placing parameters on the supports they have access to, thus reinforcing ideas of who belongs and who doesn't, alongside ideas of whose bodies and linguistic practices are valued.

We now turn to exploring how DisCrit can help to strengthen a raciolinguistic perspective, examining Rosa and Flores's (2017) conceptualization of a perceiving subject, as well as focusing on two components of a raciolinguistic perspective. Building on their previous conceptualization of a *white listening subject,* Rosa and Flores (2017) shift to "*racially hegemonic perceiving subjects* more broadly that are oriented to spoken language as well as other modes of communication and semiotic forms" (pp. 627–628, emphasis added). This perceiving subject includes "various nonspoken and nonlinguistic signs," as well as "literacy practices, physical features, bodily comportment, and sartorial style" (p. 629). Even though a *perceiving subject* can avoid audist orientations toward language by decentering listening, it dichotomizes spoken and unspoken language at the expense of signed languages. Stronger theorization of the perceiving subject vis-à-vis a producing rather than speaking subject should trouble assumptions of language production.

Both frameworks offer insights into using intersectionality as an analytical tool. In eschewing additive approaches to intersectionality, Rosa and Flores (2017) argue that "a raciolinguistic perspective can contribute to understandings of the ways that categories are intersectionally assembled and communicatively co-constituted" (p. 635). Therefore, rather than simply adding on disability or immigration status as an identity or social category for analysis, we attend to how ableism and racism simultaneously operate with, in, and through language and how this relates to the pathologization of undocumented immigrants in particular.

We thus need DisCrit for extending the third component of a raciolinguistic perspective: regimentation of racial and linguistic categories. Rosa and Flores (2017) highlight processes of *raciolinguistic enregisterment* that "involve asking how and why particular linguistic forms are construed as emblems of particular racial categories and vice versa, in what historical, political, and economic contexts, and with what institutional and interpersonal consequences" (p. 634). We need to understand ableism to understand the delegitimization of language practices of immigrants of color and the delegitimization of their personhood (Rosa, 2016). Even though sociolinguists have long theorized and promoted linguistic diversity, we must be more attuned to how language variation is often used as an indicator of disability. Not only has bilingualism been wrongly assumed to be detrimental to the education of children who grow up in multilingual families (Yu, 2016), language variation within the boundaries of named languages also leads to classification of disability, particularly for students of color (Cioè-Peña, 2017). Students of color contend with their bilingualism being qualified as nonacademic, semilingual, and so forth and also see their language proficiency called into question, even for those who are positioned as monolingual English speakers (Flores, 2020).

We, therefore, need to consider the white *normative* gaze to understand and uncover the role of ableism as a mechanism of power. Only taking on a raciolinguistic perspective ignores how ableism operates, namely through the marginalization of students who deviate from the norm of a white, cisgender, male, statistically average ability, English-speaking child in school. Language thus becomes medicalized and pathologized in ways that undergird the oppression of EBLADs.

A CDR perspective offers a centralized focus on the experiences of linguistically minoritized people of color labeled as disabled. This perspective also acknowledges how the evaluation of linguistic practice functions as a flashpoint for both racism and ableism and as a process for reproducing and enforcing the white normative gaze. While DisCrit and raciolinguistic perspectives both aim to shed light on the subversive ways that evaluation, pathologization, and intervention function as tools of oppression, a CDR perspective centers that process on how language practices are manipulated to serve as indications of a disability, a response to a disability, and a barrier to inclusion through assimilation, regardless of whether a classification of disability is present or not (Cioè-Peña, 2020). As such, a CDR perspective extends DisCrit and raciolinguistic perspectives in an effort to adequately address the multiplicity of the aforementioned communities and foreground the unique nexus among race, language, *and* disability. It is also a way to ensure that both frameworks are as inclusive as their originators intended them to be without creating opportunities for subgroup othering or erasure. Thus, a CDR perspective is not a replacement but rather an explicit and necessary integration of the two theories. This theoretical and analytical move pushes us to adequately respond rather than further contribute to existing intersectional gaps (Cioè-Peña, 2017).

METHODS

We examine the *nexus* of the co-constitution of racism and ableism in and through language in educational policies and practices at two scales: language education policies that shape the pathologization of EBLADs and their language practices and an ethnographic case study of how an undocumented mother of EBLADs navigated those educational language policies. Examining this phenomenon along multiple scales allows us to understand "the fluid and dynamic nature of relationships among discourse processes across dimensions of social organization" (Hult, 2010, p. 14).

We begin by taking a CDR perspective to explore categorizations of students and the basis for such categorizations to understand the policing and the pathologization of language practices through ableism and racism. More specifically, we examine how language is conceptualized through *specific learning disability*, the category of disability with the highest incidence in the United States; *Long Term English Language Learner (LTELL)*, a category of language learner that relies on enduring assumptions around ability and language proficiency; and the role of standardized assessment in these learner classifications. In doing so, we show how language is used to perpetuate normative and oppressive conceptualizations of ability, as well as monoglossic ideologies that prioritize English (Flores et al., 2015).

These insights serve as the context for a case study, which is part of a larger research project centered on the mothering experiences of Spanish-speaking mothers of EBLADs (Cioè-Peña, 2018). The study consisted of two phases. During the first phase, all 10 participants engaged in two face-to-face qualitative, narrative interviews. At the end of the first phase, three of the participants were invited to take part in ethnographic case studies based on their demographics, their children's educational placements, and their engagement and interests in phase one. These case studies were the basis of the second phase of the study. As part of the case studies, participants engaged in additional interviews and home observations and offered up artifacts relating to their or their children's experiences. The data shared here arose from the second phase during an interview that explored an undocumented mother's desires regarding one of her children's, an EBLAD, linguistic development. Data analysis consisted of narrative analysis of the mothers' *testimonios* using inductive codes (e.g., language, disability, school, and motherhood) as well as deductive codes that arose from the data (e.g., immigration, future, employment).

Exploring two different scales allows us to demonstrate the complex and fluctuating nature of ableism and racism in and through language, both with and without disability classifications present. Throughout, we demonstrate how using a CDR perspective can foreground the interconnectedness of race, language, disability, and immigration.

FINDINGS

We start with examining educational policy and practices to explore how racism and ableism contribute to language policing, namely through categorizations of students and the standardized testing that undergirds such categorizations. We then turn to a case study of how an undocumented mother of a child with a disability navigates language and education to demonstrate how one family negotiates such language policing.

Language Policing at School

Ties among language, race, and disability become cemented within educational structures. Disability classifications function to regiment and categorize both disability and linguistic practice, taking up linguistic practice as an indicator of normative versus deviant behavior. This can lead to disability categorizations and the reinforcement of those categorizations. Thus, linguistic practices are policed in order to cement ideas of normalcy. In this section, we examine language policing mechanisms in education, specifically (a) the *specific learning disability* (SLD) classification; (b) the *Long-Term English Language Learner* (LTELL) classification; and (c) standardized assessments.

In the 1960s, learning disability and cultural deprivation were two disability classifications used to describe students who supposedly struggled with abstract reasoning, object sorting assessments, and language deficiencies (Carrier, 1986). However, learning disability was the explanation given for behaviors of white, monolingual, English-speaking, middle-class, U.S.-born students who were considered the norm, and cultural deprivation was the explanation given for behaviors of students who deviated from those norms, such as students of color, students with a lower socioeconomic status, immigrant students, and rural students (Riessman, 1962; Snyder & Mitchell, 2006). Therefore, these categories of disability emerged to explain individual failure within educational institutions rather than examining the institutions.

Currently, cultural deprivation is no longer a disability classification, though its ideological underpinnings in situating educational problems within minoritized communities, rather than within educational structures, continues. Learning disability became Specific Learning Disability (SLD); however, the definition is embedded in color-evasive federal legislation that continues to perpetuate racism and ableism (Beratan, 2006). SLD is the category of disability with the highest incidence in public schools, with Black, Indigenous, and Latinx students overrepresented. Furthermore, these students are more likely to receive special education services in more restrictive settings, regardless of classification, than white students (Brantlinger, 2006). SLD is defined as

> a disorder in one or more of the basic psychological processes involved in understanding or in using language, spoken or written, which disorder may manifest itself in the imperfect ability to listen, think, speak, read, write, spell, or do mathematical calculations (§§ 2657–2658)

Here, language is used to reinforce both white supremacy and ableism, necessitating the lens of the white normative gaze to unpack how imperfection is attributed to individuals' language practices. Phuong (2017) highlighted the ties between the individualization and the pathologization of disability and language within special education structures as part of the white perceiving subject; the unspoken assumption is that so-called normal and able-bodied students use language *perfectly*. As Flores and Rosa (2015) rightly ask us to consider how we perceive the language practices of students of color, it is also important to consider how the white normative gaze evaluates language practices as (im)perfect, rather than solely as the white gaze.

The prioritization of English over other languages also contributes to the reification of monoglossic ideologies that pathologize imperfect language practices that deviate from some imagined norm. Monoglossic ideologies are intertwined with raciolinguistic ideologies that lead to normative ideas of fluency and language proficiency mediated by racism and ableism that converge to sort and categorize learners. Flores et al. (2015) argue that *idealized monolingualism* allows schooling systems to reify white monolingualism as an ideal, leading to the creation of labels like LTELL. In New York, LTELLs are students who are educated in the United States for at least 7 years and annually do not pass a battery of standardized assessments that purport to objectively measure a student's English language proficiency, thereby leaving them with the LTELL label. Flores et al. (215) explain that this label relies on discourses of academic and linguistic partiality that positions LTELLs in a constant state of remediation, such that their linguistic practices in any language variety are seen as deficient. Such categorizations rely on both white supremacist and normative framings of language proficiency that cannot be separated from ableism. LTELLs and linguistically minoritized students of color, in general, are often positioned as languageless (Rosa, 2016). Parallel to SLD, this lack of language proficiency is situated in the student rather than considering how students' language practices are perceived.

The white normative gaze also mediates standardized testing and its impact on linguistically diverse students of color labeled as disabled. Language proficiency exams, state reading and math assessments, and psychological evaluations rely on normative ideas of language proficiency, intelligence, and behavior. Drawing from this tradition, eugenicists used intelligence testing as a mechanism to discover individuals who were considered defective or deviant (Snyder & Mitchell, 2006). Intelligence testing was central to education policies, allowing educators and researchers to view intelligence as "a fixed trait, passed on genetically, that clearly stamped certain groups as significantly more intelligent than others" (Osgood, 2000, p. 55), thus reifying the medical model of disability. Bilingualism was also historically seen as an indicator of disability, especially for immigrant populations (Valett, 1965). These types of testing relied on normative ideas of idealized monolingual language use. This way, through standardized testing, language, race, and disability are not socially constructed but naturalized facts.

Even though scholars have shown the multiplicity and hybridity of the language practices of students of color through a heteroglossic lens (García,

2011), standards-based reforms and testing rely on monoglossic ideologies that lead to deficit-oriented views of those same language practices. Monoglossic ideologies thus intertwine with ableism and racism to create particular categories of learners that deviate from some standard (Au, 2009), which is partially determined through assessment (Kibler & Valdés, 2016). This is reflective of the medicalization and the individualization of disability, race, and language, which converge as part of the language policing of undocumented immigrants. Ultimately, rigidity in conceptualizations of linguistic boundaries and proficiency reveal how monoglossic ideologies and deficit-oriented views of bilingualism contribute to constructions of disability. We use a case study to demonstrate how educational mechanisms of language policing manifest in home practices.

Language Policing at Home[3]

This case study highlights how these structural policies eventually filter into and through families, featuring the perspective of one mother to underscore the different ways that language can function in relation to disability, citizenship, and class within the same household. At the time, Paty's social positioning was that of an undocumented Mexican national living in the United States with two of her four children: Dan, a 5th-grader EBLAD in an English-only inclusive class, and Tanya, a 4th-grade emergent bilingual student in a dual-language class. To understand how language policing works, we first explore how each language is framed.

Language and Disability: Spanish as Disability Marker; English as Disability Remediation

When asked to explain why Dan was recommended for an evaluation, Paty first spoke about issues with communication:

> Yo me sentía impotente porque no podía ayudar a mi hijo, él no podía hablar. Él no más pedía leche, "Mmhm, mmhm." Le decía, "Leche" y él me decía "Le." Algo así corto. [. . .] Y na' mas empezaba señas, o llorar, y eso era como una impotencia para mí.
>
> *I felt powerless because I couldn't help my son, he couldn't speak. He just asked for milk, "Mmhm, mmhm." I said, "milk," and he said, "me." Something like that, short. [. . .] And then he'd just start signaling, or cry, and that was like impotence for me.*

In this brief vignette, oral language or a lack thereof was used to signal a problem and resulted in Paty feeling powerless as a mother. Simultaneously, other forms of communication like *signaling* or crying were not viewed as forms of communication, thus reinforcing our need to reinterpret language as more than oral communication. Paty then continued to discuss how she first started to notice improvements:

> Cuando él empezó a ir a la escuela, el empezó a hacer muchos cambios, tanto como aquí en la casa como en la escuela. Lógico que el todas las clases las daban en inglés. Pero él podía ya pronunciarme las cosas, Ya pués decía [inglés] "Milk, water mommy, juice mommy." Lógico, mochas[4] todavía, pero ya podía.
>
> *When he started going to school, he began to make many changes, both here at home and at school. It was logical that all classes were taught in English. But he could already pronounce things for me. He was saying [English], "Milk, water mommy, juice mommy." Logical, still mangled, but he could [communicate].*

In this retelling, Paty frames her child's growth around his ability to clearly communicate his needs in English. Despite the household being Spanish-dominant, Paty's son received English-only services. Here, Paty frames English differently from Spanish—while linguistic approximation was filtered through a lens of "corto" and by extension deficient, the brevity of Dan's English discourse was held to different standards. She discusses his changes and provides examples of his expanded vocabulary, framing his English development as growth despite concluding that the words were still *mocha*. Here, we see the beginnings of dichotomous positioning of each language: Spanish signaled a disability while English signaled growth and proximity to normal.

Language, Nationality, and Class: English for the Doctor, Spanish for the Maid

Although Dan's linguistic practices are evaluated through frames of normalcy, Tanya's linguistic practices yield common tropes that relate English to power and privilege and Spanish to inferiority and othering.

> **Paty:** Yo le digo a Tanya, [. . .] "cuando tú seas grande y ya doctora, y sigas en este país, y no hay quien te limpie tu casa, y viene una señora, y te habla español, tú le puedes decir las cosas en español. Tú le puedas decir las cosas en español. Que no seas racista," le digo. "Porque tú eres mexicana. El título de que nada más porque naciste en este país, pero tú vienes de padres mexicanos." Porque Dan una vez me dijo—, bueno varias veces me dijo, "Pero yo no soy mexicano. Yo soy americano."
>
> *I say to Tanya, [. . .] "when you are big and a doctor, and you are still in this country, and there is no one to clean your house, and a lady comes and speaks Spanish to you, you can tell her things in Spanish. You can tell her things in Spanish. Don't be racist," I say. "Because you are Mexican. The title, that's just because you were born*

in this country, but you come from Mexican parents." Because Dan once said to me—well, several times he said, "But I'm not Mexican. I'm American."

In this passage, Paty—who works as a cleaning lady for English-speaking employers—frames language around communication—not to communicate with her family or her patients but rather with *the lady* who cleans her house. As such, English is associated with a higher level of education, a profession, and superior status, while Spanish is associated with domestic work and subjugation. Additionally, Paty ends by saying *"Don't be a racist,"* which reflects the idea that those who do not use a common language to communicate with others have a perspective that is inherently grounded in white supremacy.

Conversely, Paty uses language to reinforce her children's ethnic identities to them. Spanish, therefore, becomes synonymous with working-class Mexicans and English with elite, yet racist, Americans. This positioning of language is not representative of Paty's flaws as much as they are indicative of how the language ideologies of the perceiving subject are imposed upon, consumed, and adopted by the producing subject. Eventually, they become not only subject to but also enforce these ideologies.

From Policed to Policing

After numerous encounters positioning their home language as problematic at best, the children in the family then adopt the role of ideological enforcers. Here, Paty recounts a common exchange with Dan in which he both urges her to learn English and faults her for not being *fluent*:

Para mí difícil porque a veces a [Dan], más que a nadie con [Dan], me cuesta porque a veces él quiere que yo le hable más en inglés, a veces me cuesta porque yo no puedo pronunciar esas palabras, a veces le digo

"vuélvemela a repetir"

"pero es que tu no la estás diciendo bien, tu estás diciendo otra palabra,"

"okay entonces yo te la puedo contestar en español"

"si mamá pero tu también tienes que aprender inglés"

Él se enojaba al principio porque me decía "es que no es mi culpa que tu no hayas aprendido inglés, porque no aprendiste" [. . .] y yo le explicaba y le decía "hijo yo no nací en este país, yo vine grande a este país, siendo ya mamá de dos de tus hermanos," entonces a veces [responde] "pues vete a una escuela"

"hijo, es que no es tan fácil que uno que ya está más grande aprender el inglés como a ustedes que son pequeños que se les meten los idioma[s] más rápido."

A veces yo tengo que pensar luego digo "estoy aprendiendo."
[Dan] se molestaba mucho porque me decía "es que me dejaron tarea
y es tu culpa que yo no pueda porque tu no las dices bien y yo no las
escribo bien."

*For me, it's difficult because sometimes [Dan], more than anyone
with [Dan], it's hard for me because sometimes he wants me to speak
more to him in English, sometimes it's hard for me because I cannot
pronounce those words, sometimes I tell him,*

"Repeat it again."

"But you are not saying it well, you are saying another word."

"Okay, so I can answer it in Spanish."

"Yes, Mom, but you also have to learn English."

*He was angry at first because he told me, "It is not my fault that
you did not learn English because you did not learn" [. . .], and I
explained to him and said, "Son, I was not born in this country, I
came to this country, being a mother to two of your brothers," then
sometimes [he responds], "Go to school."*

*"Son, it is not as easy for one who is older to learn English as it is
for you who are children who get language[s] faster."*

*Sometimes I have to think, then I say, "I am learning." [Dan] was
very upset because he said, "It's that I have homework, and it's your
fault that I can't [do it]because you don't say them well and I don't
write them well."*

Here, we hear of how Dan chastises his mother for not learning English,
critiquing her efforts to speak English, and holding her responsible for his
inability to complete homework. Paty tries to reason with him, explaining
her late introduction to English and restating her efforts to learn as an adult.
In this retelling, we see how language policing evolves from systemic to interpersonal practice: blaming the producing subject without acknowledging
systemic barriers; associating linguistic practice with age, ability, and birth-
place; blaming the parent for their inability to engage rather than recognizing how monolingual services create a barrier; and extending the child's
inability to perform to the parent. Racism and pathology thus become
commonplace—it hides in the details and is enforced through relationships.

DISCUSSION

In this chapter, we used CDR to explore language policing in educational
structures and how a mixed-status family that includes an EBLAD navigates
those structures. Language policing occurs in schools through monoglossic
and raciolinguistic ideologies that converge in normative schooling practices, such as standardized testing. Ultimately, categorizations of learners

and subsequent language and special education services in schools rely on normative understandings of bilingualism and language proficiency and lead to language policing. Languages other than English become pathologized for producing racialized subjects, and bilingualism becomes positioned as a problem for students of color labeled as disabled in developing language proficiency as measured through standardized testing (Chaparro, 2017).

School-based deficit perspectives of language permeate the home, extending individual pathologies to families, erasing their funds of knowledge (Gonzáles et al., 2006), and restricting their ability to act agentively when navigating complex and oppressive educational structures. This was evident in Paty's experience; she was knowledgeable in her own right but regularly encountered structural barriers. A CDR perspective offers an understanding of how the perceiving subject's pathologizing of language is central to evaluating linguistic practice and measuring progression toward normalcy. Thus, in an effort to accelerate their children's qualification as normal across ability and nationality, parents like Paty inhabit the role of language police as a form of parental engagement, acting as good parents without understanding systemic structures that are being imposed on their family. The shift from language policed to language policing is critical to understanding how the racialization and pathologization that undocumented parents experience influence the educational policies and practices they support. In other words, to spare their children ongoing racism and ableism, parents seek to perfect their EBLADs' linguistic practices to accomplish racial *and* able-bodied passing.

Rather than subject their children to policing on the basis of race and immigration status, parents police their children's linguistic practices to cement their ability to pass as citizens. This desire to pass is not actually grounded in citizenship status, given that most of these children are, in fact, citizens but rather in an effort to deflect the ways in which non-English linguistic practice is used as a proxy for undocumented status. Unfortunately, this protective practice reinforces the very policing it aims to avoid. Furthermore, within one family, bilingualism can serve as an advantage for an able-bodied child, while being a potential risk for *outing* a disabled one. These dynamics reveal the complexity of discourses around immigration when considering the multitude of migrant categories, including refugees and asylum seekers, as compared to documented immigrants who arrive in the United States for work, marriage, school, and so forth; different categories evoke different treatment and policing practices (Crawley & Skleparis, 2018). Ultimately, a CDR perspective allows us to recognize how language can be perceived as a barrier to access while also serving as a "racialized signifier of cultural assimilation and immigrant worth" (Kibria & Becerra, 2021, p. 11), no matter the migrant status.

Language policing thus highlights the significance of the perceiving subject as the unit of analysis, not as a specific individual but rather the subject positions they embody as they perceive language practices. For example, Flores et al. (2020) found that teachers tied deficit descriptions of students' language practices to institutional categorizations of learners (e.g., EL status, speech-language impairment) and schooling practices (e.g., performance on literacy assessments), thereby using the labels and supposedly objective testing to rationalize such descriptions. Language, therefore, becomes a color-evasive way for teachers to find disability and reify the pathologization of disabled students.

CONCLUSION

A CDR perspective allows researchers to foreground how the white normative gaze mediates the language policing of multiply marginalized students through schooling structures and policies that focus on sorting and categorizing students. In attending to the role of language in racism and ableism, we consider the particularities of how language-minoritized communities are marginalized, as well as how language is co-constructed with race, disability, and immigrant status. This analysis ultimately emphasizes the importance of avoiding trickle-down social justice (Crenshaw, 2019) and instead centering multiply marginalized groups to extend the possibilities of DisCrit.

NOTES

1. We use the term *linguistically minoritized students of color* to account for the fact that even students of color who identify as users of English have their linguistic practices discounted through dialectical categorizations often driven by anti-Blackness.

2. Within language education, monoglossic ideologies "treat . . . languages as separate and whole, and view . . . languages as bounded autonomous systems" (García, 2011, p. 7).

3. We choose to foreground the voices of the participants in this manuscript. In a nod to Mendoza-Denton (2008), the body of the text includes participants' narratives in the original language without the use of italics. English translations can be found immediately after in italics; in-text quotation translations are italicized.

4. The word *mocha* can be seen as an alternative to short or mangled. The translation of one definition is: "that it does not have the tip, termination, or finish that it would have to have due to its nature" (Oxford Dictionary, n.d.).

REFERENCES

Annamma, S. A., Connor, D., & Ferri, B. (2013). Dis/ability critical race studies (DisCrit): Theorizing at the intersections of race and dis/ability. *Race Ethnicity and Education, 16*(1), 1–31.

Au, W. W. (2009). High-stakes testing and discursive control: The triple bind for non-standard student identities. *Multicultural Perspectives*, *11*(2), 65–71.

Banks, A. M. (2017). Respectability & the quest for citizenship. *Brooklyn Law Review*, *83*(1), 1–54.

Beratan, G. D. (2006). Institutionalizing inequity: Ableism, racism and IDEA 2004. *Disability Studies Quarterly*, *26*(2). https://dsq-sds.org/article/view/682/859

Brantlinger, E. A. (Ed.). (2006). *Who benefits from special education? Remediating (fixing) other people's children*. Lawrence Erlbaum.

Carrier, J. G. (1986). *Learning disability: Social class and the construction of inequality in American education* (Vol. 18). Praeger.

Chaparro, S. E. (2017). *Language and the gentrifying city: An ethnographic study of a two-way immersion program in an urban public school* (Publication No. 2213) [Doctoral dissertation, University of Pennsylvania]. Publicly Accessible Penn Dissertations.

Cioè-Peña, M. (2015). Translanguaging within the monolingual special education classroom. *Theory, Research, and Action in Urban Education*, *4*(1).

Cioè-Peña, M. (2017). The intersectional gap: How bilingual students in the United States are excluded from inclusion. *International Journal of Inclusive Education*, *21*(9), 906–919.

Cioè-Peña, M. (2018). *"Yo soy su Mama:" Latinx Mothers Raising Emergent Bilinguals Labeled as Dis/Abled*. City University of New York.

Cioè-Peña, M. (2020). Planning inclusion: The need to formalize parental participation in individual education plans (and meetings). In *The educational forum* (Vol. 84, No. 4, pp. 377–390). Routledge.

Cioè-Peña, M. (2021). 3 dual language and the erasure of emergent bilinguals labeled as disabled (EBLADs). In N. Flores & A. Tseng (Eds.), *Bilingualism for all? Raciolinguistic perspectives on dual language education* (pp. 63–87). Multilingual Matters.

Crawley, H., & Skleparis, D. (2018). Refugees, migrants, neither, both: Categorical fetishism and the politics of bounding in Europe's "migration crisis." *Journal of Ethnic and Migration Studies*, *44*(1), 48–64.

Crenshaw, K. (1989). Demarginalizing the intersection of race and sex: A black feminist critique of antidiscrimination doctrine, feminist theory and antiracist politics. *University of Chicago Legal Forum*, *1989*(1), 139–167.

Crenshaw, K. (2019). The marginalization of Harriet's daughters: Perpetual crisis, misdirected blame, and the enduring urgency of intersectionality. *Kalfou*, *6*(1), 7–23.

Danforth, S., & Gabel, S. L. (Eds.). (2016). *Vital questions facing disability studies in education* (2nd ed.). Peter Lang.

Delpit, L., & Dowdy, J. K. (Eds.). (2008). *The skin that we speak: Thoughts on language and culture in the classroom* (2nd ed.). The New Press.

Flores, N. (2020). From academic language to language architecture: Challenging raciolinguistic ideologies in research and practice. *Theory into Practice*, *59*(1), 22–31. http://doi.org/10.1080/00405841.2019.1665411

Flores, N., Kleyn, T., & Menken, K. (2015). Looking holistically in a climate of partiality: Identities of students labeled long-term English language learners. *Journal of Language, Identity & Education*, *14*(2), 113–132. http://doi.org/10.1080/15348458.2015.1019787

Flores, N., Phuong, J., & Venegas, K. M. (2020). "Technically an EL": The production of raciolinguistic categories in a dual language school. *TESOL Quarterly*, *54*(3), 629–651.

Flores, N., & Rosa, J. (2015). Undoing appropriateness: Raciolinguistic ideologies and language diversity in education. *Harvard Educational Review*, *85*(2), 149–171.

García, O. (2011). *Bilingual education in the 21st century: A global perspective.* John Wiley & Sons.

Gonzáles, N., Moll, L. C., & Amanti, C. (Eds.). (2006). *Funds of knowledge: Theorizing practices in households, communities, and classrooms.* Routledge.

Hult, F. M. (2010). Analysis of language policy discourses across the scales of space and time. *International Journal of the Sociology of Language*, *2010*(202), 7–24. http://doi.org/10.1515/ijsl.2010.011

Kibler, A. K., & Valdés, G. (2016). Conceptualizing language learners: Socioinstitutional mechanisms and their consequences. *The Modern Language Journal*, *100*(S1), 96–116.

Kibria, N., & Becerra, W. S. (2021). Deserving immigrants and good advocate mothers: Immigrant mothers' negotiations of special education systems for children with disabilities. *Social Problems*, *68*(3), 591–607.

Mallett, C. A. (2017). The school-to-prison pipeline: Disproportionate impact on vulnerable children and adolescents. *Education and Urban Society*, *49*(6), 563–592.

Mendoza-Denton, N. (2008). *Homegirls: Language and cultural practice among Latina youth gangs.* Blackwell.

Osgood, R. L. (2000). *For "children who vary from the normal type": Special education in Boston, 1838–1930.* Gallaudet University Press.

Oxford University Press. (n.d.) Mocha. *Oxford English Dictionary.*

Phuong, J. (2017). Disability and language ideologies in education policy. *Working Papers in Educational Linguistics*, *32*(1), 47–66.

Riessman, F. (1962). *The culturally deprived child.* Harper & Row.

Rosa, J. D. (2016). Standardization, racialization, languagelessness: Raciolinguistic ideologies across communicative contexts. *Journal of Linguistic Anthropology*, *26*(2), 162–183.

Rosa, J., & Flores, N. (2017). Unsettling race and language: Toward a raciolinguistic perspective. *Language in Society*, *46*(5), 621–647.

Snyder, S. L., & Mitchell, D. T. (2006). *Cultural locations of disability.* University of Chicago Press.

Solórzano, D. G., & Yosso, T. J. (2001). Critical race and LatCrit theory and method: Counter-storytelling. *International Journal of Qualitative Studies in Education*, *14*(4), 471–495.

Valett, R. E. (1965). A formula for providing psychological services. *Psychology in the Schools*, *2*(4), 326–329.

Yu, B. (2016). Bilingualism as conceptualized and bilingualism as lived: A critical examination of the monolingual socialization of a child with autism in a bilingual family. *Journal of Autism and Developmental Disorders*, *46*(2), 424–435.

Part III

MARGIN TO MARGIN

LatDisCrit: Exploring Latinx Global South DisCrit Reverberations as Spaces Toward Emancipatory Learning and Radical Solidarity

Alexis Padilla

This chapter builds upon my ongoing intersectional (primarily linking race and dis/ability) conceptualization of LatDisCrit, short for Latinx dis/ability/ critical intersectionality studies (see Padilla, 2018, 2021; Padilla & Tan, 2019). I am a blind Brown Latinx engaged scholar and activist. I was born and raised in the Global South, yet throughout the past three decades, I have resided and struggled in Global North contexts within the United States where the plight of Latinx students with dis/abilities and their families is at stake. For example, Latinx students with dis/abilities and their families are required to attend multiyear Individualized Education Program (IEP) meetings where education goals, objectives, and benchmarks are decided, often without genuine parent/student input and even in the absence of a basic sense of family understanding about the meaning and significance of these processes. Importantly, I am not an American citizen. Even though I have spent more than half my life paying taxes in the United States, I have not even been given the opportunity for permanent residency, which prevents me from enjoying so-called dis/ability benefits and places me without exaggeration as a Brown dis/abled person at the margin of margins. A lot of this is what LatDisCrit's explorations attempt to unearth.

I pursue a critical integration of LatCrit (e.g., Bernal, 2002; Dávila & de Bradley, 2010; Solórzano & Bernal, 2001; Valdes, 1999, 2000; Yosso, 2000) and DisCrit (e.g., Annamma et al., 2013, 2016; Annamma et al., 2018). Both bodies of literature look at the interplay of race/ethnicity, diasporic cultures, historical sociopolitics, and dis/ability with regard to multiple Latinx identities in mostly Global North contexts. In my conceptualization of LatDisCrit, Global South epistemologies are a crucial part of the equation. Decolonial Latinx and intersectionally grounded critical feminist political philosophers tend to agree (e.g., Alcoff, 2009; Castro-Gómez & Martin, 2002, 2007; Dussel, 2012; Maldonado-Torres, 2007; Mignolo, 2000, 2005; Mignolo & Walsh, 2018; Quijano, 2000, 2006; Saldívar, 1991, 2012; Sandoval, 2000; Wynter, 2003). Although thinkers such as Ghai (2015), Grech (2011, 2015), and Meekosha (2011) have linked dis/ability and Global South issues for years (see also recent decolonial work by Nguyen [2015] and the myriad of outstanding articles published in the journal *Disability Studies in the Global South*), LatCrit theorists and emerging DisCrit developments do not yet embrace these Global South paradigms (Dávila, 2015; Handy, 2018; Mendoza et al., 2016; Migliarini, 2017; and Piepzna-Samarasinha, 2018, are interesting exceptions within Global North contexts). Therefore, looking at targeted DisCrit tenets, I address what it means for upcoming DisCrit developments to deepen emancipatory learning and radical solidarity tools relevant for exilic migrant Latinx populations residing and struggling in the Global North.

Many, if not most, contemporary decolonial Global South thinkers ignore dis/ability concerns altogether. Hence, I seek to bridge DisCrit with the emancipatory work of thinkers who adhere critically to what has been clustered in recent years under the umbrella of epistemologies of the Global South, under the guidance of Boaventura de Sousa Santos (2015, 2016, 2018; see also Santos & Meneses, 2020). My aim is to propitiate a critical metatheoretical and possibilitarian dialogue whose purpose is to elevate the value of emancipatory learning and radical solidarity for Latinx dis/abled Global South agents (in the sense of people who use agentic power) of color as they transgress and resist oppressive Global North epistemologies and institutional practices of exclusion and systemic marginalization. There is a third important dimension in my conceptualization of LatDisCrit, which I only develop tangentially in the present chapter due to reasons of space (Padilla, 2021). In my view, it is paramount to ground in Global South wisdom the need to challenge in tangible ways reductionist representations of Latinx exilic migrations. This means setting the critical basis for undoing ableist and supremacist ontologies of *mestizaje*, which must be distinguished from the rich legacy of epistemological/border-crossing modes of *mestizaje* pursued by thinkers such as Anzaldúa (1987), Calderón (2014), Moraga and Anzaldúa (1981), Moya (2001), Trinidad Galván (2001, 2003, 2006, 2014), and Villenas (2005).

REVISITING INTERSECTIONAL TENETS OF DISCRIT

A few years ago, I had the opportunity to observe two parallel incidents of schooling dominance transgression attempts in a U.S. Deep South context. In both cases, the challenging actors involved intersectional marginalized/oppressed (i.e., impacting racialized and dis/ability) populations where

Black or Brown families of children with disabilities were trying to stand their ground against exclusionary acts carried out by school district administrators. Nevertheless, both the process and the outcomes of these incidents were qualitatively different.

In the case where Black communities were the protagonist, communal actors were challenging a long process of resource distribution discrimination that affected the entire community. Communal coalition-building made it indispensable for the school superintendent to come in person to pursue damage control. There was conspicuous press coverage. The event took place at a public setting located in the historically Black neighborhood victimized by long-standing acts of oppression such as divestment, racialized instances of the school-to-prison pipeline, and unequal distribution of services/material resources. The community stance was very vocal, congruent, and unified. They clearly expressed their unwillingness to tolerate further symbolic or overt acts by district bureaucrats that involve vulnerating their rights and their collective good faith as a sociopolitical whole (Bell, 2011; Frank, 2001; Williams, 2006).

In the second instance, which was located in a Brown Latinx community, most of the families affected were recent Mexican immigrants. Many of them fell within the unauthorized bureaucratic label used by school administrators and were monolingual Spanish speakers. Given these power imbalances, it was not surprising that negotiations in this case were rather secretive without public meeting venues of any sort and in the absence of future-driven accountability mechanisms. All conversations were channeled through a bilingual intermediary whose interests as a therapist, although credible to the families involved, were not entirely independent of future profit-making relational links with this particular district or other districts in the area, very much like the flexible workgroup convergent interest practices that Malcolm M. Feeley (1979) talks about in his qualitative study of a criminal court in the United States where litigating and adjudicating actors ended up displaying clique-like collective behaviors instead of those expected from their respective professional roles.

My contrast of these parallel situations does not imply that they are representative cases of the exchanges one should always expect between districts and intersectional population segments nationwide. My aim in bringing them up here is to offer preliminary metatheoretical, ethical, and strategic considerations about the dynamic placing of LatDisCrit in light of concrete DisCrit tenets and in line with what Annamma and Morrison (2018) call DisCrit classroom ecology, which involves proactively cultivating learning spaces of solidarity for resistance's sake within and beyond decolonial intersectional/subaltern groups in Global North and Global South contexts. For instance, it is important to notice the Global South/colonizing underpinnings of the observational contrast I just presented. Strategically speaking, most of the Latinx migrant families involved in the incident I observed were rurally grounded folks from Mexico and Central America, people who generally hold in high regard and who are unlikely to challenge the authority of schoolteachers and administrators. Prior to this incident, I had been told by a Chicanx (born and raised in the United States) psychologist who has been working in this urban area for almost two decades that Latinx of South American origin are perceived by rural migrants from Mexico and Central America as classist. This seems due to the overall level of education, which tends to be somewhat higher among South American groups. Instead of using this knowledge diversity to their advantage, both communities fall prey to divide-and-conquer modes of colonizing, which hurt their solidarity possibilities and their collective advancement. In terms of DisCrit, I rely in this chapter primarily on the list of seven DisCrit tenets put together by Annamma et al. (2019, p. 233). Their 2019 version constitutes a slight refinement of the DisCrit tenet version provided in two earlier publications (Annamma et al., 2013, p. 11; Connor et al., 2016, p. 20). In the following pages, I concentrate on the first two and last three of the seven DisCrit tenets, clustering them in three sections for ease of analysis.

TENETS ONE AND TWO: LATDISCRIT, GLOBAL SOUTH/GLOBAL NORTH PARAMETERS OF NORMALCY: INTERROGATING INTERLOCKING OPPRESSIVE FORCES

Resuming the discussion of ontological *mestizaje* (synonymous throughout the chapter with something deemed real and racially superior), it is important to stress that the discussion is closely linked to white supremacy as an expression of normalcy-centered hegemony (Garland-Thomson, 1997; Obourn, 2020). As such, one needs to critically disrupt *mestizaje*, especially in the cosmic race idea articulated by Vasconcelos (1997), whose implications are directly or indirectly endorsed by contemporary mainstream multicultural theorists, which requires an articulation of how the reductionist meaning of *mestizaje* has historically operated within Global North/interimperial contexts such as those of the United States. In crucial periods, it was legally convenient for U.S. hegemonic forces to classify Latinx, although the Hispanic nomenclature was preferred to emphasize Eurocentrism (see Wallerstein, 2016, for an expansive discussion), segments of the population as formally white." Formal whiteness worked as a manipulative rhetoric of pseudoprivilege. It consecrated *mestizaje* as a practical expression of white supremacy within the American legal system (López, 2004, 2006; Sandrino-Glasser, 1998). Furthermore, it always operated in deferential reference to other European empires, in this case the Spanish empire that ruled the territorial portions of Mexico, Puerto Rico, and other areas of Latin America that were subsequently transferred de facto to the control of American imperial interests during the 20th and 21st centuries.

In my work, I have come up with the notion of interimperialism, incorporating it into LatDisCrit to deal with Global North and Global South dynamics of normalcy imposition and resistance that operate through the interplay of imperial hegemony and decolonial modes of counterhegemony. In other words, the political economy and transidentitarian contours of interimperialism help make sense of the Global South/North divide in LatDisCrit's marginalization as well as resistance. Interimperialism works via power and knowledge on both sides of the divide (Holloway, 2002; Stahler-Sholk, 2010; Tremayne, 2014; Vanden, 2007). Spaces of resistance in both Global South and Global North contexts are not immune, as it became clear in the observational incident described in the previous section. The practical manifestation of interimperialism depends on two simultaneous yet complementary forces: (1) a sustaining articulation gap and (2) a crucial movement toward rupture with the vestiges of interimperialistic oppressions. The best metaphor for representing this complex functional duality is that of an articulation (Hall, 1996). As in the body, articulations unite and divide, at once bridging and demarcating. Their real force resides in not being as rigid as bones, in bridging, in not being core. They are especially vulnerable to ruptures and coordination of further links and ulterior spheres of mobilization. In the sociopolitical, sociocultural, and sociohistorical contexts of LatDisCrit's modes of interimperialism, interimperial immediacy and exchange help the enactment of these dual forces.

For instance, Latinx folks are within the borders of the imperial realities imposed by the United States, even if they do not reside within the limits of the American state, yet at the same time, the vestiges of many other empires are intrinsic to their identity and their sociopolitical embodiments of cultural and epistemological *mestizaje* (Castro-Gómez, 2007). Thus, interimperial proximity, continuity, and discontinuity exacerbate what Edwards (2003) calls a décalage (offset) dimension of diaspora, which refers to the residues of untranslatable discourse, as well as cultural, institutional, peoplehood/nationhood, and structural perception differences. Multifaceted differences open the door to the uncertainty of concrete, context-based change articulation among various imperial actors. The "notion of articulation is crucial not just because it combines the structural and the discursive but also because it has a flip side: such societies structured in dominance" are also the ground of cultural resistance (Edwards, 2003, p. 12).

As disability researchers, we must find out how modes of Latinx resistance translate into specific intersectional dis/ability expressions in the Global North. We do know that most dis/ability organizations are dominated by non-Latinx leadership (Padilla, 2018, Ch. 4), with entities such as the National Coalition for Latinxs with Disabilities (NCLD) being noteworthy exceptions to this trend. In traditional, white-dominated dis/ability organizations, Latinx actors who rise to the top often commit themselves to modes of resistance that resemble the prescribed organizational recipes salient to white dominance, as well as Global North epistemology and axiology paradigms (Grech, 2011; Meyers, 2019a, 2019b; Wildeman, 2020). It is paramount to take advantage of the work undertaken by DisCrit scholars among Latinx, Black, Asian, and First Nations folks with dis/abilities (Annamma, 2017; Bell, 2011; Piepzna-Samarasinha, 2018; Waitoller & Thorius, 2016). Doing so can help unearth innovative resistance, transcending simplistic mantras of demographic change, which creates a false aura, as if demography alone would magically give Latinx students and other Latinx populations with dis/abilities in the Global North an edge of advantage (Gándara & Mordechay, 2017; García, 2014; Irizarry, 2011). It is imperative in the current stage of epistemological development of both DisCrit and LatDisCrit to firmly incorporate intersectional dis/ability into the equity and social justice education bag of tools (Parrey, 2020). Intersectionality's strategic implications must reach beyond schooling, dovetailing with radical solidarity (Collins, 2015; Collins & Bilge, 2016; Connor, 2019; Davis, 2008; DeMatthews, 2016; Erevelles & Minear, 2010; Erevelles & Mutua, 2005; Hancock, 2007; Yuval-Davis, 2006). It must also impact sociohistorical critical interpretations, which help us understand the entire life span of individuals and groups with dis/abilities as well as their organizational, communal, and transcommunal dimensions locally and globally (Erevelles, 2011; Malhotra, 2016; Obourn, 2020).

TENETS FIVE AND SIX: BLACKNESS STUDIES, INDIGENEITY, AND TRANS-LATINX ANALYSES: DECODING WHITENESS AS PROPERTY IN LATDISCRIT'S INTERSECTIONAL DIS/ABILITY INTERROGATIONS

Interimperialism is not unique to trans-Latinx diasporas. My sense is that Pan-Asian and Pan-African Global South diasporas of color with dis/abilities in Global North contexts as well as tribal First Nations could also benefit from adopting or expanding their transgressive understanding of decolonial resistance through the lens of interimperialism. In subverting the colonialist ideology and hegemonic force of Latinx *mestizaje*, it is indispensable (1) to read various kinds of Latinxness in racial instead of purely ethnic or national origin (López, 1997, 2004, 2006; Sandrino-Glasser, 1998) and (2) to take the transgressive power of the idea a step further by placing Blackness studies (Dei, 2000, 2008, 2012, 2014, 2017; Dei & Hilowle, 2018) and Global South epistemologies at the core of LatDisCrit's radical axiological modes of decolonial solidarity (Gaztambide-Fernández, 2012).

Through the first principle, one opens the door to understanding the plight of Latinx of color with dis/abilities, those who reside and struggle in Global South as well as those of us residing and struggling in Global North contexts. Their experiences are different. Nonetheless, their bridging involves an ontology and epistemology of multiple sources of embodied wisdom (Trinidad Galván, 2006, 2014; Obourn, 2020, Ch. 1). Embodied wisdom emerges from the differential struggles faced by these populations in local and global spaces of material precarity and/or subaltern marginalization. Moreover, there is complementarity, often untapped, among various layers of wisdom, as in the example of strategies and approaches adopted by rurally grounded Mexican and Central American Latinx versus those coming from South America's urban centers. Tapping them in tandem would mean that instead of being prey to divisive traps, their complementary modes of embodied wisdom could serve to mutually enhance communal positionalities and provide rich sources for situated emancipation. The significance for radical solidarity in complementary modes of strategic wisdom resides in their bridging role between LatDisCrit's unique resistance tactics and those adopted by other peoples of color with dis/abilities and other kinds of subaltern oppressed identitarian subjectivities.

Lao-Montes's (2016) work serves as an illustration here by centering on the identitarian experiences of Afro-Latinx groups, primarily of Caribbean origin in East Coast U.S. urban centers. Some of his observations point to the need to raise key questions to pinpoint the genesis and implications of their links with Africanity and Latinidad. Lao-Montes (2016) does so by elevating Afro-Cuban and Afro-Puerto Rican sources, addressing particularly the famous Caribbean trope of Caliban (Arroyo, 2003; Fernández Retamar, 2003; Henry, 2000), yet in dealing with these issues in conjunction with LatDisCrit's radical solidarity imperatives, I prefer to draw on George J. Dei. Dei's (2017) bridging metatheoretical work is unique, linking Blackness studies and indigeneity with particular reference to global education and racialized interdisciplinary spaces of transformational knowing. Dei's framework is helpful to combat the invisibility of Afro-Latinidad, defined as the sense of Latinxness identitarian ethos driven by Blackness studies or axiological principles grounded on Blackness historicity and/or sociopolitical considerations. It also helps link decolonial Afro-Latinx identitarian axiology and epistemologies with the indigenous roots of trans-Latinidad, showing the need to overcome racially neutral stances toward Latinidad as an identitarian space completely independent from Africanity, Indigeneity, and/or Pan-Asian modes of identity (Perea, 1997). Its significance lies in creating solidarity spaces for a less divided Latinidad front (Alcoff, 2009). The truth is that unless intersectional dis/ability elements are added to the LatDisCrit equation, its ideological picture as an identity transformational force is extremely vulnerable to the internalizing perils of whiteness as property.

Harris's (1993) original formulation of the concept of whiteness as property implies material as well as symbolic dimensions of entitlement and enjoyment. In the same way that one's property rights entail the material enjoyment of real estate, precluding others from such enjoyment, whiteness as property underscores the relational basis for social exclusion. Its sole rationale is the racialized hierarchization of intersectional categories, dis/ability dimensions included (Bell, 2006; Broderick & Leonardo, 2016; Gillborn, 2015; Hernández-Saca, 2016; Thorius & Tan, 2016).

I have experienced firsthand the hierarchical implications of this process within Latinx communities. While conducting ethnographic work for my first doctoral dissertation in New Mexico, I ran into law enforcement professionals from the northern part of the state who regarded themselves as direct descendants of the first Spanish conquistadores. As such, they disdained the identitarian stance of Chicanx or darker modes of Latinxness (Nieto-Phillips, 2004). Also in New Mexico, I was fortunate to encounter folks, some of them Latinx with dis/abilities, who proudly invoked their identitarian legacy as *genízaros*. The term had demining mixed-race connotations in colonial times. It often alluded to mixed-blood Native American groups who had incorporated fugitive slaves from the Southern colonies into their communal life. It is precisely this racial fluidity and transgressive marron/fugitive/border-crossing spirit (Anzaldúa, 1987; Barclay, 2014; Ben-Moshe, 2020; Bilge, 2013; Carastathis, 2016; Clare, 2009; May, 2015) that feeds into the identitarian sources for their sense of pride. Following their example, there is a need to realize the transformational value of denouncing and disrupting the multiple layers of meaning constructed around American citizenship, which for many Latinx with dis/abilities constitute legal and widely accepted grounds for exclusion (Burtt, 2007; Michaels, 2006; Minich, 2013), as my introductory positionality note implied at the start of this chapter. It is time to confront passive perpetuations of hierarchical and exclusionary modes of nationhood. It is key to understand that their subsistence is deeply rooted in multifaceted constellations of ableist modes of whiteness as property. LatDisCrit as a transgression space of intersectional subaltern knowledges can propitiate dialogical practices of strategic rupture toward radical solidarity and emancipatory learning, opening new possibilitarian ways for bridging the interlocking work of multiple spheres of resistance and utopian imagination within and beyond DisCrit's epistemological and axiological expansions. By focusing, for instance, on resisting the exclusionary force of citizenship classroom discourses as a way to dismantle or disrupt marginalizing ecologies, a great deal of movement forward could be gained in the building of enduring solidarity and rightful presence (Calabrese Barton & Tan, 2020) spaces for emancipatory learning.

TENET SEVEN: CONCLUDING NOTES ON ACTIVISM, LATDISCRIT, AND DISCRIT'S INNOVATIVE HORIZONS

This chapter has offered an exploratory window into the diasporic, Global South epistemology possibilities of LatDisCrit, emphasizing LatDisCrit's role in enriching DisCrit's intersectional dis/ability justice agenda. Based on the practical ramifications of both LatDisCrit and DisCrit's engaged scholarship, one would expect powerful activism vestiges (Annamma et al., 2013, 2016). However, to boost dis/ability justice activism as an impending priority in LatDisCrit and DisCrit alike, it is necessary to cultivate concrete modes of intersectional transdisciplinarity. Engaged scholars and intersectional/decolonial dis/ability activists need to be radically committed to genuinely bringing activism in as an equal dialogical action partner. By definition, academic circles are likely to think that disciplines only encompass respectable academic fields. Thus, they extend their umbrella for multiple knowledges exclusively to spheres that fit squarely into reductionist epistemological and axiological paradigms (Bhaskar & Danermark, 2006; Bhaskar et al., 2017). On the other hand, disruptive intersectionality justice is at once enacted engaged scholarship and the driving work of participatory action research-savvy, scholarly cognoscenti activists. Therefore, emerging fields like DisCrit and subidentitarian fields such as LatDisCrit need to move beyond dualist conceptions of scholarship and activism. Their identitarian and networking contours need to break through, transgressing established frontiers of knowledge and embodied collective action (Carey, 2009; Farred, 2003; Mignolo, 2000).

Given my desire to elevate Latinidad and trans-Latinidades in their identitarian solidarity possibilities, my reference to dis/ability throughout the chapter has been rather cursory. It is important to stress that dis/ability was the triggering climactic source of solidarity among Latinx moms in the conflicted incident mentioned in the second section of the chapter. Mothers were used to coming to lunch with their children, mostly pre-K and other early childhood groups who had been diagnosed with diverse categories of anxiety disorders. Once the principal prevented them from doing so in an expansion of pernicious race-based classroom ecologies (almost all the moms affected were monolingual Spanish speakers), they knew that something radical needed to occur to resist this injustice, which would most likely exacerbate anxiety episodes for their children. I singled out this incident because I feel uneasy about the isolationist mechanics of the situated emancipation process chosen, although it seemed that choice may not be the right word to use in their case, since no other options were offered or considered by the mediating therapist. Perhaps looking for ways to mature conditions toward Brown-Black multiple-knowledge parent alliances would be a more sustainable/enduring strategy in a similar case, which is why I stress the value of linking Blackness studies in conjunction with LatDisCrit as a paradigm that translates into alliance-building practices of intentional resistance and transgressional knowledges. Having ways to link the spontaneous axiological and epistemological activism of these parents within an interdisciplinary engaged scholarship coalition would be ideal, yet I write this last sentence in the certainty that ideal conditions seldom present themselves, requiring proactive intersectional/decolonial solidarity carving endeavors that transgress established comfort zones of scholarship and privilege.

REFERENCES

Alcoff, L. M. (2009). Comparative race, comparative racisms. In J. J. E. Gracia (Ed.), *Race or ethnicity? On Black and Latino identity* (pp. 270–288). Cornell University Press.

Annamma, S. A. (2017). *The pedagogy of pathologization: Dis/abled girls of color in the school-prison nexus.* Routledge.

Annamma, S. A., Connor, D. J., & Ferri, B. A. (2013). Dis/ability critical race studies (DisCrit): Theorizing at the intersections of race and dis/ability. *Race Ethnicity and Education, 16*(1), 1–31.

Annamma, S. A., Connor, D. J., & Ferri, B. A. (2016). Introduction: A truncated genealogy of DisCrit. In D. J. Connor, B. A. Ferri, & S. A. Annamma (Eds.), *DisCrit: Disability studies and critical race theory in education* (pp. 1–9). Teachers College Press.

Annamma, S. A., Ferri, B. A., & Connor, D. J. (2018). Cultivating and expanding disability critical race theory (DisCrit). In K. Ellis, R. Garland Thomson, M. Kent, & R. Robertson (Eds.), *Manifestos for the future of critical disability studies* (Vol. 1, pp. 231–239). Routledge.

Annamma, S. A., & Morrison, D. (2018). DisCrit classroom ecology: Using praxis to dismantle dysfunctional education ecologies. *Teaching and Teacher Education, 73*(2018), 70–80.

Anzaldúa, G. (1987). *Borderlands/la frontera: The new mestiza.* Aunt Lute Books.

Arroyo, J. (2003). *Travestismos culturales: Literatura y etnografía en Cuba y Brasil.* Nuevo Siglo.

Barclay, J. L. (2014). Mothering the "useless": Black motherhood, disability, and slavery. *Women, Gender, and Families of Color, 2*(2), 115–140.

Bell, C. (2006). Introducing white disability studies: A modest proposal. In L. J. Davis (Ed.), *The disability studies reader* (2nd ed., pp. 275–282). Routledge.

Bell, C. (2011). *Blackness and disability: Critical examinations and cultural interventions.* Michigan State University Press.

Ben-Moshe, L. (2020). *Decarcerating disability: Deinstitutionalization and prison abolition.* University of Minnesota Press.

Bernal, D. D. (2002). Critical race theory, Latino critical theory, and critical race-gendered epistemologies: Recognizing students of color as holders and creators of knowledge. *Qualitative Inquiry, 8*(1), 105–126.

Bhaskar, R., & Danermark, B. (2006). Metatheory, interdisciplinarity and disability research: A critical realist perspective. *Scandinavian Journal of Disability Research, 8*(4), 278–297.

Bhaskar, R., Danermark, B., & Price, L. (2017). *Interdisciplinarity and wellbeing: A critical realist general theory of interdisciplinarity.* Routledge.

Bilge, S. (2013). Intersectionality undone: Saving intersectionality from feminist intersectionality studies. *Du Bois Review, 10*(2), 405–424.

Broderick, A., & Leonardo Z. (2016). What a good boy: The deployment and distribution of "goodness" as ideological property in schools. In D. J. Connor,

B. A. Ferri, & S. A. Annamma (Eds.), *DisCrit: Disability studies and critical race theory* (pp. 55–67). Teachers College Press.

Burtt, S. (2007). Is inclusion a civic virtue? Cosmopolitanism, disability, and the liberal state. *Social Theory and Practice, 33*(4), 557–578.

Calabrese Barton, A., & Tan, E. (2020). Beyond equity as inclusion: A framework of "rightful presence" for guiding justice-oriented studies in teaching and learning. *Educational Researcher, 49*(6), 433–440. https://doi.org /10.3102%2F0013189X20927363

Calderón, D. (2014). Anticolonial methodologies in education: Embodying land and indigeneity in Chicana feminisms. *Journal of Latino/Latin American Studies, 6*(2), 81–96.

Carastathis, A. (2016). *Intersectionality: Origins, contestations, horizons.* University of Nebraska Press.

Carey, A. C. (2009). *On the margins of citizenship: Intellectual disability and civil rights in twentieth-century America.* Temple University Press.

Castro-Gómez, S. (2007). The missing chapter of empire: Postmodern reorganization of coloniality and post-Fordist capitalism. *Cultural Studies, 21*(2–3), 428–448.

Castro-Gómez, S., & Martin, D. A. (2002). The social sciences, epistemic violence, and the problem of the "invention of the other." *Nepantla: Views from the South, 3*(2), 269–285.

Clare, E. (2009). *Exile and pride: Disability, queerness, and liberation.* South End Press.

Collins, P. H. (2015). Intersectionality's definitional dilemmas. *Annual Review of Sociology, 41*(1), 1–20. https://doi.org/10.1146/annurev-soc-073014-112142

Collins, P. H., & Bilge, S. (2016). *Intersectionality.* Polity Press.

Connor, D. J. (2019). Why is special education so afraid of disability studies? *Journal of Curriculum Theorizing, 34*(1), 10–23.

Connor, D. J., Ferri, B. A., & Annamma, S. A. (Eds.). (2016). *DisCrit: Disability studies and critical race theory in education.* Teachers College Press.

Dávila, B. (2015). Critical race theory, disability microaggressions and Latina/o student experiences in special education. *Race Ethnicity and Education, 18*(4), 443–468.

Dávila, E. R., & de Bradley, A. A. (2010). Examining education for Latinas/os in Chicago: A CRT/LatCrit approach. *Educational Foundations, 24*(1), 39–58.

Davis, K. (2008). Intersectionality as buzzword: A sociology of science perspective on what makes a feminist theory successful. *Feminist Theory, 9*(1), 67–85. https://doi.org/10.1177%2F1464700108086364

Dei, G. J. S. (2000). Rethinking the role of indigenous knowledges in the academy. *International Journal of Inclusive Education, 4*(2), 111–132.

Dei, G. J. S. (2008). *Racists beware: Uncovering racial politics in contemporary society.* Sense.

Dei, G. J. S. (2012). Subhuman: The trialectic space. *Journal of Black Studies, 43*(8), 823–846.

Dei, G. J. S. (2014). The African scholar in the western academy. *Journal of Black Studies, 45*(3), 167–179.

Dei, G. J. S. (2017). *Reframing blackness and black solidarities through anti-colonial and decolonial prisms.* Springer.

Dei, G. J. S., & Hilowle, S. (Eds.). (2018). *Cartographies of race and social difference* (Vol. 9). Springer.

DeMatthews, D. E. (2016). Competing priorities and challenges: Principal leadership for social justice along the US–Mexico border. *Teachers College Record*, *118*(11), 1–38.

Dussel, E. (2012). *Ethics of liberation: In the age of globalization and exclusion*. Duke University Press. https://doi.org/10.1215/9780822395218

Edwards, B. H. (2003). *The practice of diaspora: Literature, translation, and the rise of black internationalism*. Harvard University Press.

Erevelles, N. (2011). *Disability and difference in global contexts: Enabling a transformative body politic*. Palgrave.

Erevelles, N., & Minear, A. (2010). Unspeakable offenses: Untangling race and disability in discourses of intersectionality. *Journal of Literary & Cultural Disability Studies*, *4*(2), 127–145.

Erevelles, N., & Mutua, K. (2005). "I am a woman now!" Rewriting cartographies of girlhood from the critical standpoint of disability. In P. Bettis & N. Adams (Eds.), *Geographies of girlhood: Identity in-between* (pp. 253–269). Lawrence Erlbaum & Associates.

Farred, G. (2003). *What's my name? Black vernacular intellectuals*. University of Minnesota Press.

Feeley, M. M. (1979). *The process is the punishment: Handling cases in a lower criminal court*. Russell Sage Foundation.

Fernández Retamar, R. (2003). *Todo caliban*. Ediciones Callejon.

Frank, A. W. (2001). Can we research suffering? *Qualitative Health Research*, *11*(3), 353–362. https://doi.org/10.1177/104973201129119154

Gándara, P., & Mordechay, K. (2017). Demographic change and the new (and not so new) challenges for Latino education. *The Educational Forum*, *81*(2), 148–159. https://www.tandfonline.com/doi/abs/10.1080/00131725.2017.1280755

García, O. (2014). U.S. Spanish and education: Global and local intersections. *Review of Research in Education*, *38*(1), 58–80.

Garland-Thomson, R. (1997). *Extraordinary bodies: Figuring physical disability in American culture and literature*. Columbia University Press.

Gaztambide-Fernández, R. A. (2012). Decolonization and the pedagogy of solidarity. *Decolonization: Indigeneity, Education and Society*, *1*(1), 41–67.

Ghai, A. (2015). *Rethinking disability in India*. Routledge.

Gillborn, D. (2015). Intersectionality, critical race theory, and the primacy of racism, race, class, gender, and disability in education. *Qualitative Inquiry*, *21*(3), 277–287.

Grech, S. (2011). Disability and the majority world: Challenging dominant epistemologies. *Journal of Literary & Cultural Disability Studies*, *5*(2), 217–219.

Grech, S. (2015). *Disability and poverty in the Global South. Renegotiating development in Guatemala*. Springer.

Hall, S. (1996). Race, articulation, and societies structured in dominance. In H. A. Baker, M. Diawara, & R. H. Lindeborg (Eds.), *Black British cultural studies: A reader* (pp. 25–42). University of Chicago Press.

Hancock, A. M. (2007). When multiplication doesn't equal quick addition: Examining intersectionality as a research paradigm. *Perspectives on Politics*, *5*(1), 63–79. https://doi.org/10.1017/S1537592707070065

Handy, G. T. (2018). *Examining teaching activities in war-affected schools: Advancing transformative praxis* [Doctoral dissertation, University of Kansas]. ProQuest Dissertations and Theses Global.

Harris, C. I. (1993). Whiteness as property. *Harvard Law Review, 106*(8), 1707–1791. https://doi.org/10.2307/1341787

Henry, P. (2000). *Caliban's reason: Introducing Afro-Caribbean philosophy.* Routledge.

Hernandez-Saca, D. (2016). *Re-framing the master narratives of dis/ability through an emotion lens: Voices of latina/o students with learning disabilities* [Unpublished doctoral dissertation]. Arizona State University.

Holloway, J. (2002). Zapatismo and the social sciences. *Capital & Class, 26*(3), 153–160.

Irizarry, J. (2011). *Latinization of U.S. schools: Successful teaching and learning in shifting cultural contexts.* Routledge.

Lao-Montes, A. N. (2016). Afro-Latin@ difference and the politics of decolonization. In R. Grosfoguel, N. Maldonado-Torres, & J. D. Saldívar (Eds.), *Latin@s in the world-system: Decolonization struggles in the 21st century U.S. empire* (pp. 75–88). Routledge.

López, I. F. H. (1997). Race, ethnicity, erasure: The salience of race to LatCrit theory. *California Law Review, 85*(5), 1143–1211.

López, I. H. (2004). *Racism on trial: The Chicano fight for justice.* Belknap Press.

López, I. H. (2006). *White by law: The legal construction of race.* New York University Press.

Maldonado-Torres, N. (2007). On the coloniality of being: Contributions to the development of a concept. *Cultural Studies, 21*(2–3), 240–270.

Malhotra, R. (2016). The legal politics of Marta Russell: A Castoriadan reading. In R. Malhotra (Ed.), *Disability politics in a global economy* (pp. 19–39). Routledge.

May, V. M. (2015). *Pursuing intersectionality, unsettling dominant imaginaries.* Routledge.

Mendoza, E., Paguyo, C., & Gutiérrez, K. (2016). Understanding the intersection of race and dis/ability: common sense notions of learning and culture. In D. J. Connor, B. A. Ferri, & S. A. Annamma (Eds.), *DisCrit: Disability studies and critical race theory* (pp. 71–86). Teachers College Press.

Meekosha, H. (2011). Decolonising disability: Thinking and acting globally. *Disability & Society, 26*(6), 667–682.

Meyers, S. (2019a). *Civilizing disability society: The Convention on the Rights of Persons with Disabilities socializing grassroots disabled persons' organizations in Nicaragua.* Cambridge University Press.

Meyers, S. (2019b). Misrecognising persons with disabilities in the Global South: The need for a comparative disability studies framework. In K. Ellis, R. Garland-Thomson, M. Kent, & R. Robertson (Eds.), *Interdisciplinary approaches to disability: Looking towards the future* (Vol. 2, pp. 199–208). Routledge.

Michaels, W. B. (2006). *The trouble with diversity: How we learned to love identity and ignore inequality.* Metropolitan Books.

Migliarini, V. (2017). Subjectivation, agency and the schooling of raced and dis/abled asylumseeking children in the Italian context. *Intercultural Education, 28*(2), 182–195.

Mignolo, W. D. (2000). *Local histories/global designs: Coloniality, subaltern knowledges and border thinking*. Princeton University Press.

Mignolo, W. D. (2005). Huntington's fears: "Latinidad" in the horizon of the modern/colonial world. In R. Grosfoguel, N. Maldonado-Torres, & J. D. Saldívar (Eds.), *Latin@s in the world-system: Decolonization struggles in the 21st century U.S. empire* (pp. 57–73). Routledge.

Mignolo, W. D., & Walsh, C. E. (2018). *On decoloniality: Concepts, analytics, praxis*. Duke University Press.

Minich, J. A. (2013). *Accessible citizenships: Disability, nation, and the cultural politics of greater Mexico*. Temple University Press.

Moraga, C., & Anzaldúa, G. (Eds.). (1981). *This bridge called my back: Writings by radical women of color*. Persephone Press.

Moya, P. M. L. (2001). Chicana feminism and postmodern theory. *Signs: Journal of Women in Culture and Society*, 26(2), 441–483.

Moya, P. M. L. (2016). *The social imperative: Race, close reading, and contemporary literary criticism*. Stanford University Press.

Nguyen X. T. (2015). *The journey to inclusion*. Sense/Brill.

Nieto-Phillips, J. M. (2004). *The language of blood: The making of Spanish-American identity in New Mexico, 1880s–1930s*. The University of New Mexico Press.

Obourn, M. W. (2020). *Disabled futures: A framework for radical inclusion*. Temple University Press.

Padilla, A. (2018). *Race, disability, and the possibilities of radical agency: Toward a political philosophy of decolonial critical hermeneutics in Latinx DisCrit* [Doctoral dissertation, University of New Mexico]. https://digitalrepository.unm.edu/educ_lls_etds/96/

Padilla, A. (2021). *Disability, intersectional agency and Latinx identity: Theorizing LatDisCrit counterstories*. Routledge.

Padilla, A., & Tan, P. (2019). Toward inclusive mathematics education: A metatheoretical reflection about countering ableism in mathematics educational standards and curriculum. *International Journal of Qualitative Studies in Education*, 32(3), 299–322. https://doi.org/10.1080/09518398.2019.1576941

Parrey, R. C. (2020). Embracing disorientation in the disability studies classroom. *Journal of Literary & Cultural Disability Studies*, 14(1), 37–56. https://doi.org/10.3828/jlcds.2019.16

Piepzna-Samarasinha, L. L. (2018). *Care work: Dreaming disability justice*. Arsenal Pulp Press.

Quijano, A. (2000). Coloniality of power, ethnocentrism and Latin America. *International Sociology*, 15(2), 215–232.

Quijano, A. (2006). El "movimiento indígena" y las cuestiones pendientes en América Latina. *Argumentos (México, DF)*, 19(50), 51–77.

Saldívar, J. D. (1991). *The dialectics of our America*. Duke University Press.

Saldívar, J. D. (2012). *Trans-Americanity: Subaltern modernities, global coloniality, and the cultures of greater Mexico*. Duke University Press.

Sandoval, C. (2000). *Methodology of the oppressed*. University of Minnesota Press.

Sandrino-Glasser, G. (1998). Los confundidos: De-conflating Latinos/as' race and ethnicity. *ChicanoLatino Law Review*, 19, 69–162.

Santos, B. S. (2015). *If God were a human rights activist*. Stanford University Press.

Santos, B. S. (2016). *Epistemologies of the south: Justice against epistemicide.* Routledge.

Santos, B. S. (2018). *The end of the cognitive empire: The coming of age of epistemologies of the South.* Duke University Press.

Santos, B. S., & Meneses, M. P. (2020). Preface. In B. S. Santos & M. P. Meneses (Eds.), *Knowledges born in the struggle: Constructing the epistemologies of the Global South* (pp. xv–xvii). Routledge.

Solórzano, D. G., & Bernal, D. D. (2001). Examining transformational resistance through a critical race and Latcrit theory framework: Chicana and Chicano students in an urban context. *Urban Education, 36*(3), 308–342.

Stahler-Sholk, R. (2010). The Zapatista social movement: Innovation and sustainability. *Alternatives, 35*(3), 269–290.

Thorius, K. A. K., & Tan, P. (2016). Expanding analysis of educational debt: Considering intersections of race and ability. In D. J. Connor, B. A. Ferri, & S. A. Annamma (Eds.), *DisCrit: Disability studies and critical race theory* (pp. 87–97). Teachers College Press.

Tremayne, M. (2014). Anatomy of protest in the digital era: A network analysis of Twitter and Occupy Wall Street. *Social Movement Studies: Journal of Social, Cultural and Political Protest, 13*(1), 110–126. http://dx.doi.org/10.1080/14742837.2013.830969

Trinidad Galván, R. (2001). Portraits of mujeres desjuiciadas: Womanist pedagogies of the everyday, the mundane and the ordinary. *International Journal of Qualitative Studies in Education, 14*(5), 603–621.

Trinidad Galván, R. (2003). *Campesina epistemologies and pedagogies of wholeness: Transformations of the spirit in a Mexicano transnational community* [Unpublished doctoral dissertation]. University of Utah.

Trinidad Galván, R. (2006). Campesina epistemologies and pedagogies of the spirit: Examining women's sobrevivencia. In D. Delgado Bernal, C. A. Elenes, F. E. Godinez, & S. Villenas (Eds.), *Chicana/Latina education in everyday life: Feminista perspectives on pedagogy and epistemology* (pp. 161–179). SUNY Press.

Trinidad Galván, R. (2014). Chicana/Latin American feminist epistemologies of the Global South (within and outside the north): Decolonizing el conocimiento and creating global alliances. *Journal of Latino/Latin American Studies, 6*(2), 135–140.

Valdes, F. (1999). Afterword, theorizing OutCrit theories: Coalitional method and comparative jurisprudential experience—RaceCrits, QueerCrits and LatCrits. *University of Miaimi Law Review, 53*(4), 1265–1306.

Valdes, F. (2000). Race, ethnicity, and Hispanismo in a triangular perspective: The essential Latina/o and LatCrit theory. *UCLA Law Review, 48*(2), 1–41.

Vanden, H. E. (2007). Social movements, hegemony, and new forms of resistance. *Latin American Perspectives, 34*(2), 17–30. http://www.jstor.org/stable/27648007

Vasconcelos, J. (1997). *The cosmic race/La raza cósmica: A bilingual edition* (D. T. Jaén, Trans.). Johns Hopkins University Press.

Villenas, S. A. (2005). Latina literacies in convivencia: Communal spaces of teaching and learning. *Anthropology and Education Quarterly, 36*(3), 273–277.

Waitoller, F. R., & Thorius, K. A. K. (2016). Cross-pollinating culturally sustaining pedagogy and universal design for learning: Toward an inclusive pedagogy that accounts for dis/ability. *Harvard Educational Review*, 86(3), 366–389. https://doi.org/10.17763/1943-5045-86.3.366

Wallerstein, I. (2016). Latin@s: What's in a name? In R. Grosfoguel, N. Maldonado-Torres, & J. D. Saldívar (Eds.), *Latin@s in the world-system: Decolonization struggles in the 21st century U.S. empire* (n.p.). Routledge.

Wildeman, S. M. (2020). Disabling solitary: An anti-carceral critique of Canada's solitary confinement litigation. In C. Spivakovsky, L. Steele, & P. Weller (Eds.), *The legacies of institutionalisation: Disability, law and policy in the "deinstitutionalised" community* (n.p.). Hart.

Williams, D. J. (2006). Autoethnography in offender rehabilitation research and practice: Addressing the "us vs. them" problem. *Contemporary Justice Review*, 9(1), 23–38.

Wynter, S. (2003). Unsettling the coloniality of being/power/truth/freedom: Towards the human, after man, its overrepresentation: An argument. *The New Centennial Review*, 3(3), 257–337.

Yosso, T. (2000). *A critical race and LatCrit approach to media literacy: Chicana/o resistance to visual macroaggressions* [Unpublished doctoral dissertation]. University of California, Los Angeles.

Yuval-Davis, N. (2006). Intersectionality and feminist politics. *European Journal of Women's Studies*, 13(3), 193–209. https://doi.org/10.1177%2F1350506806065752

Unveiling the Intersections of Race and Disability in Students with Significant Support Needs

Nitasha M. Clark, George W. Noblit, Charna D'Ardenne,
David A. Koppenhaver, & Karen Erickson

White Americans use racism to undergird their claims to supremacy (Kohli et al., 2017). One of the ways they do this is by ascribing inability to People of Color. Racism is coupled with ableism to shore up white dominance, and this intersection then makes it possible for overt racism to be shielded by claims about lack of capability (Gillborn, 2015; Harris & Leonardo, 2018). This chapter situates white supremacy not as a relic of our sordid racial history but rather as the structural foundation for current practices regarding race and disability in the United States. We focus our analysis on schooling for students deemed eligible to receive special education services due to their being identified with variety of severe disability labels[1] (e.g., severe intellectual disability, multiple disabilities).

White supremacy is a set of practices grounded in settler colonialism (Bonds & Inwood, 2016) and the eugenics movement (Pfeiffer, 1994; Selden, 2000) that continues today to impact school practice. Over time, biased assumptions, harmful stereotypes, and irrational fears concerning race have merged with similar concerns about individuals with disabilities in what has been termed scientific racism or intellectual racism (Baynton, 2016; Fallace, 2016). Social Darwinism and eugenics historically justify policies for conquest, enslavement, extermination, and isolation of *others* (Bashford & Levine, 2010).

In this chapter, we reflectively re-examine a case study of a school that serves only students with significant support needs (SSN).[2] In this chapter, we focus primarily on the first two tenets of Disability Critical Race Theory (DisCrit): (1) "DisCrit focuses on ways that the forces of racism and ableism circulate interdependently, often in neutralized and invisible ways, to uphold notions of normalcy"; and (2) "DisCrit values multidimensional identities and troubles singular notions of identity such as race or dis/ability or class or gender or sexuality, and so on" (Annamma et al., 2016, p. 19).

Our case reveals how ableism and disability are used to construct color-evasiveness (Annamma et al., 2017) in the education of students with SSN. As Annamma et al. (2017) argue, "Color-evasiveness as an expanded racial ideology acknowledges that to avoid talking about race is a way to willfully ignore the experiences of people of color and makes the goal of erasure more fully discernible" (p. 156). Artiles (2013) asserts that "disability arises out of society's ableist assumptions and practices about what is considered normal" (p. 335). Our argument is that under ableism, disability—or the need for significant supports in education—is used by white educators in this school to willfully *veil* how racism is at play in the school, as they construct singular identities of their students as disabled. We conceptualize the intersection of racism and ableism in this study as a case of multiple forms of oppression (Harris & Leonardo, 2018), with ableism serving as a powerful and singular formation of difference that veils racism from view.

Our use of *veil*, or more correctly *veiling*, is centered in Du Bois's (2008/1903) theory of double consciousness, the psychological manifestation that Black Americans experience due to racialized oppression and devaluation in a white-dominated society.[3] Dubois developed the metaphor of a veil to depict the color line that results when white educators structure schools as white institutions on one side of a veil, or color line, that is purposely constructed to segregate and oppress Black students. This veiling by whites enables them to construct narratives that blame the victim rather than acknowledging the power of their racism. In turn, they willfully ignore the effects of white supremacy on society, including its effects on the ways that Black students regard themselves. In this chapter, we assert that such veiling is at work in the school where we conducted our research.

INTERSECTIONALITY IN CRITICAL RACE THEORY

Intersectionality was first articulated within Critical Race Theory and has been elaborated there and in Black feminist studies (Crenshaw, 1989). Some have argued that intersectionality has been co-opted, but Black women thinkers have a long history of confronting intersectionality. In 1851, Sojourner Truth, in her unique oratorical style, delivered her "Ain't I a Woman?" speech that questioned racial, gender, and ability discrimination (Minister, 2012). Later, the works of Anna Julia Cooper (1892), Ida B. Wells (1892, as reported in Royster, 2016), and Mary Church Terrell (1940) laid the foundation for African American legal scholars and Critical Race theorist Kimberle Crenshaw (1989) to elaborate and coin the term *intersectionality*. Rice et al. (2019) have argued that scholars need to ensure that intersectionality (and in our view DisCrit, as an intersectional theory) is not diluted or misappropriated. Rice and colleagues (2019) argue that intersectional work requires that researchers: (a) center community interests; (b) consider

diverse, aggrieved voices; (c) account for social positions and shifting intersections; (d) address social forces through a political lens; (e) enact research
reflexivity and attend to power relations; and (f) adopt social justice as the
primary commitment. This is a tall order, but our team has tried to embrace
each of these commitments. Focusing on Students of Color with SSN, we
sought to understand the politics of the forces, social positions, and shifting
intersections at play.

Our team is diverse in race, gender, and intellectual perspectives and
continually addresses issues of our positionalities and reflexivity, including
the fact that the students in our research cannot directly speak for themselves. As a result, we are positioned as speaking for them both in terms of
their situation and what social justice might mean for them. This is a situation fraught with the potential for misappropriation and misunderstanding.
Thus, one of our long-term goals is to facilitate society's ability to access
students with SSN and enable their voices to be expressed and heard. Our
team and its positionalities are described as follows.

Nitasha, a rural, working-class daughter of the African diaspora, was educated in Black-majority Title I public schools. A first-generation college graduate, she has taught and researched in general education and special education
settings with a focus on inclusion, research-based interventions, and equity.

George, from a white, Appalachian, working-class, father-only household, was a scholarship boy who eventually earned his PhD in sociology.
He is new to research on dis/ability but has a long history of studying race
in education.

Charna, from a white, working-class, single-parent family, completed
college on scholarships, loans, and work-study, and earned a PhD in education after teaching elementary grades and ESL in urban public schools for
10 years. Her research has centered on critical theory and issues of equality
around race, second language, and class constructions.

David, son of two first-generation white college graduates, taught in
a rural Title I public school before earning his doctorate. His research addresses literacy learning in students with SSN.

Karen, from a white, suburban home, has always sought opportunities
to teach and improve understandings of students with SSN. Her research
has been marked by seeing possibility where many see only disability.

RESEARCH METHOD

For 3 years, we have been conducting a postcritical ethnography (Noblit
et al., 2004) in a school for students with SSN with funding from the
Spencer Foundation. We have used standard ethnographic data collection
techniques of observation in classrooms and close, detailed observations
of and interactions with students, interviews with teachers (the students

can vocalize but generally do not have speech or other conventional means of communication), and document review of curricula and classroom, school, and school district documents. In response to critiques by Scholars of Color that critical ethnography valorized the white, male critic and rendered those studied as cultural dupes (hooks, 1990; McCarthy & Apple, 1988; Rosoaldo, 1989; Villenas, 1996), proponents of postcritical ethnography argued that the tools of critique needed to be applied to the critic as well, problematizing researchers' positionality, objectivity, reflexivity, and modes of representation. As part of the postcritical ethnographic process, we observed, recorded, and examined the thinking and learning of students with SSN in a school, but we were also informed by critical, interpretivist, and postmodern theories (Anders, 2019). We acknowledge and allow our positionality and reflexivity to inform our practice of ethnography. Multiple experimental expressions were produced to analyze and critique dominance, oppression, and inequity in the educational experiences of school-age students with disabilities and in our own interpretations and critiques.

In this postcritical ethnography, we locate the study in a school and with the students, teachers, and administrator experiences in that school. The school offered classes for some 85 school-aged students—about 60% low income, 58% male, and 55% Students of Color (Black, Latinx, and Asian). The 11 teachers for the school-age students were 81% female and 91% white. Two of the 11 teachers had visibly altered gaits, but they did not require mobility or other supports.

Our focus was on developing theories of thinking and learning for students with SSN, embracing possibilities in the face of many who see only disability. Employing postcritical ethnography allowed us to recognize that in our work, and in the school itself, the focus on ableism veiled race from our and their purview. Our own color-evasiveness (Annamma et al., 2017) hampered our ability to understand how ableism was constructed and how race was made all but invisible. We were chastened by our complicity, and this chapter is one way we are working to embrace DisCrit more seriously in our research and lives.

This chapter details the ways that we returned to our data collection and analysis to examine white supremacy, color evasiveness, and the intersectionality of racism and ableism. We conducted new observations and interviews, reread, and recoded transcripts, field notes, and documents to better understand these issues, and in the process, we learned how influential the construction of disability was in this school. It is so powerful, in fact, that teachers and administrators did not, and seemingly could not, see race as meaningful to the lives of Students of Color, who are the majority of students. In what follows, we show how in this school discourse and practice focused on disability-veiled race and racism from view in both educator discourse and in classroom practice.

RACE AND SCHOOLS IN THE SOUTHERN UNITED STATES

The Crossover School District (a pseudonym) is in a southern U.S. state with a long and devastating history of enslavement, segregation, white terrorism of African Americans, and begrudging accommodation to school desegregation and the civil rights movement. The district, after resisting school desegregation, complied decades ago with a court order to desegregate by employing pupil transportation and revamped attendance zones to physically desegregate many of the schools, at least minimally. White flight to the surrounding county district confounded these efforts, and the district created a magnet school program to attract white families to urban schools with enhanced curricula and smaller teacher–student ratios.

The state later initiated a standardized testing program that required schools to address disparities in achievement by race and published these results. While the tests are racially biased, the disparities that were revealed forced the district and each school to focus on reducing them. One superintendent required each principal to present an explanation as well as submit new plans to address disparities. The disparities remained a persistent problem, and thus the district and the schools became increasingly attendant to issues of race. Testing preparation programs, culturally relevant curricula, and teacher anti-bias training were instituted and continue today. School reform efforts were employed and included the only Black-designed school reform initiative. Today, the district has a dedicated equity staff and a central office-level department, regular anti-bias training for teachers, district and school performance plans that require culturally relevant curricula, low-performing school turnaround efforts that require racial disparities be addressed, and so on. While we have critiques of these efforts, the salient points are that race is prominent in the educational discourse in Crossover School District, and school personnel in general education school sites know race must be addressed, even if they have little record of doing so effectively.

A COLOR-EVASIVE SCHOOL

Obscura School (a pseudonym) is a separate school within the district that exclusively serves students with SSN. While other schools in the district acknowledge that race must be addressed, in Obscura School, there is no mention of race in either official or informal discourses. School personnel do not reflect on the fact that this is a segregated school, even though the law requires the least restrictive environment for students with disabilities, including those with SSN. The school is racially identifiable as well. The lead administrators and 91% of the teachers in the school are white. The predominantly white teaching staff serve a majority Student of Color student body, but this is never remarked upon. In fact, the staff rarely speak about the race of their students even in interviews that might prompt such comments. The administration also did not speak of race in either everyday discourse or in interviews with the research team. Instead, students are characterized in terms of ableism, with disability alone defining their identity. For example, the principal stated in one interview, "We have students from 3 to 22 years of age. All have a disability but many abilities. Many are medically fragile."

School personnel regard their approach to teaching their students as successful. Their singular focus is on disability, which they acknowledge creates a level of complexity that requires an individualized response. As one teacher put it, "Each kid is different, even the same diagnosis. They present in different ways, are worlds apart." Another teacher elaborated about how she knew her students were learning:

> [It is] dependent on the student. Most of the time if they are
> responding, then you know that they are at least open to what you're
> presenting to them, eye gaze, touching, speaking, making their body
> move in the direction you are. . . . if there is a particular learning
> activity that you are modeling to them, and they are able to reciprocate
> over a certain amount of times, and then in different sessions, then you
> know that they have got what you are trying to teach them.

The teachers commonly downplay the importance of professional development (PD) addressing race offered by the school district. Moreover, based on our interviews, teachers participated in little professional development related to race. As the school curriculum coordinator noted, "Don't know if anyone takes it." One teacher noted that diversity PD "didn't apply to our students and their learning. It was more about district diversity. Stuff that was common sense to me." Another teacher agreed and explained that the school's focus on relationships overrode the focus on diversity: "Whole-district things often don't apply to us, but we always try to make it apply to us by talking about relationships as key." The principal concurred that the district's diversity and inclusion discussions "are not talking about us." Thus, the school staff explicitly use disability to inoculate themselves from the very PD that would challenge their veiling of race and its salience in the school.

As noted by Annamma and colleagues (2016), under the oppressive formation of ableism, disability justifies the segregation of students with SSN in this school even when educational history and law require educational entities to eschew it. Moreover, this segregation and the overarching focus on disability as the students' salient identity reveal color evasiveness. A teacher summarized the staff's view of race and diversity by saying, "It is good to be aware of differences in that manner, but I don't feel it is as necessary here. We know every family in this building. We don't have to make broad assumptions because of their culture." To evade race, the predominantly white teaching staff speaks of relationships, individualized instruction, and the complexity of teaching students with SSN.

Color evasiveness also plays out in the classroom. Although we have many examples across the classrooms we observed, due to space we focus on examples from one classroom to illustrate how color evasiveness was at work. We present the classroom vignettes with a level of depth and richness to allow readers to evaluate the veracity of our analysis as well as form their own interpretations.

THE CLASSROOM AND PARTICIPANTS

Ms. Torie and Her Classroom

Ms. Torie (pseudonym) is a white elementary teacher. As a veteran special educator with over 10 years of teaching experience, Ms. Torie confidently implements the Individualized Education Programs (IEPs) for seven students, three white and four Black/African American. The teacher assistant (TA), another white female, and Ms. Torie support students in personal care and educational activities. Two of the students have medical needs that necessitate full-time certified nursing assistants who support their personal care.

Ms. Torie uses a variety of assistive technologies and communication supports throughout the school day. She has participated in a variety of PD activities focused on augmentative and alternative communication (AAC) and ways to help students with SSN develop symbolic communication. Throughout the day, she presents her students with graphic symbols and simple technologies that produce preprogrammed messages (e.g., "that's the one I want") when touched. During educational activities, students generally have a display of four to nine graphic symbols clamped on the table or the desk in front of them. Students in Ms. Torie's class do not have independent access to AAC devices with voice output, but students in the school generally receive AAC devices after they demonstrate independent use of graphic symbols and the kinds of simple technologies Ms. Torie uses.

Morning educational activities consist of the seven students in the class gathering in a semicircle around the brightly colored interactive bulletin board where Ms. Torie leads instructional routines (i.e., calendar, morning sign-in, weather, read aloud, and other activities). The adults position students in wheelchairs, therapeutic chairs, or equipment that helps them stand. The teaching assistant and other adults sit beside or behind students to provide individualized support. Ms. Torie sings songs and asks didactic questions to elicit student participation, with students petitioning for a turn. Ms. Torie prepares modified materials for each student and provides prompts, ranging from gestures to hand-over-hand assistance, to compel student responses. At midmorning, students travel to the gym or media center activities led by specialist teachers or remain in the semicircle, small-group format for a communication activity led by a speech and language pathologist or an art and/or music activity led by other specialist teachers. For the remainder of the day, students engage in lunch and personal care, free play with toys, school jobs, gross motor therapies in different positions and equipment, and watch videos. Special theme-based activities occur related to seasonal, school, or community activities. Race is at play throughout the entire day, as we will demonstrate by comparing the treatment of Freedom and Missy in separate interactions.

Freedom

Freedom (pseudonym), age 6, is a Black student who recently immigrated to the United States. Her home language is French, and she receives special education under the Individuals with Disabilities Education Act (IDEA) disability category of developmental delay. She walks independently but often leans her slender, above-average height frame toward nearby adults for support and affection. Her sociable and playful personality shows on her face with a warm, broad smile and frequent laughter. Freedom communicates through a variety of facial expressions, vocalizations, and gestures. During instructional routines, she has access to graphic symbols in a communication book that is clamped to the tray of the therapeutic chair she sits in throughout the day. She gently reaches toward people or objects to indicate interest. She wears her natural, textured hair in a short-tapered hairstyle that she rubs while she thinks.

Missy

Missy (pseudonym), age 7, enjoys echolocation or making noises that echo off walls and objects to help her detect them and singing with her favorite adults. She is a white student who has a severe visual impairment. She is learning to navigate with a long cane to improve her orientation and mobility in the school environment. She receives special education services under the IDEA disability category of multiple disabilities. Missy persistently communicates her needs and emotions with a mixture of speech (i.e., single words and short phrases), vocalizations, and a simple, sequenced message AAC device. Throughout the day, she sits in a chair at a desk like you might find in any primary grade classroom. She wears her brunette, shoulder-length hair pulled away from her face to prevent irritation or sensory overload.

COMPARING THE TREATMENT OF FREEDOM AND MISSY

Although Freedom and Missy demonstrated similar skills and behavior, their school experiences are very different. Across observations, researchers noted the ways that adults interact with, redirect, ignore, and otherwise manage the experiences of the two girls. Here we draw excerpts from field notes to illustrate these differences. We draw connections from what follows to DisCrit's tenets one and two in the discussion and conclusion.

Missy

Ms. Torie and the TA in the classroom prioritize making meaning from Missy's efforts to communicate. In this way, they are likely increasing her engagement and building her communication skills (Cress et al., 2007).

> Missy calls out. The TA responds, "You're fine." Then follows, "No, no, that's not going to work. I know you're mad. I'm sorry, sit up in your seat. That's just [another student] making noise. That's fine."
> Missy vocalizes, "Nnnnnnnn." It looks like she is fed up. She touches her hair and pulls on the poof ponytail that she has on top of her head. She puts her hands in her lap and the TA moves them to the table. Missy holds her hands together and whines. The TA repeats, "It's just [another student] making some noise. It's okay." Missy hoots (in a protesting way). The TA adds, "I know you don't like that. I'm sorry, we are done with circle."

This example shows the teaching staff working diligently to attribute meaning to Missy's communication attempts.

On another occasion, the meaning of Missy's communication attempt may have been misinterpreted by staff.

> Missy vocalizes, rocks back and forth, hits the switch to activate her communication device, and it says, "Want." The TA says "Want? Want? Want? [she repeats it in a questioning way, like she is trying to figure out what it might mean] Do you want your water?" Missy shakes her head side to side, but the TA brings her water, and she drinks.
> Missy hits her switch again and says, "Hi." Ms. Torie responds, "Missy, are you saying you want a turn? Do you want a turn, too? You said, 'Hi.' Missy, maybe you can help me count. Would you like to help me count? Missy, [the TA] is there, she is back." (TA has returned from telling [another student] to stop putting hands in his mouth.) The TA asks, "Do you want a turn? You're shaking your head no. Do you NOT want a turn?" Ms. Torie presses "not" on Missy's communication device. She then turns to the TA and says: "No, I think she just wanted to know where you were."

Though there is clear confusion about what Missy needs, what is clear is that the event demonstrates a level of adult responsivity. This same attention in attributing meaning to Missy's communication efforts is evident outside of structured group or work time. For example:

> Missy, who is still sick and sitting with her head down, waiting for someone to get her, calls out every once in a while. This time, it sounds like she said her name. The TA also interpreted the same thing and said, "I hear you Missy. You rest." Then Missy says another word that both the TA and teacher interpret as "water." The teacher says, "You can have some water," and the TA goes to the cubbies in the corner and gets Missy the water bottle that has her name on it (it is the kind that comes in a child's lunch box). The TA hands it to Missy, who reaches for it and begins drinking. After a few sips, she puts her head back down.

Adults embrace Missy's communication attempts and interact with her as if she were a competent communicator. This appears to give Missy confidence to continue, which increases her communication attempts and subsequently the amount of feedback from and interaction with adults.

However, the ongoing attention from adults is not without its costs for Missy. Often, Missy is cut off from interacting with or building relationships with peers. Her severe visual impairment keeps her from connecting with them visually. The fact that none of the other students use speech to communicate prevents her from talking with them, and the use of spacing and specialized seating keeps her from physically interacting with them. This excerpt highlights the type of adult hovering that we often observed:

> The TA is seated behind Missy holding her hands, touching the front of her throat, putting her arms around Missy's body, and talking to her softly. . . . Often when Missy vocalizes with her own voice, the TA tells her "no," and "we're not going to do that today." At other times when the TA or teacher asks a direct question, Missy vocalizes or uses her communication device to respond, and the adults do not tell her to be quiet but attribute meaning and respond to their interpretation of Missy's efforts.

The hovering by the teaching staff does sometimes result in denial or redirection, but it also leads to Missy's actions being regarded as meaningful and worthy of staff approbation. While hovering and adult responsivity are ongoing features of Missy's school day, Freedom's experience is characterized by avoidance and redirection. The following excerpt from an art lesson highlights the fact that Freedom and a male classmate, who is also African American, sit and wait for extended periods of time while adults interact with Missy and her white classmates. The researcher noted:

> Where is Freedom's card? The students are being offered choices of different colored duct tape to add to the cards they are making, but

Freedom has yet to get an initial piece for her card. She doesn't even have her card in front of her. The TA knows I'm watching Freedom; I told them when I came in. Freedom is watching the art teacher move around. Another student and Freedom have nothing yet. Finally, the art teacher puts a piece of tape on the other Black student's card but then takes it away. He watches her. Freedom still has nothing on her desk. The TA continues to work with Missy. She puts hands over Missy's hands and works. Freedom leans forward, all the way down, almost putting her head on her desk.

The instance alone could be one event of overlooking a child. However, the multiple events suggest that vestiges of racial discrimination have not disappeared. While the teacher and the TA work hard to attribute meaning to the communication efforts of some students, this is not consistent across students. In fact, Freedom's attempts to communicate are often interpreted as aggression. For example, in a small-group lesson, we see this occur:

Ms. Torie is paying attention to everyone else and not Freedom, who is sitting right in front of her. In fact, Ms. Torie turns her back on Freedom to look at another child. Freedom hits Ms. Torie on the back. It is unclear if was intended to be a smack, but it is interpreted as deliberate. Ms. Torie says, "That's not nice."

Another example comes from an interaction between Freedom and Missy.

Freedom reaches out to touch Missy's hair and laughs. The TA responds, "Get out of her hair. No, I do not like that." Freedom laughs and touches Missy's hair again as soon as the TA looks away. The TA points to the graphic symbol for "finished" in Freedom's communication notebook. As she does, the TA says, "That is FINISHED." Freedom stops smiling and closes her book. Then she looks up and smiles and vocalizes, kind of giggling and waiting, watching as the TA works with Missy.

Consistent with the literature regarding Black girls, Freedom's school experience is shaped by the intersections of race, gender, and femininity (Annamma et al., 2019; Blake et al., 2010; DeBlase, 2003). Since some Black girls are viewed as threatening and less innocent, they experience excessive surveillance and punishment in school environments. This appears to extend to Black girls with SSN like Freedom.

At no point did we observe adults working to attribute meaning to the various ways in which Freedom attempted to interact with them or other students. She was consistently given directives and redirected, unlike Missy who adults continually attempted to understand. Even when she was clearly vocalizing in ways that paralleled Missy's vocalizations, adults did not make efforts to understand Freedom. Instead, they diverted her to another activity and, in doing so, repeatedly missed opportunities for teaching and learning. For example, the following observation was recorded during a transition from circle time to playtime:

> Freedom is in her seat talking (unintelligibly) and vocalizing but otherwise patiently watching while everybody moves around. She laughs and says "Kaheh" and watches Ms. Torie come to her. Ms. Torie says, "Freedom, I'm going to let you go check your schedule." Then she pulls Freedom's seat away from the table. Freedom leans forward and grins excitedly. Ms. Torie puts her shoes on.

Ms. Torie makes no effort to understand or respond to what Freedom is saying, to her body language, or to any other efforts to communicate. Instead, she focuses on directing Freedom's next steps in the school day.

Missy and Freedom are treated quite differently despite their similar learning profiles and disability labels. The teaching staff attend and respond to Missy in ways that attribute meaning to her interactions, while Freedom is controlled and redirected. The teaching staff, by denying the salience of race in the school, are unable to recognize how their classroom practices enact differential treatment by race. From this comparison, we can see that there is a complex technology to the veiling of race in this classroom and school. Color evasiveness is enacted via specialized equipment, adapted materials, and structured interventions intended to address the students' disabilities. The veiling of race that this technology enables is so effective that the teacher and TA are seemingly unaware that they enact racism.

DISCUSSION AND CONCLUSION

This chapter engages the first two tenets of DisCrit: (1) "DisCrit focuses on ways that the forces of racism and ableism circulate interdependently, often in neutralized and invisible ways, to uphold notions of normalcy;" and (2) "DisCrit values multidimensional identities and troubles singular notions of identity such as race or dis/ability or class or gender or sexuality, and so on" (Annamma et al., 2016, p. 19).

Our research documents that the teachers and administrators in Obscura School have created a discourse that denies the salience of race in education and that predominates in the wider school district as well as the wider Black Lives Matter movement, which is coincidental with the timing of this study. In their view, the complexity of disabilities, the necessity of individualized responses, and a focus on family relations mean that it is not *necessary* to attend to race and culture. Denying the salience of race, a form of color evasiveness, is a common discursive practice among white Americans in the United States. Annamma and colleagues (2017) argue:

"Color-evasiveness, an expanded racial ideology, acknowledges that to avoid talking about race is a way to willfully ignore the experiences of People of Color, and makes the goal of erasure more fully discernible" (p. 156). Color evasiveness allowed white educators in the study to deny the fact that they were actively constructing racial differences in their interactions with Missy and Freedom.

This study also shows how the ableism of a largely white teaching staff and administration used disability singularly to define student identity, while obscuring how racism was at work in their separate school for students with SSN. The willful veiling of race by white teachers enabled racist treatment of students because the differences in treatment were justified by the students' need for significant educational supports. The comparison of Missy and Freedom is but one example of what we saw repeatedly in the school. The treatment of white students with SSN led to more opportunities for communication and engagement, while the treatment of Students of Color with SSN was restrictive and controlling, similar to Ferguson's (2001) critique. Race was veiled from view by the primary discourse constructed around disability. As a result, the teachers perceived neither race as salient nor difference in treatment by race as problematic or racist. The veiling of race *debilitated* teachers' perceptions about the ways they perpetrated racism in their teaching (Annamma et al., 2020). Some might see this as a case of implicit bias, but in our view, it was explicit and enacted color evasiveness, thinly but explicitly veiled by a singular focus on disability.

This willful veiling has real costs to white students and Students of Color. For both Freedom and Missy, the veiling by white teachers sends the message that preferring some (white) students and ignoring other (Black) students is acceptable—the norm for school experiences. Not only are Freedom and the other Students of Color in the classroom lacking adequate and culturally relevant educational experiences every day, but also, toxic classroom experiences jeopardize the long-term academic achievement and functional performance of Students of Color. Many students spend their entire academic career in this school. The academic and social consequences of being in a hierarchical educational system of institutional racism perpetuate white supremacy and deny an equitable education to Students of Color. As Du Bois (2008/1903) noted, the willful veiling by whites means that Students of Color have to see themselves in terms of how white educators treat them—as less valued than white students.

There are no simple solutions to this problem. The veiling can be revealed and critiqued, as we have done here. Teachers can be educated to attend to race in critical ways, but the lesson of Critical Race Theory is that racism is ubiquitous, and white educators will align with Students of Color only when it serves their own, white, interests (Ladson-Billings & Tate, 1995). We can hope that special educators embrace the intersection of racism and ableism and see that their students require them to embrace diversity in all its facets. White teachers of children with disabilities will likely need to conclude that their own race benefits when those seen as being of Color and with disabilities are treated equitably and honorably in a way that recognizes the multidimensional nature of their identities.

AUTHORS' NOTE

We have no known conflict of interest to disclose. The research reported in the chapter was made possible by a grant from the Spencer Foundation (#201800037). The views expressed are those of the authors and do not necessarily reflect the views of the Spencer Foundation.

NOTES

1. We use the term *severe disability labels* to note IDEA eligibility for special education services.

2. We use *SSN* advisedly because the deficit construction does not address the students' capabilities, but it does signal our solidarity with parents and others (e.g., Sheldon, 2019) who advocate tirelessly for this group of students and the ways we can collectively support their needs to change this history of exclusion and segregation (Erickson & Geist, 2016).

3. We find Du Bois's conceptualization powerful in that it is imposed via white domination. We also recognize that this metaphor can be read as equating veil with ignorance in the current anti-Muslim context and are grappling with both.

REFERENCES

Anders, A. D. (2019). Post-critical ethnography. *Oxford Research Encyclopedia of Education*. https://doi.org/10.1093/acrefore/9780190264093.013.342

Annamma, S. A., Anyon, Y., Joseph, N. M., Farrar, J., Greer, E., Downing, B., & Simmons, J. (2019). Black girls and school discipline: The complexities of being overrepresented and understudied. *Urban Education*, *54*(2), 211–242. https://doi.org/10.1177/0042085916646610

Annamma, S. A., Connor, D. J., & Ferri, B. A. (2016). Introduction: A truncated genealogy of DisCrit. In D. J. Connor, B. Ferri, & S. Annamma (Eds.), *DisCrit: Disability studies and critical race theory in education* (pp. 1–8). Teachers College Press.

Annamma, S. A., Handy, T., Miller, A. L., & Jackson, E. (2020). Animating discipline disparities through debilitating practices: Girls of color and inequitable classroom interaction. *Teachers College Record*, *122*(5), 1–46. https://www.tcrecord.org/Content.asp?ContentId=23280

Annamma, S. A., Jackson, D. D., & Morrison, D. (2017). Conceptualizing color-evasiveness: Using dis/ability critical race theory to expand a color-blind racial ideology in education and society. *Race Ethnicity and Education, 20*(2), 147–162. https://doi.org/10.1080/13613324.2016.1248837

Artiles, A. J. (2013). Untangling the racialization of disabilities: An intersectionality critique across disability models. *Du Bois Review, 10*(2), 329–347. https://doi.org/10.1017/S1742058X13000271

Bashford, A., & Levine, P. (Eds.). (2010). *The Oxford handbook of the history of eugenics*. Oxford University Press.

Baynton, D. C. (2016). *Defectives in the land: Disability and immigration in the age of eugenics*. University of Chicago Press.

Blake, J. J., Butler, B. R., Lewis, C. W., & Darensbourg, A. (2010). Unmasking the inequitable discipline experiences of urban black girls: Implications for urban educational stakeholders. *The Urban Review, 43*(1), 90–106. https://doi.org/10.1007/s11256-009-0148-8

Bonds, A., & Inwood, J. (2016). Beyond white privilege: Geographies of white supremacy and settler colonialism. *Progress in Human Geography, 40*(6), 715–733. https://doi.org/10.1177/0309132515613166

Cooper, A. J. (1892). *A voice from the south*. Aldine Printing House.

Crenshaw, K. W. (1989). Demarginalizing the intersection of race and sex: A black feminist critique of antidiscrimination doctrine, feminist theory, and antiracist politics. *University of Chicago Legal Forum, 1989*(1), 139–167. https://chicagounbound.uchicago.edu/cgi/viewcontent.cgi?article=1052&context=uclf

Cress, C. J., Arens, K. B., & Zajicek, A. K. (2007). Comparison of engagement patterns of young children with developmental disabilities between structured and free play. *Education and Training in Developmental Disabilities, 42*(2), 152–164. https://www.jstor.org/stable/23879992

DeBlase, G. L. (2003). Missing stories, missing lives: Urban girls (re)constructing race and gender in the literacy classroom. *Urban Education, 38*(3), 279–329. https://doi.org/10.1177/0042085903038003002

Du Bois, W. E. B. (2008). *The souls of black folk*. Oxford University Press. (Original work published 1903)

Erickson, K. A., & Geist, L. A. (2016). The profiles of students with significant cognitive disabilities and complex communication needs. *Augmentative and Alternative Communication, 32*(3), 187–197. http://doi.org/10.1080/07434618.2016.1213312

Fallace, T. D. (2016). Educators confront the "science" of racism, 1898–1925. *Journal of Curriculum Studies, 48*(2), 252–270. https://doi.org/10.1080/00220272.2015.1088067

Ferguson, A. A. (2001). *Bad boys: Public schools in the making of black masculinity*. University of Michigan Press.

Gillborn, D. (2015). Intersectionality, critical race theory, and the primacy of racism: Race, class, gender, and disability in education. *Qualitative Inquiry, 21*(3), 277–287. https://doi.org/10.1177/1077800414557827

Harris, A., & Leonardo, Z. (2018). Intersectionality, race-gender subordination, and education. *Review of Research in Education, 42*(1), 1–27. https://doi.org/10.3102/0091732X18759071

hooks, b. (1990). *Yearning race, gender, and cultural politics*. South End Press.

Kohli, R., Pizarro, M., & Nevárez, A. (2017). The "new racism" of K–12 schools: Centering critical research on racism. *Review of Research in Education, 41*(1), 182–202. https://doi.org/10.3102/0091732X16686949

Ladson-Billings, G., & Tate, W. (1995). Toward a critical race theory of education. *Teachers College Record*, *97*(1), 47–68.

McCarthy, C., & Apple, M. W. (1988). Race, class, and gender in American educational research: Towards a nonsynchronous parallelist position. In L. Weis (Ed.), *Class, race, and gender in American education* (pp. 9–39). SUNY Press.

Minister, M. (2012). Female, black, and able: Representations of Sojourner Truth and theories of embodiment. *Disability Studies Quarterly*, *32*(1). https://doi .org/10.18061/dsq.v32i1.3030

Noblit, G. W., Flores, S. Y., & Murillo, E. G. (Eds.). (2004). *Postcritical ethnography: Reinscribing critique*. Hampton Press.

Pfeiffer, D. (1994). Eugenics and disability discrimination. *Disability & Society*, *9*(4), 481–499. https://doi.org/10.1080/09687599466780471

Rice, C., Harrison. E, & Friedman, M. (2019). Doing justice to intersectionality in research. *Cultural Studies Critical Methodologies*, *19*(6), 409–420. https://doi .org/10.1177/1532708619829779

Rosoaldo, R. (1989). *Culture and truth: The remaking of social analysis*. Beacon Press.

Royster, J. J. (2016). Southern horrors: Lynch law in all its phases. In J. J. Royster (Ed.), *Southern horrors and other writings: The anti-lynching campaign of Ida B. Wells, 1892–1900* (pp. 49–72). Macmillan Learning.

Selden, S. (2000). Eugenics and the social construction of merit, race and disability. *Journal of Curriculum Studies*, *32*(2), 235–252. https://doi.org /10.1080/002202700182736

Sheldon, E. (Host). (2019, November). *#044 Erin Sheldon on removing barriers to learning* [Audio podcast]. Good Things in Life. https://goodthingsinlife.org/044/

Terrell, M. C. (1940). *A colored woman in a white world*. GK Hall.

Truth, S. (1851, June 21). Women's rights convention. *Anti-slavery Bugle*. https:// chroniclingamerica.loc.gov/lccn/sn83035487/1851-06-21/ed-1/seq-4/

Villenas, S. (1996). The colonizer/colonized Chicana ethnographer: Identity, marginalization, and cooptation in the field. *Harvard Educational Review*, *66*(4), 711–732. https://doi.org/10.17763/haer.66.4.3483672630865482

CHAPTER 11

Theorizing the Curriculum of Colonization in the U.S. Deaf Context

Situating DisCrit Within a Framework of Decolonization

Gloshanda Lawyer

Disability Critical Race Theory (DisCrit) has revolutionized our ability as scholars, activists, and scholar–activists to frame and analyze dis/ability and race, particularly in the education context. This chapter is extracted from the author's dissertation, where DisCrit was placed within what the author coined the decolonizing–intersectionality framework to address the "curriculum of colonization" (Lawyer, 2018). Placing DisCrit in dialogue with colonization and the role that schooling has played and continues to play in the indoctrination and reification of dis/ability and other forms of oppression provides a lens that allows for addressing both the colonized and the colonizer; the oppressed and the oppressor; the subordinated and the superordinated (Fiorenza, 2001). This chapter specifically analyzes the schooling experiences of multiply marginalized Deaf, DeafBlind, DeafDisabled, and Hard of Hearing individuals. The curriculum of colonization shows how pervasive colonization is and how schools function as its tool (Lawyer, 2018). Considering DisCrit within this framework of addressing colonization and in conjunction with other critical theories not only allows for an examination of dis/ability, race, class, language use, sexual orientation, and gender constructs but more. The expansion of DisCrit was used as one of the tools of analysis for addressing the curriculum of colonization and the ways injustice is maintained and sustained at all levels of education—K–12 schooling, higher education (including teacher preparation and research), and educational policy, especially in the case of Deaf, DeafBlind, DeafDisabled, and Hard of Hearing students.

A LONG OVERDUE ENCOUNTER

Throughout history, multiply marginalized peoples within the United States have been theorizing toward liberation. With each generation, we have arrived closer to naming the forces that deny us existence in our full humanity. Hints toward disability and colonization have appeared in previous writings of our departed activists and scholar–activists such as Audre Lorde and Frantz Fanon and indigenous scholar–activists such as Swadener and Mutua (2008), as well as the work of grassroots disability rights and disability justice leaders in the United States such as Talila "TL" Lewis, Dustin Gibson, and Lydia X. Z. Brown, among others. Fanon (1952/1967) serves as an example of one of the earliest international scholars of color to connect the experience of Black peoples, a racialized group, to imperialism and colonization around the globe. I mention Fanon's work here because he dove into the psychological effects of colonialism and the repercussions for racial relations within the context of colonization, which is important for understanding that one of the effects of colonization is disability. Therefore, the need to make explicit connections between colonization and disability, particularly in the United States, is long overdue. From the foundation laid by the previously mentioned scholar–activists, I found it necessary to put colonization, the construction of dis/ability, intersectionality, and the U.S. schooling system in direct dialogue. I do this by first putting forth the curriculum of colonization, described later. I then describe the decolonizing–intersectionality framework that I believe is a path toward addressing the curriculum of colonization. I explain how I applied the decolonizing–intersectionality framework to multiply marginalized U.S. Deaf, DeafBlind, DeafDisabled, and Hard of Hearing individuals. Last, I address why DisCrit is necessary for the curriculum of colonization and the decolonizing–intersectionality framework, potential tensions and affordances of placing them in dialogue, and future areas of exploration.

THEORIZING THE CURRICULUM OF COLONIZATION

Colonization constitutes all ideologies, behaviors, institutions, policies, and economies that are employed to dehumanize, subordinate, and/or exploit peoples, lands, and resources (Fanon, 1963/1969; Sartre, 1969; Waziyatawin & Yellow Bird, 2005). The curriculum of colonization refers to the ways in which colonialism has instituted and secured its position in all fabrics of Western-based life, including schooling in the United States, while simultaneously remaining elusive to the vast majority of people (Lawyer, 2018). This theory was developed to describe how the system uses schooling as one of the primary processes for constructing dis/ability in tandem with racializing, gendering, and imposing identities to indoctrinate students into superordinated (unmarked) and subordinated (marked) positions. This theory also accounts for how colonization functions as a multilevel and multifaceted process that operates like a well-oiled machine that is self-sustaining at the macro (system) and micro (individual) levels.

One of the primary motivations for developing the curriculum of colonization was to shift the frame from the "other," specifically the present-day dis/abled, raced, gendered body, including those who do not use English and/or are considered to exist outside what has been constructed as the normative standard. Moving away from analyzing these marked positions in isolation and ahistorically, this theory positions dis/ability as co-constructed within and a result of colonization. Highlighting this process of construction, colonization employs different mechanisms in order to sustain itself, while often remaining elusive to those who are superordinated (unmarked). These mechanisms have repercussions for dis/ability that include but are not limited to (1) assignment and evacuation from humanity; (2) schooling and science; (3) stratification of peoples (and in capitalist societies, this stratification is often linked to the perceived ability to contribute to/be productive in the capitalist system); and (4) erasure or rewriting of colonial processes.

Withers et al. (2019) stated, ". . . disability isn't a discrete identity; disabled people are also people of colour, queer people, women, trans-people and poor people" (p. 180). This is an important point because within colonization any identity or compilation of identities that have been pushed outside of the normative standard are expected to disappear into said standard. Reflecting on Gordon's (1997) conceptualization of anti-Blackness, we understand how multiply marginalized individuals are forced into the normative standard. Analyzing from the lens of anti-Blackness, humanity is gauged by one's relation to whiteness. Whiteness is judged to be human, and its negation—blackness—as "human nothingness" (Woods, 2013, p. 126). In the same way, dis/ability has been framed through colonization as another onto-epistemic condition of negation. The human race is "normatively [abled], [disabled] human beings . . . a subspecies of humanity are not [abled]" (Woods, 2013, p. 126). Therefore, proximity to [the normative standard] [becomes] a vehicle for their onto-epistemic genocide by forcing them to "disappear into [the normative standard]" (Smith, 2014). The further and more multiply marginalized an individual is, the more devastating the genocide of oneself.

Ladson-Billings and Donnor (2008) point out that discourses tend to be dichotomized—us and them, colonizer and colonized, and so forth. Those who are devalued as not being fully human are not the only victims in colonialism. As the colonizers acted upon the colonized, they too lost their own humanity (Freire, 1970). Fanon's (1967) argument also advanced the idea that there is both a dual and interactional impact of colonization on both the colonizer and the colonized. He cautioned that this is a reason why imperialism and colonization should not be reduced to simply a colonized/

colonizer binary. Both the colonized and the colonizer are mutual constructions within the curriculum of colonization. Reducing the discourse to a colonized/colonizer binary ignores the effects of colonization within as well across both groups, as well as how shifting contexts and spaces allow for one to exist as both colonized and colonizer. In other words, we must thoroughly address how disability is constructed as well as how ability is constructed and how the mechanisms of colonization are useful in violently stripping us of our humanity, while simultaneously distracting us from these historical and present-day processes.

THE DECOLONIZING-INTERSECTIONALITY FRAMEWORK

The decolonizing-intersectionality framework (Lawyer, 2018) was developed as a way to respond to the curriculum of colonization within educational teaching, research, and policy. I conceptualized the decolonizing–intersectionality framework as a type of disruptive methodology (Bhattacharya, 2018). It is an approach to theory, research, teaching, and advocacy that challenges colonization and the multiple forms of subordination enacted in schooling contexts in the United States. This framework has several purposes. First, the goal is to shift the frame from the oppressed body to systems and unnamed forces that maintain normative standards. Second, this framework is intended to address intersectionality as it manifests at each level of schooling for dis/abled students. I identified these levels as educational policy, higher education (including teacher preparation and research), and K–12 schooling. DisCrit was a primary lens for this part of the framework but with the additional goal of decolonization. Third, the framework places the action on the teacher, researcher, and/or policymaker to make themselves accountable for doing the work of self-analysis and understand where they are positioned (e.g., uplifted or superordinated in relation to their students or research participants).

The historical forefronting of one or both race and dis/ability is a way the curriculum of colonization functions by allowing other sites of marginalization and oppression to be backgrounded. I outline four steps that are necessary in the decolonizing–intersectionality framework and give an example of how this was accomplished with my research with U.S. Deaf People of Color (POC) and schooling and also to set an example of how a given experience should be analyzed emphasizing the multiple ways the system is impacting a student instead of forefronting race *and/or* ability. In the context of educational research, the four steps are: (1) identifying the colonizer's coat (McCaslin & Breton, 2008, p. 513) or how we embody and enact colonizer behaviors in their historical and current manifestations; (2) removing the colonizer's coat through critical self-assessment (Bhattacharya, 2018) into how one's behavior is implicated in colonization historically and currently;

(3) exploring research frameworks, methods, and teaching pedagogies that address colonization and intersectionality (Crenshaw, 1991); and (4) coding, analyzing, interpreting, and presenting data with decolonial and intersectional lenses. Within the aforementioned outlined steps, DisCrit was applied in identifying the colonizer's coat, removing the colonizer's coat, and as a framework that addressed intersectionality of the dis/abled and Deaf POC experience in the United States.

The decolonizing–intersectionality framework is intended to be used as an analytical tool and a decolonizing praxis methodology created from the marriage of Critical Race Theory (CRT) in education (Ladson-Billings & Tate, 1995; Lynn & Dixson, 2013) and Critical Indigenous Pedagogy of Place (CIPP; Darder et al., 2008). Waziyatawin and Yellow Bird (2005) define decolonization as "the intelligent, calculated, and active resistance to the forces of colonialism that perpetuate the subjugation and/or exploitation of our minds, bodies, and lands, and it is engaged for the ultimate purpose of overturning the colonial structure and realizing Indigenous [and other colonized peoples'] liberation" (p. 5). I envision DisCrit as an integral and necessary part of the framework in order to address how dis/ability is deployed within the curriculum of colonization.

When first theorizing a framework to address colonization across identities and dis/ability, I used the U.S. Deaf, DeafBlind, DeafDisabled, and Hard of Hearing population to describe the curriculum of colonization and the role of schooling. I sought to understand how Deaf, DeafBlind, DeafDisabled, and Hard of Hearing people living at the intersections of additional marginalized/racialized identities describe the experiences they have had in formal schooling spaces. The decolonizing–intersectionality framework was applied at the research level—methodological implications—and the K–12 and higher education levels. Figure 11.1 shows the steps involved in enacting the decolonizing–intersectionality framework (left box), the levels it is applicable to (center), and the experiences analyzed from the stories shared by U.S. multiply marginalized Deaf, DeafBlind, DeafDisabled, and Hard of Hearing Peoples of Color (right box).

Identifying the Colonizer's Coat

The first step of the model involves what I am calling "identifying the colonizer's coat." This step involves what Bell (2011) calls recovery and detection work, and it requires both decolonization and DisCrit. Enacting a project of decolonization requires radical love and humanization to remove what colonization seeks to erase and to keep all aspects of the dis/abled person's identity in conversation with one another. Working with DisCrit afforded a critical analysis of how: (a) historically dis/ability was imposed on the U.S. Deaf, DeafBlind, DeafDisabled, and Hard of Hearing population, (b) how this population has been more concerned with abled, white

Figure 11.1. Decolonizing-Intersectionality Framework and U.S. DDBDDHOH Peoples of Color

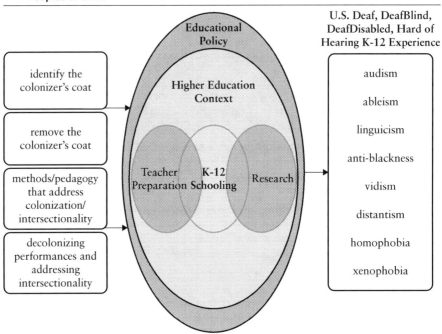

Deaf bodies, and (c) how educational systems that are assumed to be neutral can actually be sites of oppression for Deaf, DeafBlind, DeafDisabled, and Hard of Hearing bodies/minds. The result has been years of this community resisting the dis/ability label and researching, writing, and talking back to hegemonic forces to claim themselves as a cultural/linguistic minority (see Gertz, 2007; Reagan, 1985). In this act of resistance, however, they further essentialized Deaf culture into whiteness and ableness, making disability mutually exclusive with being Deaf, and further marginalizing DeafBlind and DeafDisabled individuals within the community. DisCrit gives individuals from these communities a lens to analyze how and what purpose it serves society to disable them (i.e., the use of sign languages means breaking out of the monolingual English ideology of the United States, not being able to contribute to capitalism without changes in the system, and/or being resistant to indoctrination in the same way as others).

Identifying the colonizer's coat involves tracing the history of how colonization has been and continues to be active in the U.S. Deaf, DeafBlind, DeafDisabled, and Hard of Hearing communities and in the schooling context. One of those ways is by painting a singular "Deaf" community (see Lane, 1992) or only addressing race within the community (see Wrigley, 1996), failing to address the diversity within the communities even by those who discuss colonization. Another way colonization can be revealed is by analyzing how hearing people continue to problematize the Deaf existence within policy—requiring the use of the Americans with Disabilities Act (ADA) to receive interpretation in American Sign Language (ASL); situating Deaf Education within Special Education and considering the least restrictive environment (LRE) as a placement with typically developing hearing peers as much as possible; and requiring that individualized education plans (IEP) specify how deafness disables and/or presents limitations in learning in a regular/general education classroom. Identifying the colonizer's coat with a DisCrit lens analyzes that while these practices may be strongly opposed by white abled Deaf individuals, for many Deaf POC attending a Deaf residential school with Deaf peers often means being in a predominantly white environment with signing peers but isolated from their ethnic/racial peers who are often schooled in general education settings. Therefore, Deaf POC are forced to choose between a linguistic environment with cultural deprivation or schooling within their ethnic/racial communities with linguistic deprivation, a dilemma that is rarely discussed.

Removing the Colonizer's Coat

This step within the framework moves beyond simply exploring positionality and into how one's behavior is implicated in colonization historically and currently. My critical self-assessment involved analyzing how, having received educational training through a special education teacher preparation program (with bilingual emphasis), I was trained through a pathological or deficit lens. Therefore, my teaching methods and approaches in many ways reflect this, particularly in relation to dis/abled students. The goal was to force my students to disappear into ableness, meaning become more proximal to what special education refers to as typically developing peers. For example, when working with Deaf autistic preschoolers, I would support bilingual or multilingual access and development, resisting against linguicism. I would support my students' right to access their diverse home cultures and languages, yet I pathologized their autism and used applied behavioral analysis (ABA) principles to suppress socially undesirable behaviors. It wasn't until I was taught by dis/abled adults that I realized how I had been an agent of and complicit in the colonization processes of Deaf, DeafBlind, DeafDisabled, and Hard of Hearing students in formal school settings. I used science (i.e., ABA), a common tool historically and currently employed in colonization of marginalized populations to condition children into socially desirable behaviors. I wore the colonizer's coat. I was an example of how divided our social movements have been through colonization. I supported persons of color and linguistic diversity while simultaneously oppressing dis/abled persons. My actions demonstrate the importance of examining issues of colonization from an intersectional lens, to address the experiences of colonization by multiply marginalized individuals.

Therefore, the step of removing the colonizer's coat necessitates that we analyze the ways in which we maintain and serve as tools of colonization. My own experiences stress the importance of examining our teaching pedagogy and approaches to advocacy, as well as our research methods. In all the aforementioned categories, we have field guidelines or acceptable practices that reflect minimum standards. Often those standards are a barometer of what systems of power are willing to permit in order to keep colonization illusive. Therefore, when removing the colonizer's coat, important questions to consider are: (a) Do my pedagogy, advocacy, and research approaches benefit the most marginalized of the marginalized? (b) Why are these pedagogies and methods uplifted in this context? (c) How did I come to inherit and implement these pedagogies and methods? (d) If I rejected these pedagogies and methods, who would be harmed? and (e) What would or could be reimagined in their place?

Methods: Addressing Colonization and Intersectionality

Though I envision methods to refer to teaching pedagogies, advocacy approaches, and research methods, the original iteration of the decolonizing–intersectionality framework was in research. In my dissertation (Lawyer, 2018), I used counterstorytelling as a tool (Atwood & López, 2014; Bell, 1992; Delgado, 1995; Griffin et al., 2014) to understand how schools reproduce social inequities along ability, sexual orientation, immigration status, language use, and racial and class lines. Using counterstorytelling as a research tool centered the stories of Deaf, DeafBlind, DeafDisabled, and Hard of Hearing students and placed their stories in contrast to the current dominant narratives in Deaf Education teaching and research. These stories gave both the Deaf, DeafBlind, DeafDisabled, and Hard of Hearing (and me as the researcher) the "power to construct and influence understandings" of multiply marginalized Deaf, DeafBlind, DeafDisabled, and Hard of Hearing students' confrontations with intersectionality within the curriculum of colonization (Griffin et al., 2014, p. 1355).

In the second step of the method (removing the colonizer's coat), I sought out contributors (commonly referred to as participants) who could be considered to be among the marginalized of the marginalized. It was essential to examine schooling in the United States from the perspective of individuals living at the intersections of multiple sources of marginalization, including those who identified as Deaf, DeafBlind, DeafDisabled, or Hard of Hearing who were also Black, Indigenous, or People of Color; part of the LGBTQI community; gender nonbinary/nonconforming; raised in a family that used a language other than English in the home; and/or used ASL, Black ASL, and/or Tactile ASL as one of their primary languages. Table 11.1 shows a breakdown of the contributors' demographics.

Table 11.1. Contributor Demographic Data Overview

Age Range	Gender	Home Language	Immigration Status	Self-Identified Ethnicity	Parent Hearing Status	Parent Level of Involvement in School
20–25 years: 5	Non-binary: 0	Sign language only: 3	1st generation: 5	African: 6	Deaf (signer): 2	High: 8
26–30 years: 10	Female: 10	Spanish: 2	1.5 generation: 3	Asian: 2	Deaf (non-signer): 1	Medium: 6
31–35 years: 4	Male: 15	Creole: 2	2nd generation: 2	Black/Afro-Latinx: 1	Hearing (signer): 0	Low: 2
36–40 years: 3		Multiple spoken languages: 4	U.S.-born: 14	Brown Latinx: 1	Hearing (non-signer): 19	Undisclosed: 5
41–45 years: 0		Sign and spoken languages: 2	Undisclosed: 1	Black/African American: 13	Undisclosed: 3	Not applicable: 4
46–50 years: 3		English only: 12		Haitian American: 1		
				Multi-ethnic (Black Native American): 1		

I also designed research questions and data collection methods that engaged intersectionality and colonization. Focus groups and one-on-one interviews were selected as the method of collecting and documenting the study contributors' stories. Roulston (2010) described six types of interviewing orientations, and two of the interview types were within what Roulston called a critical theory orientation: the transformative interview and the decolonizing interview. Of these, I chose the decolonizing interview for the study. Roulston (2010) described the decolonizing interview as one that focuses on restorative justice and privileging the research agenda of the colonized. The decolonizing interview is one that centers "the processes of decolonization, transformation, mobilization, and healing" (Roulston, 2010, p. 68). This is consistent with Darder et al.'s (2008) description of decolonizing inquiry as involving the "performance of counter-hegemonic theories that disrupt the colonial and the postcolonial" and an inquiry that should be "ethical, performative, healing, transformative, decolonizing, and participatory" (pp. xi, 2). Twenty-five contributors shared their experiences in a total of 30 hours of recorded conversations. Ten composite characters (Lawyer, 2018) were created that elucidate the violence, harm, and dehumanization enacted upon them through the curriculum of colonization and the impacts they continue to experience today, even as many of them have transitioned out of schooling and into their careers.

Data Analysis: Decolonizing and Intersectional Performances

In this step of the decolonizing–intersectionality framework, I focused on decolonizing (Swadener & Mutua, 2008) and intersectional performances. A notable characteristic of decolonizing performances is challenging the "colonizing ways in certain research that studies, produces and silences specific groups . . . through the ways it constructs and consumes knowledge and experiences about such groups" (Swadener & Mutua, 2008, p. 35). Taking this further, a decolonizing and intersectional performance challenges the ways that certain aspects of a group may be backgrounded or foregrounded and how this is normalized to facilitate essentializing said group for colonizing purposes. Unessentializing the group, highlighting their unique experiences, and privileging voices are also a part of decolonizing and intersectional performance. For this research study, I applied this step at the data coding, analysis, and presentation phases. I coded the data for frequency of the types of experiences, extensiveness, intensity, and contributor perception of importance. I used constant comparative analysis (Glaser & Strauss, 1967) to explore and highlight the differences in experiences with intersectionality related to the various constructed identities individuals embodied, as well as the similarities across marginalized groups. Using CRT and CIP, I developed composite narratives based on common and recurring experience types. To develop the 10 composite narratives, I selected themes related to experience types across each contributor's interview stories. Some examples of experience types included racialization; being gendered; the intersections of gender and dis/ability; language socialization; and the intersections of gender, disability, and racialization, among others. I presented three major themes and several subthemes in the form of composite counterstories with my analytical commentary to connect back to how the curriculum of colonization was being enacted on the composite characters. The full composite stories and description of how I developed them can be found at Lawyer (2018). In the following section, I make connections between specific tenets of DisCrit and how each is applied within the framework.

SITUATING DISCRIT WITHIN A FRAMEWORK OF (DE)COLONIZATION

In the original iteration of DisCrit, Annamma et al. (2016) proposed seven tenets. Each of the tenets I applied in my conceptualization of addressing colonization in U.S. schooling with Deaf, DeafBlind, DeafDisabled, and Hard of Hearing Students of Color are discussed in this section. I reflect on why DisCrit was a necessary part of the decolonizing–intersectionality framework for my study. I elaborate on how each tenet affirmed or supported what is described in the curriculum of colonization and/or how the tenet was expanded on within the curriculum of colonization and/or the decolonizing–intersectionality framework.

DisCrit Tenet One

This tenet holds that forces of racism and ableism circulate interdependently. The theory of (de)colonization expands on this tenet in two ways. First, step one of the decolonizing–intersectionality framework involves identifying the colonizer's coat. This was accomplished by putting dis/ability in direct dialogue with colonization by theorizing the curriculum of colonization. The onto-epistemic negation of the racialized and dis/abled body explains one of the ways that DisCrit tenet one is compatible with a theory of colonization. Evidence of this onto-epistemic negation can be found even in our daily use of language. Racialized and dis/abled beings continue to serve as a linguistic negation in English (see Annamma et al., 2017 and Schalk, 2013, respectively, e.g., "black sheep," "blacklist," "black market," "crazy," "insane," "blind to the truth," "fall on deaf ears"). The way language is used signals how U.S. society positions these groups of people and reifies the inferior social position (May & Ferri, 2005). The use of one linguistic form sustains the use of the other. This is a form of legitimized and systemic violence. This is also apparent in eugenic efforts that targeted Black people regardless of dis/ability and dis/abled people regardless of race within the United States (Selden, 1999). Second, the curriculum of colonization expands on tenet one by including other epistemic sites of oppression that circulate interdependently with racism and ableism. In other words, normativity extends beyond race and ability into sexuality, class, language use, gender, and so on. Schools are the sites of indoctrinating members of society into the stratified humanity belief system (Coleman-King, 2014), wherein humanity does not apply to people who do not fit the normative standard, including dis/abled peoples (of color).

DisCrit Tenet Two

Tenet two values multidimensional identities and troubles singular notions of identity. The curriculum of colonization explored how the U.S. Deaf, DeafBlind, DeafDisabled, and Hard of Hearing community has historically been essentialized as the "Deaf community" (Lawyer, 2018). Often there was a "Deaf trumps all other identities" sentiment held by white Deaf members. This essentializing was a way of forcing all other members to assimilate into white U.S. Deaf, abled, middle-class culture (Ladd & Lane, 2013). However, like any cultural or linguistic group, there is diversity in language use, ability, race/ethnicity, class, and other backgrounds of individuals who also identify as Deaf. In the decolonizing–intersectionality framework, step two focused on removing the colonizer's coat, specifically by working with contributors who identified as having multiply marginalized positions in society. Therefore, this step was essential because those who live at multiple points of marginalization have qualitatively different experiences from those who identify as (white, abled) Deaf.

DisCrit Tenet Three

Tenet three emphasizes the social constructions of race and ability yet recognizes the material and psychological impacts of being labeled as raced or dis/abled. Within the curriculum of colonization, colonization accounts for how identities are constructed within and outside the normative standard. It is not enough to only focus on marked identities (raced, dis/abled, gendered, etc.). We must also focus on the unmarked identities and how they are constructed as the normative standard (e.g., white, straight, man, abled, etc.; Leonardo & Broderick, 2011).

DisCrit Tenet Four

Tenet four privileges voices of the marginalized populations traditionally not acknowledged within research. This is a major part of the decolonizing–intersectionality framework. Approximately 90% of educators and researchers in deaf education are white, hearing, and grew up monolingual (Andrews & Jordan, 1993; Ausbrooks et al., 2012; Simms et al., 2008).

The majority of research *on* the Deaf, DeafBlind, DeafDisabled, and Hard of Hearing populations is through a hearing gaze. The composite counter-stories served as a recentering by privileging the voices and perspectives of the 25 contributors; Swadener and Mutua (2008) state that "valuing, reclaiming, and foregrounding" colonized voices through critical personal narratives is one decolonizing performance (p. 31). Whereas, traditionally, hearing people have been privileged as the experts on deafness and how to (re)habilitate Deaf, DeafBlind, DeafDisabled, and Hard of Hearing children through special education, the decolonizing-intersectionality framework leveraged DisCrit's fourth tenet by allowing Deaf, DeafBlind, DeafDisabled, and Hard of Hearing adults to research back and talk back to hearing-dominated narratives. Their voices remove the benevolent mask of what I term the hearing helper and reveal schools as a site of struggle for their intersectional identities in ways in which oppression distances them from their culture and ethnic communities and teachers, interpreters, and other professionals as agents in their oppression.

DisCrit Tenets Five and Six

Both tenets five and six closely align with a theory of (de)colonization. Tenet five considers the legal and historical aspects of dis/ability and race. This was primarily addressed in the curriculum of colonization by tracing the mechanisms of colonization and how they work together to (re)construct race and disability. However, the curriculum of colonization expands on this by also examining how these legal and historical aspects implicate other identity markers. Fanon (1963/1969) stated that "colonialism is not satis-fied with merely holding a people in its grip . . . but by a kind of perverted logic, it turns to the past of an oppressed people, and distorts, disfigures, and destroys it" (p. 170). This distortion of the past has permitted very few to use colonization to capture the experience of multiply marginalized and minoritized groups, including dis/abled individuals. Therefore, the curricu-lum of colonization shows how the historical aspects are often erased or reconstructed to hide how their mechanisms serve to perpetuate oppression and maintain the normative standard.

Tenet six in many ways connects to tenet five when considering how legal gains have been made when it benefits whiteness and ability. Tenet six recognizes whiteness and ability as property. As previously stated, within a capitalist society, ability is ascribed to those whose bodies and minds can produce or contribute to society. Those bodies and minds are valued more and as a result given access to full humanity. The constructed nature of dis/ability and its connection to capitalism are evident in how dis/ability and race have shifted over time based on how the construction benefited white-ness and ability. An example of a racial shift that benefited whiteness can be found in the 1940s when Mexicans were to be reported and considered as white in the U.S. census for political reasons—the need for their labor to work on railroads and for immigration policy changes to support the U.S. economy (Hayes-Bautista & Chapa, 1987). When there is a benefit to whiteness and ability, laws such as the ADA are often passed in order to provide accommodations to individuals who are dis/abled by society so that they can be productive citizens.

DisCrit Tenet Seven

DisCrit tenet seven requires activism and supports all forms of resistance. The decolonizing–intersectionality framework is designed to be a praxis methodology. The goal is to forefront the experience of multiply marginalized individuals so that we can shift the gaze and begin to tackle colonization by provoking self-analysis on the part of dominant, superordinated groups. Using counterstorytelling and other methods from the point of the subordinated groups, the hope is to reclaim humanity for all implicated in the system. Baszile (2015) described counterstorytelling as the first movement for social justice in the United States. Therefore, counterstorytelling can be used as a form of activism and resistance. Darder et al. (2008) describe decolonizing methodologies as "embody[ing] activist agendas working toward social justice, sovereignty, self-determination, and emancipatory goals," further confirming the compatibility of DisCrit with a decolonization agenda (p. 23). In the following section, I discuss affordances of situating DisCrit within a framework of colonization and potential tensions that may arrive from placing the two in dialogue together.

AN IMPERFECT BUT NECESSARY UNION

As shown in Figure 11.1, the curriculum of colonization resulted in experiences of audism, ableism, linguicism, anti-blackness, vidism,[1] distantism,[2] homophobia, and xenophobia for the multiply marginalized Deaf, DeafBlind, DeafDisabled, and Hard of Hearing contributors. As a result, when using the decolonizing–intersectionality framework to address the various manifestations of colonization, I had to use various critical frameworks in addition to critical indigenous pedagogy and DisCrit to avoid oversimplifying these manifestations and their impacts on the contributors. There are two primary affordances for leveraging multiple frameworks. First, using multiple frameworks to address colonization affords us as educators, researchers, and scholar–activists the potential to address the whole person. We can push beyond examining race *and* disability alone and move to consider all axes of privilege and oppression an individual or group experiences. Second, multiple frameworks would help to address both the colonized and the colonizer experiences and the dual and multiplicative impact on both. Each could reflect from their own perspectives/lenses based on their own identities, experiences of privilege, and experiences of oppression within colonization, if any. In this way, the burden is no longer on the subordinated to rise up. The burden is now on all of society to move toward restoring full humanity for all.

There are also potential tensions to using multiple frameworks together. First, there may be possible redundancies or overlaps in the frameworks, with differences in schools of thought that make the theories incompatible. Second, by focusing so intensely on describing colonization of a multiply marginalized group and highlighting their stories, one may wonder if this approach successfully shifts the gaze to provoke self-analysis in dominant group researchers, teachers, advocates, and scholars. Last, there are many groups who reject the label of dis/ability; many individuals within the U.S. Deaf and Hard of Hearing communities reject this label, causing tension with DeafBlind and DeafDisabled communities. Though the curriculum of colonization further explicates how experiences of anti-Blackness, for example, can have dis/abling effects on Black, Indigenous, and People of Color, many within these communities are still resistant to embracing the label of dis/abled. In that case, who determines when it is right to apply a lens of DisCrit? Similarly, when is it right to apply a lens of decolonization? Swadener and Mutua (2008) believe that decolonizing performance in research is an interrogation of the research process but also the outcomes/outputs. Echoing the same sentiments, Patel (2015) shows that educational research is a central site of coloniality that perpetuates colonial relationships. Therefore, applying decolonization in non-Indigenous geopolitical contexts must be done with intentionality, addressing ways colonization is ongoing in sociopolitical contexts (Swadener & Mutua, 2008), in order to avoid using decolonization imprecisely and weaponizing it as a tool of reinforcing white settler privilege (Tuck & Yang, 2012). These are tensions that are constantly being wrestled with within our communities.

MOVING FORWARD/CONCLUSION

Connecting DisCrit to a theory and framework that address colonization in U.S. schooling allows for unique possibilities in addressing injustices. First, using this framework at the higher education level as a dialogue space for teaching potential future teachers of the Deaf, DeafBlind, DeafDisabled, and Hard of Hearing would open up several lines of inquiry. These lines of inquiry could involve examining future teachers' journeys toward critical consciousness (Freire, 1973) and how it impacts their teaching pedagogies. Second, applying this framework as a tool of analysis for special education policy is another way I envision this framework being used. Third, this framework could be applied to other dis/abled populations within the

United States and other educational contexts, not just Deaf, DeafBlind, DeafDisabled, and Hard of Hearing students. For example, DisCrit has been used to interrogate teacher candidates' literacy practices in preschool classrooms (see Beneke & Cheatham, 2020); however, I would like to address early childhood special education (ECSE) programs that have the expressed goal of (re)habilitating dis/abled infants and toddlers. As the first grounds of exposure into colonization for dis/abled babies/toddlers and their families, applying a lens of colonization in tandem with DisCrit would allow for the creation of a transformative and disruptive decolonizing pedagogy within these programs. Last, I would like to see this pedagogy move beyond academic and schooling contexts and become a dialogue space of collaboration with Disability Justice movements.

NOTES

1. Vidism refers to the ways the sighted world understands blind, visually impaired, and DeafBlind people through what their eyes are (not) capable of and the expectation that they conform to the sighted world; see Bryen Yunashko (2015).

2. Distantism refers to ways that sighted, hearing people maintain the world out of reach of DeafBlind individuals by denying them access to touch and forcing them to operate as though they were sighted and hearing; see John Lee [J.D. in Refs.] Clark (2017).

REFERENCES

Annamma, S. A., Connor, D. J., & Ferri, B. A. (2016). Introduction: A truncated genealogy of DisCrit. In D. J. Connor, B. A. Ferri, & S. A. Annamma (Eds.), *Disability studies and critical race theory in education* (pp. 1–8). Teachers College Press.

Annamma, S. A., Jackson, D. D., & Morrison, D. (2017). Conceptualizing color-evasiveness: Using dis/ability critical race theory to expand a color-blind racial ideology in education and society. *Race Ethnicity and Education*, 20(2), 147–162. https://doi.org/10.1080/13613324.2016.1248837

Andrews, J. F., & Jordan, D. L. (1993). Minority and minority-deaf professionals: How many and where are they? *American Annals of the Deaf*, 138(5), 388–396.

Atwood, E., & López, G. R. (2014). Let's be critically honest: Toward a messier counterstory in critical race theory. *International Journal of Qualitative Studies in Education*, 27(9), 1134–1154. https://doi.org/10.1080/09518398.2014.916011

Ausbrooks, M., Baker, S., & Daugaard, J. (2012). Recruiting deaf and diverse teachers: Priorities of preservice teachers in deaf education. *Journal of the American Deafness & Rehabilitation Association*, 46(1), 369–398.

Baszile, D. T. (2015). Rhetorical revolution: Critical race counterstorytelling and the abolition of white democracy. *Qualitative Inquiry*, 21(3), 239–249. https://doi.org/10.1177%2F1077800414557830

Bell, C. M. (2011). Introduction. In C. M. Bell (Ed.), *Blackness and disability: Critical examinations and cultural interventions* (pp. 1–7). Michigan State University Press.

Bell, D. (1992). *Faces at the bottom of the well: The permanence of racism.* Basic Books.

Beneke, M. R., & Cheatham, G. A. (2020). Teacher candidates talking (but not talking) about dis/ability and race in preschool. *Journal of Literacy Research, 52*(3), 245–268. https://doi.org/10.1177%2F1086296X20939561

Bhattacharya, K. (Host). (2018, April 25). *Learning to do "woke" qualitative research: How to break the master's rules and tools* [Video webinar]. Weebly. https:// https://wokeresearch.weebly.com/dr-kakali-bhattacharya.html

Clark, J. D. (2017). Distantism. https://wordgathering.syr.edu/past_issues/issue43/essays/clark.html

Coleman-King, C. (2014). *The (re-)making of a Black American: Tracing the racial and ethnic socialization of Caribbean American youth.* Peter Lang.

Crenshaw, K. (1991). Mapping the margins: Intersectionality, identity politics, and violence against women of color. *Stanford Law Review, 43*(6), 1241–1299.

Darder, A., Mirón, L. F., Denzin, N. K., Lincoln, Y. S., Guba, E., Olesen, V., & Spivak, G. C. (2008). Part I: Locating the field: Performing theories of decolonizing inquiry. In N. K. Denzin, Y. S. Lincoln, & L. T. Smith (Eds.), *Handbook of critical and indigenous methodologies* (pp. 21–29). Sage Publications, Inc.

Delgado, R. (1995). *The Rodrigo chronicles: Conversations about America and race.* New York University Press.

Fanon, F. (1967). *A dying colonialism* (H. Chevalier). Grove Press, Inc.

Fanon, F. (1967). *Black skin, white masks.* Grove Press, Inc. (Original work published 1952)

Fanon, F. (1969). *The wretched of the earth* (C. Farrington). Grove Press, Inc. (Original work published 1963)

Fiorenza, E. S. (2001). *Wisdom ways: Introducing feminist biblical interpretation.* Orbis Books.

Freire, P. (1970). *Pedagogy of the oppressed.* Herder & Herder.

Freire, P. (1973). *Education for critical consciousness.* Continuum.

Gertz, E. N. (2007). Dysconscious audism: A theoretical proposition. In H. L. Bauman (Ed.), *Open your eyes: Deaf studies talking* (pp. 219–234). University of Minnesota Press.

Glaser, B. G., & Strauss, A. L. (1967). *The discovery of grounded theory: Strategies for qualitative research.* Aldine.

Gordon, L. R. (1997). *Her Majesty's other children: Sketches of racism from a neocolonial age.* Rowman & Littlefield.

Griffin, R. A., Ward, L., & Phillips, A. R. (2014). Still flies in buttermilk: Black male faculty, critical race theory, and composite counterstorytelling. *International Journal of Qualitative Studies in Education, 27*(10), 1354–1375.

Hayes-Bautista, D. E., & Chapa, J. (1987). Latino terminology: Conceptual bases for standardized terminology. *American Journal of Public Health, 77*(1), 61–68.

Ladd, P., & Lane, H. (2013). Deaf ethnicity, Deafhood, and their relationship. *Sign Language Studies, 13*(4), 565–579. https://doi.org/10.1353/sls.2013.0012

Ladson-Billings, G., & Donnor, J. K. (2008). Waiting for the call: The moral activist role of critical race theory scholarship. In N. K. Denzin, Y. S. Lincoln,

& L. T. Smith (Eds.), *Handbook of critical and indigenous methodologies* (pp. 279–301). Sage Publications, Inc.

Ladson-Billings, G., & Tate, W. F. (1995). Toward a critical race theory of education. *Teachers College Record, 97*(1), 47–68.

Lane, H. (1992). *The mask of benevolence: Disabling the deaf community.* Knopf.

Lawyer, G. (2018). *Removing the colonizer's coat in deaf education: Exploring the curriculum of colonization and the field of deaf education.* [Unpublished doctoral dissertation]. University of Tennessee Knoxville.

Leonardo, Z., & Broderick, A. A. (2011). Smartness as property: A critical exploration of intersections between whiteness and disability studies. *Teachers College Record, 113*(10), 2206–2232.

Lynn, M., & Dixson, A. D. (2013). *Handbook of critical race theory in education.* Routledge.

May, V. M., & Ferri, B. A. (2005). Fixated on ability: Questioning ableist metaphors in feminist theories of resistance. *Prose Studies, 27*(1–2), 120–140.

McCaslin, W. D., & Breton, D. C. (2008). Justice as healing: Going outside the colonizer's cage. In N. K. Denzin, Y. S. Lincoln, & L. T. Smith (Eds.), *Handbook of critical and Indigenous methodologies* (pp. 511–530). Sage Publications, Inc.

Patel, L. (2015). *Decolonizing educational research: From ownership to answerability.* Routledge.

Reagan, T. (1985). The deaf as a linguistic minority: Educational considerations. *Harvard Educational Review, 55*(3), 265–277.

Roulston, K. (2010). *Reflective interviewing: A guide to theory and practice.* Sage Publications, Inc.

Sartre, J. (1969). Preface. In F. Fanon (Ed.), *The wretched of the earth* (C. Farrington; pp. 7–31). Grove Press, Inc.

Schalk, S. (2013). Metaphorically speaking: Ableist metaphors in feminist writing. *Disability Studies Quarterly, 33*(4).

Selden, S. (1999). *Inheriting shame: The story of eugenics and racism in America.* Teachers College Press.

Simms, L., Rusher, M., Andrews, J. F., & Coryell, J. (2008). Apartheid in deaf education: Examining workforce diversity. *American Annals of the Deaf, 153*(4), 384–395.

Smith, A. (2014, June 20). The colonialism that is settled and the colonialism that never happened. *Decolonization, Indigeneity, Education and Society.* http://decolonization.wordpress.com/2014/06/20/the-colonialism-that-is-settled-and-the-colonialism-that-never-happened/

Swadener, B. B., & Mutua, K. (2008). Decolonizing performances: Deconstructing the global postcolonial. In N. K. Denzin, Y. S. Lincoln, & L. T. Smith (Eds.), *Handbook of critical and indigenous methodologies* (pp. 31–43). Sage Publications, Inc.

Tuck, E., & Yang, K. W. (2012). Decolonization is not a metaphor. *Decolonization: Indigeneity, Education & Society, 1*(1), 1–40.

Waziyatawin, A. W., & Yellow Bird, M. (Eds.). (2005). *For indigenous eyes only: A decolonization handbook.* School of American Research Press.

Withers, A. J., Ben-Moshe, L., Brown, L. X., Erickson, L., da Silva Gorman, R., Lewis, T. A., McLeod, L. & Mingus, M. (2019). Radical disability politics. In

R. Kinna & U. Gordon (Eds.), *Routledge handbook of radical politics* (pp.178–193). Routledge.

Woods, T. P. (2013). Surrogate selves: Notes on anti-trafficking and anti-blackness. *Social Identities*, *19*(1), 120–134. https://doi.org/10.1080/13504630.2012.753348

Wrigley, O. (1996). *The politics of deafness*. Gallaudet University Press.

Yunashko, B. (2015). *Deaf interpreters: The weapon against vidism.* [Plenary session]. Deaf Interpreter Conference for Street Leverage, Saint Paul, MN.

Conclusion

Reflections on the Inquiries, Reverberations, and Ruptures of DisCrit

Beth A. Ferri, David J. Connor, & Subinni A. Annamma

The grounding assumption that animates DisCrit is that racism and ableism are mutually constituted and collusive, circulating across histories and contexts in interconnected ways. Drawing on a long and interdisciplinary lineage, in crafting DisCrit, we sought to provide a framework for examining and addressing how racism and ableism structure the educational experiences of multiply marginalized youth. Several years after we published the initial DisCrit article in *Race, Ethnicity and Education* (Annamma et al., 2013), we decided to publish an edited book (Connor et al., 2016) in which we invited scholars across education to engage with the tenets of DisCrit. From the beginning, it has always been our hope that DisCrit would be a living framework—open to diverse contexts and wide-ranging analyses. This has certainly been the case. In the space of the just 5 years, for instance, we couldn't help but take note of how far DisCrit had traveled—traversing discipinary divides and geographic borders, taking up a growing list of topics, identities, marginalizations, and structures. We documented the reverberations of DisCrit in *Review of Educational Research* (Annamma et al., 2018). Since that publication, the scope of DisCrit informed scholarship has expanded even further. In this book, we asked scholars to take up the framework, add to it, complicate it—even rupture it if need be. DisCrit is, in this sense, an invitation and a call to action.

WHAT'S IN THE BOOK?

In structuring this book, we decided to craft the call to invite scholars to consider outward, inward, and margin-to-margin inquiries of DisCrit. These sections were intended to be flexible, but we sought to have each contributor invite the reader to think about ways in which an intersectional framework of racism and ableism, along with other interlocking oppressions, can bring forth new knowledge that has been neglected, uncultivated, underutilized, hidden, and blocked.

Organizing the book around three sections, we sought to look at the myriad and expansive ways that DisCrit was being taken up in scholarship. Specifically, we wrote a call for papers that invited scholars to engage in inward, outward, or margin-to-margin inquiries. In section one of the book, we look at how contributors engage in outward inquiries or what we called reverberations. In this first section, we see how DisCrit has the potential to expand and grow yet retain its core focus on accounting for the interlocking nature of racism and ableism, along with other forms of oppression. In section two, we invited contributors to turn the gaze inward, asking critical questions of ourselves and others. As Alfredo Artiles notes, ruptures signal a kind of break or disharmony that is required when we ask the hard questions that demand or invite critical self-reflection of ourselves and one another. Finally, in section three, we asked authors to engage in inquiries that are not directed from margin to center but instead involve analyses that move sideways across differences or divides. In this concluding chapter, we look at the range of topics and trace ways that the contributors engage in a dialogue throughout the text. We also look at issues they raise that point the way forward to future work that warrents further study. Finally, we consider what we take away from these contributions in terms of the framework of DisCrit itself. Its been an absolute pleasure and an honor to bring these thoughtful and insightful papers together within the pages of this text.

It is fitting that Morgan makes a case for a DisCrit approach to American Law, the field that gave birth to Critical Race Theory (Crenshaw et al., 1995), illustrating the beauty and the power of interdisciplinary analyses exploring how racism and ableism are firmly entrenched in the law. Critical engagement with legal doctrine offers ways to reexamine legacies of racism and ableism in law, along with analyses of their contemporary manifestation associated with highly vulnerable citizens such as apprehending, restraining, and killing individuals of color, supporting people with psychological disabilities (who are often homeless), the denial of reproductive/parental rights, and so many other violent dis-locations (Adams & Erevelles, 2016).

Related to law, the focus on migration, citizenship, and DisCrit in the work of Migliarini et al. brings a global lens also informed by emotions, discourses, and material realities through which to view the experiences of disabled migrant children within Italian and American schools. Their research raises questions about exclusions within inclusive education, which are based on white norms and deficit-based perceptions of educational evaluators and teachers. Their chapter provokes us to think about how ableism is imbued in how we recognize (il)literacy and who fits within the schema of schooling. Likewise, Phuong and Cioè-Peña reveal ways in which ableism and racism operate within language and culture, illustrating how linguistic practices and a white normative gaze stratifies and (de)values people. Their introduction of a Critical Disabilities Raciolinguistics perspective provides an important heuristic to dig deep into the experiences of bilingual children and their families.

In keeping with a global theme, Padilla shares the personal marginalization experienced within Latinx exilic migrations. He underscores how Latinx families are afforded quite circumscribed and abated roles within U.S. school communities. Padilla's work offers a fascinating glimpse into the possibilities for DisCrit within the Global South, emphasizing the need for racial solidarity *within* Latinx communities and conceptualizing the Latinx world as ". . . not just ethnic or racial in phenomenon." Further exploring the ability of DisCrit to travel, Sarkar et al. ponder the affordances and constraints of exporting DisCrit beyond U.S. contexts. They caution against an uncritical adoption of DisCrit, within an Indian context for instance, and argue that the historical, national, and local contexts must be considered within DisCrit analyses.

Moving from the global to the personal, several contributors centered intersectional identities as sites of knowledge and agency. Culling in part from a reclamation of history, Banks et al. center ways that members of oppressed groups name but also navigate oppressive structural barriers. They encourage us to consider how a focus on counter narratives must not ignore or minimize the ways individuals from marginalized groups develop self-affirming and decolonized identities and exhibit cultural agency. Eschewing labels and emphasizing strengths of young women of color with disabilities, Miller et al. reveal ways in which racism, ableism, and linguicism interweave to impact educational experiences. Using an assets-based approach, they seek to reposition young women not as passive recipients of teacher actions but rather as informed generators of knowledge who constantly reposition themselves through discourse. Similarly, the stories of Freedom and Missy told by Clark et al. reveal how dyconscious racism and ableism circulate within segregated classrooms and special schools, revealing the race evasiveness within the field of special education (Connor et al., 2019). By revisiting their original research through a DisCrit lens, the authors illustrate the complex identities of raced, gendered, disabled girls and how interlocking oppressions shape, in part, the teaching and learning process.

Extending beyond classroom practices, several contributors focused on ways that students are positioned in and by schools and by the larger project of schooling. Payne-Tsouros and Johnson offer a timely call for police-free schools, revealing how structures and practices that are ostensibly intended to help manage schools become tools of hypersurveillance and containment. Specifically, they point to how school resource officers place Black and Brown students at a very high risk of being ensnared within the school-to-prison nexus. Instead of school resource officers wearing the three hats of educator, counselor, and law enforcement, it is the latter role that subsumes their time, often creating a no-win situation for students with disabilities forced to function in a zero-tolerance environment.

At the college level, Shallish and Taylor point out how often-unacknowledged benefits of whiteness intersects with disability, affording opportunities to deploy disability in the service of whiteness and vice versa. This slippery terrain of claiming disability when it suits an individual's goals is leveraged by white, middle-class students to maximize their chances of success—even if it means falsification of disability—in a highly competitive world. In the final chapter, Lawyer's quest to decolonize intersectionality in the U.S. Deaf context asks us to complicate our thinking even further, to push beyond race and disability alone, taking into account all axes of privilege to better understand the impact of those negotiating the intersections. As she writes, "Deaf PoC are forced to choose between a linguistic environment with cultural deprivation or be schooled within their ethnic/racial communities with linguistic deprivation; a dilemma that is rarely discussed." Lawyer reminds us of a key aspect of an intersectional framework—that the oppressed in one realm can be the oppressor in another, which is why it is critical for all educators to reflect upon bodies, meanings, and structures situated at the site of multiple axes.

In sum, it has been satisfying to see DisCrit continue to remain grounded in schools and universities, in the daily work of teaching and learning, inclusion and exclusion. At the same time, we have seen that DisCrit can be taken up and applied to other fields of study in the United States such as law and used to develop new perspectives on issues such as migration and immigration—stretching into the global realm. Exploring DisCrit in Asia and Central and Latin America reveals greater potential for imagining its use, carefully contextualized, throughout regions of the Global South. Maintaining an awareness of the multiple, moving axes, not only of race and ability but of gender, language, sexual orientation, nationality, and so on, reminds us of the complex, ongoing, shifting nature of intersectional oppressions yet gives us insights into how all of our identities are constituted and (re)shaped.

WHAT'S BEYOND THE BOOK?

It is inevitable that for every issue explored, theorized, researched, and discussed even more questions have been raised. Here, while recognizing many connections between what has been said and what more needs to be said, we share some observations and personal anecdotes. Morgan's work, for instance, calls upon us to further analyze the situations of some of the most vulnerable people in society—those who are situated as Padilla states, "at the margin of margins." Their words reverberate in the story of how, after an alleged assault by police on her Black son with autism, a mother wrote in large black letters on the side of her home, "Autistic Man Lives Here Cops No Excuse." She shared with a news reporter that, her son "doesn't understand words, what a gun is" (Garcia, 2016). No parent should have to live in fear of their son being shot for not following police directions that they cannot understand or comprehend. As we write this chapter, Walter Walace, a 27-year-old Black man struggling with mental health issues and brandishing a knife, was fatally shot by Philladelphia police despite the fact that his family had called 911 to ask for medical intervention (not the police) to help to deescalate what was clearly a mental health crisis. In Columbus, OH, a 16-year-old, Ma'Khia Bryant's sister called 911 to ask for help and instead, Ma'Khia was fatally shot by police outside her home while lunging at two other girls and holding a knife. These are two recent examples of police killings, but it links to the story of Deborah Danner, Natasha McKenna, Charleena Lyles, and so many others mentioned in the introduction who have been murdered by police. All of these stories and so many others illustrate the huge disconnect between police responses to Black and disabled people. Instances like these reveal problematic biases among police officers and policing itself across race, ethnicity, social class, gender, and sexuality, which are further compounded by a lack of knowledge about intellectual, sensory, and psychological disabilities.

Migliarini et al.'s contemplation of immigrant students being viewed by default through a lens of cultural deficits and general illiteracy call to mind Baynton's (2016) retelling of American eugenics-influenced immigration practices featuring official procedures used to weed out defectives. Sadly, in the Trump era, which championed almost all white crowds at rallies as having good genes, his desire that the United States should entice more Norwegians rather than people from African countries (referred to as shit holes), and the placing of Central American children indefinitely in cages at the U.S.–Mexican border reflect whose lives are valued and whose are not. These are three of countless examples in which demarcations are drawn along racial lines that elevate white supremacy using eugenicst notions of ability as justification. Who belongs in the United States, as Phuong and Cioè-Peña's work illustrates, is determined by social class, language, and documented status, all coalescing in ways to illustrate *processes* of enabling and debilitating (Annamma et al., 2020) that simultaneously construct notions of superiority and inferiority. Those processes open or foreclose access to material realities such as education and other property rights of whiteness and ability. Phuong and Cioè-Peña's work calls us to develop different, more nuanced, and political understandings of bilingual special education that have been advanced to date. Padilla's work, too, features a tale of monolingual Spanish-speaking parents with unrecognized cultural capital, excluded from decisionmaking processes in their children's schools and classrooms, echoing Cioè-Peña's (2020) previous findings of them being distanced from authentic participation in the Individualized Educational Program meetings. Framed within explorations of the Global South, Padilla brings us to the threshold of further possibilities, making a case for Black Studies and LatDisCrit to interanimate one another in their shared quest for a more equitable world, suggesting a robust challenge of colorism—something we hope to see addressed in future DisCrit work. Like Padilla, Sarkar et al. are keenly aware of colonializing forces within theoretical work, urging for greater awareness and opportunities to dismantle colonial thinking while purposefully resisting neo-colonializing new theoretical models. In doing so, they invite increased engagement between the Global North and South, believing it would be mutually informative.

As we have seen, notions of disability identity have been complicated by several authors in this volume. Speaking from their personal experiences, Banks et al. claim the value of a distinct positionality at the intersections of race and ability, empowering those who have historically been disempowered. We, too, hope to see a greater centering of student voices of color with disabilities in educational research, along with researchers at these intersections, sharing their observations and insights. The issue of *interpreting* students' disabled and raced identity by teachers and researchers is also of great importance. Both Miller et al. and Clarke et al. provide very different framings of disabled girls of color with multiple and severe disabilities than is customarily found in educational research, foregrounding their agency, decisionmaking skills, and active maneuverings within the dynamics of teaching and learning. By foregrounding the competence of disabled Girls of Color, they raise questions of: What can an educator's disposition combining anti-racism and anti-ableism look like within restrictive school environments, and, importantly, what might be found if researchers revisit work with a purposeful attention to the dynamics of racism, ableism, and power?

Following in the tradition of Reid and Knight (2006), Sleeter (2010), Ong-Dean (2009), and Brantlinger (2003), Shallish et al. explore how disability rights provisions can be leveraged in the service of whiteness. Exploiting loopholes in the system, they show how privileged and savvy families often enlist disability accommodations as "an unwilling—and unlikely—co-conspirator serving white supremacy." Many of us in the field could likely recount instances in which white, middle-class parents are able to similarly leverage special education services and supports in ways that further reproduce inequities in schools (Ong Dean, 2009). In IEP meetings, informed parents, sometimes accompanied by a lawyer or advocate, may request a less stigmatizing disability label (e.g., Speech and Language Disorder) or push for particular programs or specialized placements (private schools or programs). In high schools for gifted students, it's not uncommon to see high number of requests for 504 plans for Attention Deficit Hyperactivity Disorder and/or Anxiety Disorders that, when granted, provide increased time on examinations. It is not surprising, then, that the majority of students with disabilities who are admitted to college are white students with learning disabilities (Reid & Knight, 2006). We should be clear it is not that parents should not advocate for necessary services and accommodations for their children, but wide disparities between what special education eligibility means or affords children of more and less priveged circumstances might well reflect another example of how property rights of whiteness can be maneuvered in schools to maintain privilege in a highly competitive society. All these examples speak to the need for paying more attention to the benefits of whiteness that continue to inhabit practices of (special) education (Leonardo & Broderick, 2010).

In contrast, schools with school resource officers have been shown to hyper-surveil, hyper-label, and hyper-punish Black, Brown and disabled students (Annamma, 2017). Those at the intersections of race, gender, and disability are more likely to be identified as contravening rules and receive harsher punishments, including suspension, leading to a higher likelihood of entering the juvenile justice system. Athough less studied, Black girls are six times as likely to be suspended than white females. Black girls also report feeling more unsafe in schools where there are resource officers (Crenshaw et al., 2015). Attending to the experiences of LGBTQ+, gender nonconforming youth of color (Burdge et al., 2014), as well as Black girls with and without disabilities in relation to resource officers is needed (Payne-Tsoupros & Johnson). It is clear that in schools, as well as the larger society, those with minoritized identities are subject to interlocking oppressions (Crenshaw, 1989). Given the mistrust between communities of color and the police force, schools should move away from using zero-tolerance policies and inadequate systems that are unfair and unbalanced, rethinking ways to support students having difficult times, eliciting input from student councils, and learning from restorative justice practices. Simply put, we need to work toward better ways of creating a safe climate in schools, which ultimately may require abolition of SROs in schools (Payne-Tsoupros & Johnson). Additionally, we need to ensure that any replacements for punitive discipline (e.g., restorative practices, mindfulness, behavioral supports) are not color evasive, those that purposefully evade race but instead are created with recognition of racism, ableism, and other interlocking oppressions.

Lastly, Lawyer urges educators to move away from the pervasive pathological lens that still dominates educational thought about disability and, as has been argued, also race (Annamma, 2017; Bell, 1992). She invites us to challenge inappropriate, restrictive, ill-fitting practices in schools by pushing beyond race and disability alone to consider the implications of all axes of privilege and oppression pertinent to a context, with a view to our responsibility in cultivating a sense of the full humanity in all of us. We welcome her conceptualization of intersectionality, the potential benefits of decolonizing its current limitations in some circumstances, and ways it can advance in helping us understand the completeness of every individual. The work of individual and collective authors in this volume has expanded our knowledge of how DisCrit can and has been used to date. The outstanding questions these chapters raise also provides explicit and implicit suggestions for its continued growth.

WHAT'S NEXT?

The value that scholars have placed in DisCrit as a critical friend (Sarkar et al.) or guide (Migliarini et al.) is both heartening and instructive. As scholars, we too are continually reminded to operate from a DisCrit informed perspective in our own work. Once we selected the proposals, for example, we asked that each author/writing team reflect on its make up and then potentially invite a multiply marginalized co-author, not simply for representation but because their expertise would make work more robust and expansive. Our goal was to encourage those who use DisCrit as a theory to engage in its axiology by examining our own commitments and practices. The value of this is hard to quantify, but it was important that the book reflect the lived experiences of both race and disability and that we use our own privilege to make space for multiply marginalized scholars.

It is always true that we learn a great deal from scholars who have taken up DisCrit in their work. The authors in this text, for example, map out several areas that call for greater attention and focus within DisCrit and DisCrit analyses. As such, contributors point to places where DisCrit can expand and develop far beyond our initial focus on racism and ableism. Migliarini et al., for instance, call for more attention to the affective within DisCrit scholarship. Others point to issues impacting Latinx (Padilla) and Indigenous (Payne-Tsoupros & Johnson) students, including issues related to immigration, language, and citizenship (Phuong & Cioè-Peña) that must be explicitly named and accounted for, particularly as white nationalism is once again gaining traction in the United States and beyond. Accounting for the reverberating effects of colonialism and globalization, Sarkar et al. points to ways that DisCrit can support and extend efforts towards transnational solidarity and coalition in order to destabilize colonialist and imperialist logics (Padilla).

Rejecting any expectation that disabled people "disappear into ableness" (Lawyer), contributors explicate how DisCrit must reject the expectation that assimilation is a necessary precursor to inclusion (Phuong & Cioè-Peña). Scholars, too, remind us of the need to account for the full and heterogeneous nature of disability experience, not by universalizing disability experience, but by attending to its specificity. Subverting hegemonic notions of disability (Banks et al.,) thus remains a central project of DisCrit. Embracing abolition over reform (Payne-Tsoupros & Johnson), scholars in this volume also illustrate how civil rights laws, because they were not forged within an intersectional politic, often fall short of achieving equity (Morgan) and run the risk of being coopted in the service of white supremacy (Shallish et al.). Taking seriously researcher reflexivity and centering community interests (Clark et al.), scholars must also look for ways to account for the experiences and insights of those living "at the margin of margins" (Padilla). By supporting schools and educators to cultivate solidarity-driven learning spaces, DisCrit serves as a "disruptive methodology" (Lawyer).

FINAL THOUGHTS

A productive and unresolved tension that we are left with is whether the seven tenets of DisCrit as we initially crafted them are sufficiently broad and flexible enough to account for multiple and transmogrifying forms of oppression and resistance. Does DisCrit invite revision and rearticulation, and, if so, do we have a responsibility to ensure that DisCrit is not coopted or misused, diluted or misappropriated, applied without substantive engagement in the actual tenets (Clark et al.). We wonder if we individually and collectively have a responsibility for how DisCrit is taken up or suggesting when is it right to apply DisCrit (Lawyer)? Like our contributors, we wonder how well DisCrit travels and what baggage does it need to claim upon arrival (Sarkar et al.)? Does it make sense to add or modify tenets or frameworks? How far can DisCrit expand and stretch while keeping its central focus on the collusive nature of racism and ableism? When we find ourselves needing to combine DisCrit with other theoretical frameworks, how do we account for irreconcilable differences or ways that these theories might be incompatible (Lawyer) or at least in tension?

We might think about our initial decision to outline seven tenets of what we would come to call DisCrit as purposeful in some way. Seven is, after all, an odd number. Why not round up to an even eight or 10 tenets? Perhaps we envisioned DisCrit as purposefully incomplete, open to revision, and always in process—rendering it a living, breathing theory rather than authoritative discourse. Each of those seven tenets are also rearticulated anew with each application—taking on fresh insights as they are applied to diverse contexts and experiences. At the same time, there is a fullness to DisCrit that we want to honor and recognize. DisCrit comes from someplace, and it reverberates with the many voices and perspectives that first animated it. We take that lineage of struggle and insight seriously, and we hope that as DisCrit grows and matures those voices continue to inform and transform.

REFERENCES

Adams, D. L., & Erevelles, N. (2016). Shadow play: DisCrit, dis/respectability, and carceral logics. In D. J. Connor, B. A. Ferri, & S. A. Annamma (Eds.), *Disability studies and critical race theory in education* (pp. 131–144). Teachers College Press.

Annamma, S. A. (2015). Whiteness as property: Innocence and ability in teacher education. *Urban Review*, 47(2), 293–316.

Annamma, S. A. (2017). *The pedagogy of pathologization: Disabled girls of color in the school-prison nexus*. Routledge.

Annamma, S. A., Connor, D., & Ferri, B. (2013). Dis/ability critical race studies (DisCrit): Theorizing at the intersections of race and dis/ability. *Race Ethnicity and Education*, 16(1), 1–31.

Annamma, S. A., Ferri, B. A., & Connor, D. J. (2018). Disability critical race theory: Exploring the intersectional lineage, emergence, and potential futures of DisCrit in education. *Review of Research in Education*, 42(1), 46–71.

Annamma, S., Handy, T., Miller, A. L., & Jackson, E. (2020). Animating discipline disparities through debilitating practices: Girls of color and inequitable classroom interactions. *Teachers College Record*, 122(5), 1–46. https://www.tcrecord.org/Content.asp?ContentId=23280

Baynton, D. C. (2016). *Defectives in the land: Disability and immigration in the age of eugenics*. University of Chicago Press.

Bell, D. (1992). *Faces at the bottom of the well: The permanence of racism*. Basic Books.

Brantlinger, E. A. (2003). *Dividing classes: How the middle class negotiates and rationalizes school advantage*. Psychology Press.

Burdge, H., Licona, A. C., & Hyemingway, Z. T. (2014). LGBTQ youth of color: Discipline disparities, school push-out, and the school-to-prison pipeline. *Gay-Straight Alliance Network*. https://www.njjn.org/uploads/digital-library/GSA-Network_LGBTQ_brief_FINAL-web_Oct-2014.pdf

Cioè-Peña, M. (2020). Planning inclusion: The need to formalize parental participation in individual education plans (and meetings). *Educational Forum*, 84(4), 377–390. https://doi.org/10.1080/00131725.2020.1812970

Connor, D., Cavendish, W., Gonzalez, T., & Jean-Pierre, P. (2019). Is a bridge even possible over troubled waters? The field of special education negates the overrepresentation of minority students: A DisCrit analysis. *Journal of Race, Ethnicity & Education*, 22(6), 723–745.

Conner, D. J., Ferri, B. A., & Annamma, S. A. (2016). *DisCrit: Disability studies and critical race theory in education*. Teachers College Press.

Crenshaw, K., Gotanda, N., Peller, G., & Thomas, K. (1995). *Critical Race Theory: The key writings that formed the movement*. The New Press.

Crenshaw, K., Ocen, P., & Nanda, J. (2015). *Black girls matter: Pushed out, overpoliced, and underprotected*. Center for Intersectionality and Social Policy Studies, Columbia University.

Garcia, F. (2016, September 2). *Mother posts huge sign on house to 'protect black, autistic son from police.'* Independent. https://www.independent.co.uk/news/world/americas/autistic-man-police-mother-paints-sign-las-vegas-judy-mckim-mental-health-a7221231.html

Hanna, J. & Shah, K. (2016, August 23). *North Carolina deaf man police shooting*. CNN.

Leonardo, Z., & Broderick, A. (2011). Smartness as property: A critical exploration of intersections between whiteness and disability studies. *Teachers College Record*, 113(10), 2206–2232.

Ong-Dean, C. (2009). *Distinguishing disability: Parents, privilege, and special edu-cation*. University of Chicago Press.

Reid, D. K., & Knight, M. G. (2006). Disability justifies exclusion of minority stu-dents: A critical history grounded in disability studies. *Educational Researcher, 35*(6), 18–23.

Sleeter, C. (2010). Why is there learning disabilities? A critical analysis of the birth of the field in its social context. *Disability Studies Quarterly, 30*(2).

About the Authors

Prior to her doctoral studies, **Subini A. Annamma** was a special education teacher in both public schools and youth prisons. Currently, she is an associate professor at Stanford University whose research critically examines the mutually constitutive nature of racism and ableism, how they interlock with other marginalizing oppressions, and how intersectional injustice impacts education in urban schools and youth prisons. To do this, she positions multiply marginalized students and their communities as knowledge generators, exploring how their trajectories can inform liberatory education. Dr. Annamma's book, *The Pedagogy of Pathologization*, focuses on the education trajectories of incarcerated disabled girls of color and has won the 2019 AESA Critic's Choice Book Award & the 2018 NWSA Alison Piepmeier Book Prize.

Joy Banks, Ph.D., is an associate professor and Anti-Racist and Inclusive Excellence faculty in the Division of Special Education and disAbility Research at George Mason University. Dr. Banks is a recent award recipient of the Elizabeth Hurlock Beckman Award, which is designed to benefit academic faculty members who have inspired their students to make a significant contribution to society. Her publications appear in *Disability & Society*, *Remedial and Special Education*, *Journal of Diversity in Higher Education*, *Journal of Transformative Education*, and *Multiple Voices for Ethnically Diverse Exceptional Learner*. Recent publications include *Gangbangers and Wheelchairs: Urban Teachers' Perceptions of Race and Disability* as well as *Invisible Man: Examining the Intersection of Disability, Race and Gender in Urban Communities*.

D'Arcee Charington Neal is a doctoral student in English and disability studies at The Ohio State University. He also has a double master's degree in rhetoric and creative writing. His area of study focuses on the intersection of digital media composition, audionarratology, and the intersection of Black and disability identities. Noting the absence of digital work by and about Black and disabled persons, he is currently producing an immersive audio narrative alongside his dissertation research. Current research in progress includes an essay in *College, Composition, and Communication* titled "Hidden Disabled Black Technoculture" and a chapter in *Futures of Cartoons Past: The Cultural Politics of X-Men: The Animated Series* which discusses Storm's oft-overlooked role as a Black disabled woman.

Maria Cioè-Peña is a bilingual/biliterate researcher who examines the intersections of disability, language, school–parent partnerships, and education policy. She focuses specifically on Latinx bilingual children with dis/abilities, their families, and their ability to access multilingual and inclusive learning spaces within public schools. María's two-time award-winning dissertation focused on the experiences of Spanish-speaking mothers raising emergent bilinguals labeled as disabled. Maria's work is featured in multiple journals including *Urban Review, Education Forum, Bilingual Research Journal, International Journal of Inclusive Education*; she has also contributed to multiple edited volumes. María is an assistant professor and community-engaged teaching fellow at Montclair State University.

Nitasha M. Clark, Ph.D., is a postdoctoral research associate with the Center for Literacy and Disability Studies (CLDS). Her research interest focuses upon three lines of inquiry: social context of rural education, teacher implementation of instructional practices for equity and access, and qualitative/mixed-method research methodology. Prior to joining CLDS, Nitasha spent over 24 years in various educational positions supporting adult and child learners as a school and district instructional coach, university lecturer, research project coordinator, elementary and middle school special education teacher, and preschool teacher. She has been a contributing author to book chapters and peer-reviewed journal articles.

David J. Connor, Ed.D., is professor emeritus, Hunter College (learning disabilities program) and the Graduate Center (urban education program), City University of New York. David is the author/editor of numerous articles, book chapters, and books, including *DisCrit: Disability Studies and Critical Race Theory in Education* (2016) co-edited with Beth Ferri and Subini Annamma; *Contemplating Dis/Ability in Schools and Society: A Life in Education* (2018); *Rethinking Disability: A Disability Studies Approach to Inclusive Practices* (2019), 2nd edition, co-authored with Jan Valle; and *How Teaching Shapes our Thinking about Disabilities: Stories From the Field* (2021), co-edited with Beth Ferri. He also writes fiction. For more information, see www.hunter-cuny.academia.edu/DavidJConnor

Charna D'Ardenne is an assistant professor at the Center for Literacy and Disability Studies in the division of Allied Health Sciences at the University of North Carolina at Chapel Hill School of Medicine. She is the project director for *Understanding Thinking and Learning Among Students with Severe Disabilities*. Previously, D'Ardenne taught in public schools in New

York, California, and North Carolina. D'Ardenne's research interests include disability studies in education, qualitative methodology, literacy, critical theory, and sociocultural theories of learning. She is first author of a chapter on the discursive construction of Dis/Ability to be included in an upcoming book, *Discursive Psychology & Disability*, edited by Lester et al.

Karen Erickson, Ph.D., is the director of the Center for Literacy and Disability Studies, a professor in the division of speech and hearing sciences, and the David E. and Dolores "Dee" Yoder Distinguished Professor in the department of allied health sciences in the School of Medicine at the University of North Carolina at Chapel Hill. Karen is a former teacher of students with significant support needs. Her research addresses literacy and communication for students with significant support needs, with recent projects focused on creating open-source implementation models including professional development, implementation supports, and numerous instructional supports and technologies.

Beth A. Ferri, Ph.D., is a professor of inclusive education and disability studies at Syracuse University, where she also coordinates the doctoral program in special education. She has published widely on the intersection of race, gender, and disability. In addition to over 50 articles and chapters, she has also published a number of co-authored and co-edited books, including: *Reading Resistance: Discourses of Exclusion in Desegregation and Inclusion Debates* (2006, with Connor, Peter Lang), *Righting Educational Wrongs: Disability Studies Law and Education* (2013, with Kanter, SU Press), *DisCrit: Critical Conversations Across Race, Class, & Dis/ability* (2016, with Connor & Annamma, Teachers College Press), and *Stories from our Classrooms: How Working in Education Shapes Thinking about Dis/Ability* (2021, with Connor, Peter Lang).

Anjali Forber-Pratt, Ph.D., is an assistant professor in the department of human and organizational development with secondary appointments in the department of special education and department of physical medicine and rehabilitation at Vanderbilt University in Nashville, Tennessee. Her primary area of research relates to disability identity development. She presents regularly at state, national, and international conferences and is author on 31 peer-reviewed journal articles and numerous chapters. As a wheelchair-user for over 30 years, and a two-time Paralympian and medalist, Dr. Forber-Pratt is nationally and internationally recognized as a disability leader and has secured over $700,000 in disability research support.

David I. Hernández-Saca, Ph.D., is an assistant professor of dis/ability studies in education within the department of special education at the University of Northern Iowa. His scholarship agenda is problematizing the commonsense assumptions of what learning dis/abilities (LD) are at the intersections of power, emotionality, and identities. His lines of inquiry include: (1) the emotional and social impact of LD labels on conceptions of self, (2) the role of emotionality in teacher learning about social justice issues, (3) transition programming for historically multiply marginalized youth with dis/abilities, and (4) interrogating violence within the academy against nonhegemonic scholars for well-being and healing.

Najma Johnson (they/them/theirs), M.A., a BlackDeafBlindPanQueer folk, is the executive director of DAWN, whose mission is to promote healthy relationships and end abuse in the deaf community in the Washington, DC, area. Najma is an antiviolence community collectivist and adjunct professor at Gallaudet University and Rochester Institute of Technology National Technical Institute for the Deaf. They offer spaces and facilitate dialogue within the deaf community about interpersonal violence, antiviolence, survivor-centric based accountability, and healthy/safe relationships. They have worked with DDDDBHH BIPOC sex workers, trafficking survivors, victims of law enforcement violence, domestic violence survivors, and sexual violence survivors who have experienced cultural challenges that arise from seeking deaf services due to intersectional identities.

David A. Koppenhaver is a professor in the reading education and special education department at Appalachian State University. His research focuses on literacy in students with significant disabilities, and he co-founded the Center for Literacy and Disability Studies at the University of North Carolina at Chapel Hill with David Yoder in 1990. He has received a distinguished lecturer award from the International Society for Augmentative and Alternative Communication and has been a Fulbright Scholar to the University of Queensland. With Karen Erickson, he recently co-authored *Comprehensive Literacy for All: Teaching Students with Significant Disabilities to Read and Write.*

Gloshanda Lawyer is an assistant professor of deaf studies and interpreting education at Utah Valley University. She holds a master's degree in special education with dual teaching licenses in deaf education and early childhood special education. She has a Ph.D. in special education with emphasis on deaf education and educational interpreting. She is a former PK–12 teacher of the deaf and former birth–3 early interventionist. Her research interests focus on multilingual and multimodal development in young children, colonization and intersectionality within U.S. schooling systems, and theorizing decolonizing methodologies and pedagogies in teacher/interpreter preparation programs. She practices disability justice and language justice in her professional and community spaces using them as guidance towards creating authentically human and inclusive spaces.

Valentina Migliarini, Ph.D., is a assistant professor in educational studies in the School of Education at the University of Birmingham. She is a member of the interdisciplinary research network *Citizenship, Race and Belonging (CRaB)*. She coordinates the committee *Decolonizing EDSOC*. Her research sits at the crossroads of inclusive education, bilingual special education, justice and equity studies, culturally sustaining and trauma-informed pedagogies for disabled, migrant and refugee children. She was a Fulbright-Schuman Visiting Fellow at the department of special education, University of Kansas. She published a number of manuscripts in the *International Journal of Qualitative Studies in Education*, the *International Journal of Inclusive Education*, and *Race, Ethnicity and Education*.

Amanda L. Miller is an assistant professor of inclusive education at Wayne State University. Her scholarly interests focus on the lived experiences of multiply marginalized youth, particularly disabled girls of color. She also studies teacher preparation for culturally responsive and sustaining inclusive education and family–school–community partnerships with and for families from diverse backgrounds. Amanda's research has appeared in journals such as *International Journal of Inclusive Education, International Journal of Qualitative Studies in Education*, and *Teachers College Record*. Recently, she was awarded the 2020 Outstanding Dissertation Award from the AERA Disability Studies in Education SIG and the 2020 Dissertation of the Year Award from the University of Kansas School of Education.

Jamelia N. Morgan is an associate professor of law at the University of Connecticut School of Law. Her teaching and current scholarship focus on issues at the intersections of race, gender, disability, and criminal law and punishment. Her research examines the development of disability as a legal category in American law, disability and policing, overcriminalization and the regulation of physical and social disorder, and the constitutional dimensions of the criminalization of status.

Carlyn Mueller is an assistant professor of special education at the University of Wisconsin-Madison. Her research focuses on disability identity development in youth with disabilities, including development of disability community solidarity in special education and disability representation in curriculum. Her work is deeply informed by her lived experience as a person with physical and learning disabilities. Dr. Mueller's dissertation received the Outstanding Dissertation Award from the Special and Inclusive Education Research Special Interest Group of the American Educational Research Association.

George W. Noblit is the Joseph R. Neikirk Distinguished Professor of Sociology of Education Emeritus at the University of North Carolina at Chapel Hill.

He specializes in the sociology of knowledge, race and equity studies, and qualitative methods. He has won numerous awards for his scholarship, culminating in a Lifetime Achievement Award for Distinguished Contributions to Social Contexts in Education Research by Div. G of American Educational Research Association in 2019. His last two books are: *The Oxford Encyclopedia of Qualitative Research Methods in Education* (2020) and *Cultural Constructions of Identity: Meta-ethnography and Theory* (2018), both with Oxford University Press.

Sylvia N. Nyegenye is a doctoral candidate at the University of Kansas, department of special education. Sylvia's research focuses on examining systemic processes and individual practices that produce or disrupt academic and social opportunities for African immigrant students with dis/abilities in U.S. schools, exploring culturally responsive and sustaining pedagogies that support effective learning for African immigrant students with dis/abilities and building professional, equitable family–school–community partnerships with African immigrant families from former British colonies.

Alexis C. Padilla is a blind brown Latinx scholar/activist and a Ph.D. graduate from the language, literacy, and sociocultural studies department at the University of New Mexico, Albuquerque. Dr. Padilla is also a lawyer, sociologist, and conflict transformation-engaged scholar whose work explores emancipatory learning and radical agency in the context of decolonial Latinx theorizing and critical disability studies. In December 2019, NCTM published one of his co-authored volumes titled "Humanizing Disability." Dr. Padilla's published contributions emphasize the activist/disability advocacy vantage point combined with actionable dimensions of inclusive equity research. His postsecondary teaching experience encompasses almost three decades, plus more than two decades of advocacy and conflict resolution work with Spanish-speaking families and English language learning students with disabilities in various U.S. settings. Since spring 2020, Dr. Padilla has been affiliated with Phillips Theological Seminary to expand his research agenda and his activism scope into intersectional disability theology.

Christina Payne-Tsoupros (she/her/hers), J.D., M.Ed., is an academic success instructor at the University of the District of Columbia David A. Clarke School of Law. She is cis, white, hearing, and sighted. Her research interests center around increasing access and equity across a learner's educational career from early childhood through higher education. Her recent publications include "Lessons from the LEAD-K Campaign for Language Equality for Deaf and Hard of Hearing Children" in the *Loyola University Chicago Law Journal* and "A Starting Point for Disability Justice in Legal Education" in the *Journal Committed to Social Change on Race and Ethnicity*.

Jennifer Phuong is a Ph.D. candidate at the University of Pennsylvania Graduate School of Education in the educational linguistics division. Prior to starting her doctoral degree, she was a high school special education English language arts teacher in Brooklyn, New York, and was involved in teacher activism. Jennifer uses qualitative research methods to center the experiences of students and educators considering the intersection of race, language, and disability in multilingual educational contexts, with her dissertation focusing on teacher collaboration and learner categories in bilingual special education.

Tanushree Sarkar is a doctoral student in community research and action at Peabody College, Vanderbilt University. Her research examines the links between teachers, education policy, and pedagogy for inclusive and equitable education in India. Her work draws on critical disability studies, decolonial theory, critical policy analysis, and participatory research methods. Tanushree's research is embedded in her experiences as a privileged, disabled woman in India. She graduated with an MSc in social and cultural psychology from the London School of Economics and Political Science.

Lauren Shallish is an associate professor at The College of New Jersey. Her work has appeared in *Disability Studies Quarterly*, *Disability & Society*, and *Critical Readings in Interdisciplinary Disability Studies*. She most recently received a state grant award for The Troublemaker Project, a student-led coalition that addresses the ethno-racialized and gendered organizing concepts of behavior and motivation in schooling. Her work focuses on racial justice and disability liberation in secondary and higher education. She previously worked as chief of staff at Hobart and William Smith, in DC Public School's Office of Special Education, and as a qualitative research assistant for Columbia University's Center for Institutional and Social Change.

Michael D. Smith is an associate professor in the department of special education, language, and literacy at The College of New Jersey. His scholarship has been published in *Teacher Education Quarterly*, *Teacher Education and Special Education*, *The Teacher Educator*, and *Multiple Voices for Ethnically Diverse Exceptional Learners*. During doctoral study, he developed a keen interest in the pedagogical processes and course products associated with culturally responsive teacher education. Since then, his scholarship and teaching have focused on the intersections of social identity, teaching, and learning—with particular attention on empowering teachers to act as social change agents within their spheres of influence.

Phillandra Smith, M.S., is a doctoral candidate in special education also pursuing a Certificate of Advanced Studies in disability studies at Syracuse University. She is originally from The Bahamas and has taught English as a second language in Japan. Her research interests include cultural representations of disability, the recruitment and retention of racially and ethnically diverse teacher candidates to inclusive education teacher programs, and the experiences of Caribbean migrant students with disabilities in U.S. schools. Her publications are scheduled to appear in the edited book titled *Narrating Higher Education: Intellectual Disability* (edited by Gill and Myers) and a chapter in the edited book titled *Diversity, Autism, and Developmental Disabilities: Guidance for the Culturally Responsive Educator* (edited by Harkins et al.).

Chelsea Stinson is a Ph.D. candidate in special education at Syracuse University and an assistant professor of education at Utica College. Her research is focused on the social, political, and instructional contexts of emergent bilingual and multilingual students and their communities in the field of inclusive (special) education. She recently co-authored, "Inclusive Education in the (New) Era of Anti-immigration Policy: Enacting Equity for Disabled English Language Learners," which is published in *International Journal of Qualitative Studies in Education*.

Ashley Taylor is an assistant professor of educational studies at Colgate University. Her recent scholarship appears in *Disability & Society, Harvard Educational Review, Educational Theory,* and *Theory and Research in Education* as well as the book volume *Critical Readings in Interdisciplinary Disability Studies*. Taylor is interested in the gendered and racialized meanings of able-mindedness as they inform epistemic practices in education. She teaches educational foundations, disability studies, and women's studies and offers a formally inclusive praxis course on disabled citizenship and social activism in partnership with a local organization serving students labeled with intellectual disability.

Index